Walking for Peace

~ an inner journey ~

D0731665

Walking for Peace

~ an inner journey ~

Mony Dojeiji
Alberto Agraso

Awards

Winner
2012 Global Ebook Awards
Action/Adventure

Finalist
2012 National Indie Excellence Book Awards
Adventure

Finalist
2012 Global Ebook Awards
New Age

Honorable Mention
2012 Global Ebook Awards
Religion/Faith

To those who fearlessly follow their hearts, and
To those who do the work of peace—both inner and outer—despite the
odds against them.

You are not alone.

Acknowledgments

Our first thanks must go to those "ordinary" people who through their extraordinary acts of kindness helped us to keep walking. This story would not have been possible without their generosity of spirit. You all hold a special place in our hearts. Thank you. *Grazie, huala, faleminderit, efharisto, tashekkur, shukran, toda.*

To Fra Ante Logara, our angel in Croatia. *Huala, za moj dragi prijatelj.*

To Johanna van Fessem and Jeannette Albers, my Dutch oracles, *hartelijk dank*!

To our families and dear friends, many of whom didn't understand what we were doing, but who still loved and supported us unconditionally throughout this grand adventure.

To Diana Shaw-Malvern, Lesley Gilbert and all those who gave us their feedback throughout the story creation process, thank you.

Our sincerest thanks go to Sue Kenney, Camino pilgrim and author, whose skillful coaching encouraged me to find my voice as a writer, and who, with the help of Bruce Pirrie, guided us through the earliest stages of the creation of this book.

To our friend Lucy No, whose editing insights gave shape to the final story. Thank you, Snoopy!

Finally, to my husband, walking companion, and writing partner Alberto Agraso; this book would not be what it is today were it not for your insistence that it be authentic, and your persistence in making it so. *Te quiero.*

Mony

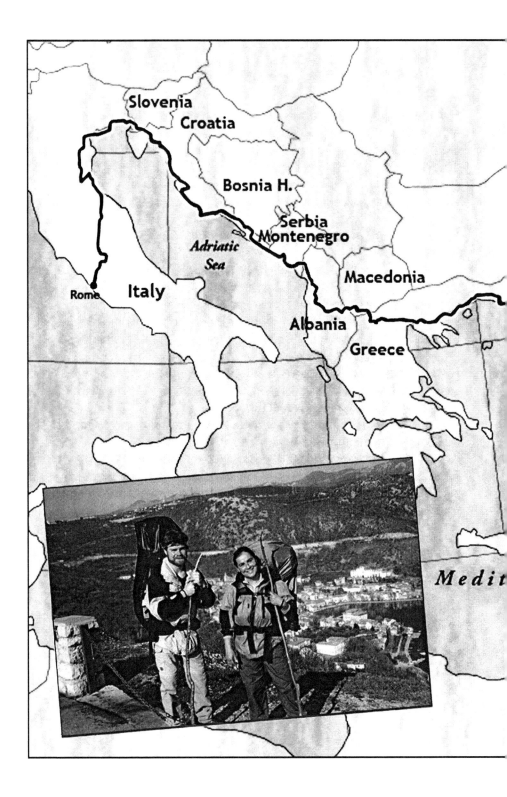

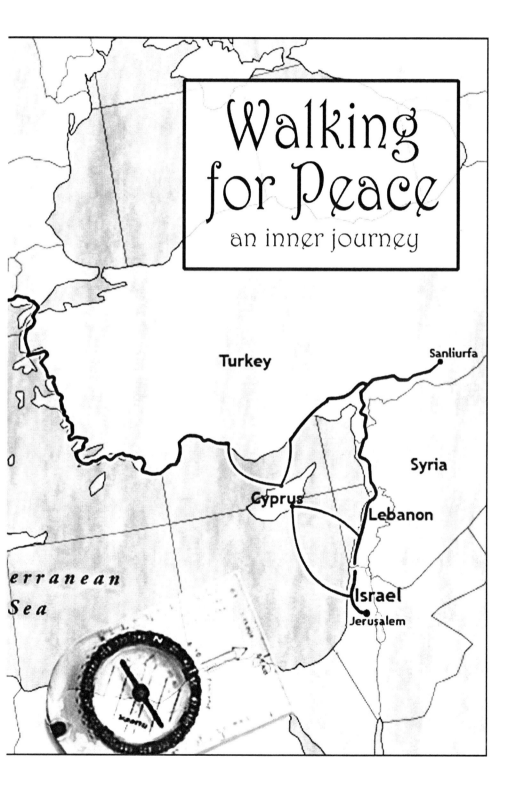

Walking
for Peace
an inner journey

"Why are you walking? Wouldn't it be easier to just take a bus or a plane?"

"Yes, it would. But I never would have met you otherwise."

Table of Contents

Introduction

When we began the process of writing this book, we each relied heavily on our diaries. In the early versions, we described every city, every person, every kilometer, every experience. The more we wrote, however, the more that we appeared to be creating an adventure travelogue, which in part it was, but one that had not captured the full spirit of the walk or, more importantly, the driving force behind all these experiences.

It was at this stage that I balked. I preferred to speak about the places and people, and keep the full extent of what was happening within me to myself. My deepest fears, curiously the same ones that I walked into Jerusalem with, now played out on a grander scale. What would people say if I revealed my insecurities and judgments, if I told them what I was really thinking? And if I told them that the biggest decisions of my life I made following signs and omens; that I didn't necessarily think through each situation, but merely jumped in and winged it, trusting that the Universe would guide me through it? Would people, especially those I hold dear, think I was nuts? If I mentioned I was on a spiritual journey, a quest to know myself, would they think I had become a religious fanatic? The more I thought about it, the more vulnerable I felt. So I resisted.

The forces of the Universe, however, were relentless and kept tugging at me to speak from the heart, to have courage to speak about my inner journey; but I wasn't prepared. I fought with them, with myself, and especially with Alberto. With each story, he would try to reason with me, explain, cajole, anything, to get me to write about what was happening "behind the veil", as he often referred to it. When I eventually did, I saw the beauty of the experience from a perspective I had not considered before. It was in those moments that I felt especially inspired, or perhaps guided, and when the words seemed to flow through me like a current. I eventually stopped resisting and allowed that flow to continue.

The people and events we describe are all true. In certain situations, we changed the names when we felt we needed to tell the story to demonstrate an important point in our journey, but we didn't want to unintentionally offend the individuals involved. We also had to remove a great number of stories, and although they are not yet available, you can still visit our website www.walkingforpeace.com to see our exact route, day-by-day, along with photos, anecdotes, and interviews we granted along the way.

Having two people come to agreement on every aspect of one book has not been an easy task. In many ways, it too was a journey. This may not be the book I would have written alone, or that Alberto would have written alone, but this final product has exceeded our wildest expectations. It is an entirely new creation, not a compromise of creations. Nothing has been lost; on the contrary, both visions have expanded.

Perhaps this book, in some small measure, can stand as an example of what can be accomplished when the intention is to unite and transcend differing views rather than keep them separated. Perhaps this can show a path towards a peace that is lasting.

We live in moments of great change, where a consciousness of peace is emerging and taking form. In this nascent state, it is still fragile and easy to dismiss as utopian. But all great journeys begin with a single step. And no matter how tentative these first steps may seem, they all inevitably lead to their destination, one that may even surprise us.

I invite you to take that first step with me now.

Mony

Prologue

"I would love for you to join me on my walk for peace to Jerusalem," I enthused.

"What? I'm still recovering from the Camino to Santiago," Hannah joked.

The candlelight flickered, accentuating the warmth of that already unforgettable evening. I had arrived in Bonn, Germany, that very afternoon, and stepped into the welcoming arms of my pilgrim friends Hannah and Alberto, with whom I now shared a wonderful meal. My imminent departure on my pilgrimage for peace, along with their budding romance and future plans, gave us great cause to celebrate.

"I appreciate you asking," Hannah added, "but I just started a new job and can't leave so quickly."

I looked over at Alberto. "Well, if you're interested, you're welcome to join me," I politely offered.

Alberto stared at me, looking visibly shaken. The moment passed, and the conversation continued well into the late hours of the evening. Alberto, however, appeared sad when we said our goodnights.

I awakened the next morning to find an anxious-looking couple wanting to speak with me. Hannah's eyes were red and swollen. "Last night, when you asked us…" Hannah started, then buried her face in her hands and began to weep. Alberto placed his arms around her shoulders, and looked at me gravely.

"I believe that I must walk with you," he said.

"Oh," I replied. "That's great, right?"

"I can't go," Hannah said through her tears. "I've just come back from a year's sabbatical." I waited for the explanation that was causing such grief.

"Mony," Alberto finally said, looking at me earnestly, "since arriving in Germany, I have been receiving signs, synchronicities, telling me that something important was about to happen, a big jump in my inner journey. When you arrived yesterday, the signs intensified and pointed clearly for me to go with you to Jerusalem." Hannah sobbed and shook her head. Alberto looked at her with concern.

"I am happy here with Hannah and excited about our plans to build a future together," he continued. "However, last night the signs were constant. I tried to ignore them and convince myself that they were my unconscious desire for adventure; but they kept coming. I finally decided that I would consider the possibility of walking with you if you asked me directly. And last night, you did."

"Yeah, but," I stammered, "I only meant for you to walk a couple of weeks with me, not the whole way."

"Still...my sign was clear," Alberto persisted.

"What about all our plans?" Hannah spat out. "What will happen now? How long will you be gone? I can't wait for you. I need you here. And what if you hear about another pilgrimage two years from now? Are you just going to go every time you receive strong signs? I can't live like that. I need to know that you will be here."

"I still haven't made my final decision," Alberto replied. "Besides, I can't give you that kind of guarantee. No one can." His eyes searched hers for understanding. "You can come too, you know," he added.

"What do you want me to do?" she retorted. "Quit my job and not think about my future? Where will the money come from? What will we do when we come back? We would need to start from zero again."

"But, Hannah, you hate your job," Alberto persisted. "How many times have we said that when we follow a dream or a call, all that we need comes to us? It's not a nice idea from a fairy tale. It's true. I've lived it, and so have you." A heavy silence hung in the air. I didn't know what to say or do, and so sat quietly, hoping for some quick end to this agony.

"I'm turning forty, Alberto," Hannah finally said. "I want to start a family. I want a man waiting for me when I come home. I don't think it's too much to ask."

"I'm only trying to live what I believe," Alberto responded softly. Hannah looked at him sadly.

"I don't feel any attraction for Jerusalem," she whispered. "It's not my calling."

Hannah and Alberto continued speaking in Spanish, and so I left them to get some fresh air. I had expected to walk to Jerusalem alone and didn't know how I felt about having company. Alberto seemed likeable enough, but I knew little about him. We had only spent a few days together, and always with Hannah who acted as our translator when my sparse Spanish and his high-school English failed us. How would we communicate without her? We seemed to hold similar views about peace, but he didn't appear interested in peace in Jerusalem. I didn't know what other differences were waiting to reveal themselves, or if I wanted to find out. This was my walk, and I wanted to do it my way.

As I breathed the night air, my runaway thoughts began to slow and the whispers of my intuition to become less faint. These events were no coincidence. We were all brought together in a web of circumstances whose purpose I didn't understand, much less control, no matter how desperately I wished to. I needed to trust and allow whatever was happening to unfold. Determined to do exactly that, or at least try, I returned to find Alberto waiting for me.

"I'm going with you," he announced. "I only need a few days to prepare."

"I'm leaving for Rome tomorrow, and will meet you when you're ready," I responded.

"I have something to show you," Alberto said, holding out his hand. In it was a silver pendant of an eagle. "This used to be my totem. I think it will bring you luck for the way." I took the pendant, trying to contain my astonishment.

In that moment, I understood that my meeting Alberto was fated, and that we indeed had a journey to make together.

1. Destiny

I had met Alberto and Hannah at the end of the world, in Finisterre, a town in northern Spain that was the ending point of the eight hundred kilometer pilgrimage route called the Camino. I had arrived there by chance, or design, depending on the point of view. Two years earlier, I had fallen into an emotional black hole that I didn't know how to crawl out of. My ordinary life, the one I had worked so hard to construct, had tumbled around me when my husband of seven years announced he was leaving for another woman. We hadn't even finished unpacking the boxes in our dream home. What had I done to deserve this? I had played by society's rules. I had done all that was expected of me; I had an MBA, a great career at an international software firm, money, and friends. I was well-liked and respected. I paid my taxes. Why did this happen to me?

My search led me from psychologists to psychics, but it was the self-help and spirituality sections of my local bookstores that ultimately changed me. They opened my eyes to perspectives that I longed to embrace: that I was the creator of my life, not its victim; that I attracted people and experiences to help me grow emotionally and spiritually; and, most prophetically, to change the world, I needed to change myself first. The ideas resonated with me deeply, but how to live them while working in the competitive business world? How to be love when a client was yelling at me? Or to be peace when deadline after deadline loomed? I felt increasingly dissatisfied and unhappy, unable to reconcile my burgeoning beliefs with my work life. So I decided to quit. It was August of 2000.

On my last day at work, while packing up my office, I received a phone call, inviting me to attend a workshop dedicated to helping people discover the life work that lights them up. The creators of this technique, the Walkers, traveled extensively with their seminar schedule; but because of a misprint on their brochure, they were unexpectedly in town, holding a session that weekend in a location that was a mere two-hour drive from my home. When I called, they had one final spot available. I registered without hesitation, believing all this to be a sign.

What emerged at the end of this intense process was the picture of a woman who desperately craved peace and who wanted to dedicate her life to it. The Walkers commented that not only did my entire face light up when I spoke about peace, but an area appeared on my forehead that was lighter than the rest of my face and shaped like a six-sided star. More curiously, they also heard an eagle's call, which they admitted was a rare occurrence. They knew that an eagle lived in the mountains nearby, but had only ever seen it once before. They took this as an important omen, an invitation for me to accept the eagle as my totem, or power animal, and my guide in the next stages of my life.

I sat by the river during a break, contemplating these unusual events. I found it all intriguing, but resisted accepting a totem as powerful as the eagle, which I knew to be the symbol of spiritual vision and reaching for higher realms. After all, I reasoned, who am I?

Suddenly, I heard several people gasp. I looked and saw an eagle flying past, gliding low over the waters, its majestic wings cutting through the air, slowly, powerfully, and eventually disappearing over the mountainous horizon. In those eternal seconds, I was speechless. Was this a sign? Was the eagle speaking with me directly?

I struggled to give meaning to this encounter, and eventually convinced myself that no, the eagle had not come to me personally and that this sighting was nothing more than a happy coincidence...until I returned to the same location two months later. To my astonishment, the same eagle landed a few short meters ahead of me and stared directly into my eyes, as if defying me to ignore his call. This time, I couldn't. That day, I accepted the eagle as my totem.

But I still had so many questions about my life and how to live it. I wanted to put into practice the spiritual principles I was learning, and so thought a long trip would help me accomplish that. With enough savings to able to travel indefinitely, I booked a one-year open ticket, starting in Egypt. I climbed the pyramids at night and rode through the desert by day. I meditated in the caves of Cappadocia and, in Istanbul, straddled two continents. I whiled away the hours on the beaches of the Mediterranean. They all whispered their secrets and offered tantalizing glimpses; but it was the Camino to Santiago in northern Spain that finally revealed my path.

It had been a long day's walk along the arid plains of the *meseta*, and I was looking forward to a good night's sleep. I sat on a bench massaging my feet, listening to a group of pilgrims sitting nearby speaking about the day's experiences.

"I heard that this Camino is called the Way of the Sword," one of them enthused. "It's where you battle your fears and demons, and find your strength." I eavesdropped a little more. "There is also another pilgrimage to Rome called the Way of the Heart, of Love," she continued, "and then finally, there is the path to Jerusalem, called the Way of the Soul, the soul's journey to God."

My heart lurched. Jerusalem, Israel, land of the six-sided star. Although I was born in Canada, my parents were Lebanese, so the Middle East conflict was ever near. As a child, while the women huddled in the kitchen, I sat quietly on the sidelines with the men, listening to them analyzing and debating the latest happenings in the region. I was fascinated with the complexity and antiquity of the conflict, the twists and turns, the friend one day becoming foe the next. I heard every conspiracy theory imaginable, most of which dehumanized the Israelis and their western allies, and made them the root of all problems in the region. I grew up believing that armed struggle was a justifiable means of defeating tyranny and oppression, and that the only way to peace was through justice.

With my spiritual awakening, however, fighting injustice no longer seemed the ideal way to achieve lasting peace; but how to create the latter without fighting against the former? Those thoughts haunted my every step until that unknown pilgrim revealed that the Way of the Soul led to Jerusalem. I knew then that I would walk that path to know my soul, to understand what peace means, and to carry it to that divided land. Two months later, the events of 9/11 would crystallize my plan—I would walk to Jerusalem for peace.

I searched the Internet for ancient routes to Jerusalem, all in vain; but I did find a Dutch woman named Johanna van Fessem who had walked from The Hague to Jerusalem a year earlier. I traveled there to meet her, my oracle, before beginning my walk. She understood my call, and advised me to trust this path and be assured that the forces that were calling me to Jerusalem would also stand as my guides and protectors.

I left Johanna feeling more powerful than ever, intending to start my walk in Rome. My fateful decision to visit Hannah in Germany would bring Alberto back into my life and change the course of my walk in ways I could not possibly imagine.

2. Walking Alone

I arrived in Rome, ready to walk, and carrying what I believed to be winter essentials: sleeping bag, tent, fleece sweater, thermal tights, hat, gloves, one change of socks, shirt, and underwear, and basic toiletries. I also carried a detailed roadmap of central Italy and one of the Mediterranean area. I would buy other maps along the way.

The Vatican, final destination of the Way of the Heart, was my starting point. It too was a sacred site, a holy place imbued with the hopes, dreams and faith of fellow pilgrims. To me, it was an energy that was real, and I wanted to carry it with me, and to have it sustain me along the Way of the Soul to Jerusalem.

I spent that evening in my hotel room, obsessively unpacking and repacking my backpack. Without food or water, it weighed about seventeen kilograms. I had never carried that much weight before and worried how my body would respond.

My physical preparations complete, I now turned inwards to emotionally and mentally prepare for the journey ahead. I lit a small candle and sat cross-legged on my bed, my breathing the only sound in the dark room. It took a long time for my body to relax, and even longer for my mind to stop racing.

"Thank you bringing me here," I whispered. *"Thank you for the opportunity to use my life in this way. Help me to stay open. Help me to surrender and trust. With these, I know I can make it to Jerusalem. Now, show me the way."*

* * *

On a warm and sunny Roman afternoon, I took my first steps to Jerusalem. It was November 21, 2001.

My map indicated that the Via Flaminia, following the Tevere River, was the main road out of the city. It led into the heartland of Italy, stretching over the Apennine Mountains to the coastal city of Rimini. I would later learn that the Via Flaminia was the ancient road that carried pilgrims to and from Rome. The route was laden with history, and without knowing it or planning it, my steps would lead me through the towns and villages that made up this time-worn path.

I walked slowly, feeling the weight of my backpack straining my knees and ankles. My destination was a campsite about ten kilometers away. I resisted the temptation to check into a hostel because I wanted to directly face my deepest fear: that of being attacked, raped, and even killed. I was a woman walking alone on the open road and easy prey for any passing car. No one, me included, knew my exact route. No one was waiting for me at the end of the day or calling to make sure I arrived safely. If I disappeared, no one would know.

I camped that night, alone in my dark tent, without incident. When I awakened the next morning, it was to find the site being boarded up for the season that very day. Had I arrived one day later, the site would have been closed; one day earlier, I would not have witnessed this amazing coincidence. I understood profoundly then that I was not alone. My way was being facilitated by an invisible hand, and all I needed to do was walk.

My plan was to go northwards towards Venice, then down the other side of the Adriatic Sea and follow the Mediterranean coast towards Jerusalem. The first few days were difficult. This wasn't like walking the Camino with beautifully marked trails. I was on fast, busy roads with little or no shoulder. I walked facing traffic, and felt the wind and exhaust in my face all day. I couldn't find a natural rhythm and wasted a great deal of energy watching oncoming cars and trucks. People honked and angrily gestured for me to get off the road. I felt drained by the end of each day.

Conditions improved when I found quieter country roads. There, in the foothills of Monti Sabini, I began to relax. Orchards, vibrant with fall colors, extended as far as the eye could see. People worked the fields, harvesting the remains of the season, and balancing precariously on tall ladders to hand-pick olives off the branches. I breathed in the smell of ripe fruit and chuckled at the animated exchanges among the workers. In this world of heightened senses and connection with nature, I began to enjoy my walk once more.

I averaged between ten to fifteen kilometers a day, on terrain that was increasingly mountainous. I slept in hostels, convents and, one night, on the floor of a restaurant in front of a roaring fire. Some people invited me to coffee, curious to speak with the woman they had seen on the road. I had several cars drive by slowly, their male occupants offering me lifts and following me as I walked. I refused them politely but firmly, and continued purposefully ahead. These incidents were few but they scared me. On the whole, however, people were respectful and helpful when I asked.

My greatest obstacle was communication. To my surprise, most people I met only spoke Italian. I spoke English, passable French, some Arabic and a smattering of Spanish. The extent of my Italian was limited to what I had learned from popular television such as *ciao*, *grazie*, and *buongiorno*. Of course I knew words such as spaghetti, lasagna, and *vino*, so I was confident I wouldn't go hungry or thirsty. Whenever I met someone who spoke English, I asked them how to say basic phrases such as: my name is Mony. Is there a hostel here? Where is it? How many kilometers to the next town? I am walking to Jerusalem for peace. I wrote down these phrases and practiced them as I walked.

So I could order food and ask for directions, but not explain why I was walking. When I could explain, people either smiled or politely changed the conversation. I wanted them to embrace this walk, this noble idea of walking for peace, and felt terribly insecure when they didn't. I realized then the loneliness of this road I was walking, and wondered if I had made the right choice.

It was my fifth day, and I had stopped at a small café in the hilltop town of Nazzano. It had been an especially arduous day emotionally and my doubts were more debilitating than ever. I sipped my tea at the bar and dejectedly asked the bartender for the nearest hostel. An older gentleman sitting nearby moved closer and introduced himself as Franco.

"*Hablas español?*" he asked.

"*Si*," I replied excitedly, as if I had spoken Spanish my entire life.

"What are you doing here?" He enunciated in Spanish.

"I'm walking from Rome to Jerusalem for peace," I muttered.

Without warning, Franco's eyes began to water, and tears started trickling down his cheeks. I stared at him in shock, feeling the flow of my own tears. "Please, let me buy you lunch," he sniffed, wiping his face with a handkerchief and leading me by the hand to a table. "You must be tired, thirsty, hungry."

I acquiesced without thought, allowing this kind-hearted man to care for me. Franco reached across the table and lightly touched my hands. "I think what you are doing is tremendous and so important. The world needs thousands of people like you, following their hearts, trying to make a difference. Maybe some people think what you are doing is crazy, but pay no attention to them. Believe in yourself."

That day, Franco gave me the emotional sustenance I couldn't yet give myself. Remembering to always look within to fill my emotional needs would be one of the greatest challenges of my inner journey.

But for now, I was ready to move on. Alberto called soon after to say he was ready to join me. We agreed to meet in Rieti. I arrived there a few days later feeling a sense of accomplishment. I had only walked one hundred and twenty kilometers in twelve days; but I had done them by myself, in conditions that were quite unlike anything I had experienced before. If I had to, I now knew that I could continue to Jerusalem on my own.

3. Walking with Alberto

"Everything has been flowing so smoothly since I decided to join you," Alberto enthused, in my hostel room in Rieti. "A family gave me their tent and camping supplies to support our walk. Some books I sold gave me more money than I imagined. Even the trains and buses to get me here were all on time." Although I still harbored doubts, I was happy to see Alberto and to share the sometimes lonely road.

Finding my hostel too expensive, Alberto decided to look for other accommodations that night. We met later at a café. Alberto looked disheartened. "Hotels, like everything in Italy, are more expensive than I thought they would be," he confessed. "I have enough money for essentials like food, but I can't stay in hostels or eat in restaurants every day."

"So what are you going to do?" I asked.

"Since this is a pilgrimage, a spiritual way," Alberto replied, "I was thinking I could sleep in churches and monasteries. I met an old man on the Camino who had no money, and so called on the churches for help. They usually gave him food and shelter. I won't ask for food, money or even a bed, only for a roof over my head. I can sleep on the floor. If they refuse me, I can always sleep in my tent."

"I don't know..." I started skeptically.

"I know you're accustomed to sleeping in hostels," Alberto responded earnestly. "I don't want to take you away from that. Don't worry about me. I'll find my way."

I didn't like asking for help when I didn't need it; but I also couldn't picture myself in a warm bed knowing Alberto was sleeping on a cold floor somewhere. If I wanted to walk with Alberto, it was becoming clear that I needed to make certain concessions.

"Go back to your hostel," Alberto urged. "I'll find something on my own."

"Let me help you look," I offered.

"I will be fine," he reassured. "I'm receiving signs as we speak. I'm going to follow them to see where they lead me."

"What kinds of signs?" I asked, looking around.

"I can't explain them to you easily because they only make sense in my head," he responded, "in my way of seeing things, in the connections that they have with past experiences, with my intuition. I trust them, just like you trust your signs."

"What if I pay for your hostel tonight?" I insisted.

"Thank you, but no," Alberto retorted firmly. "I will find my own way." I reluctantly agreed.

An impatient hour later, Alberto called my room. "Where are you?" I asked, hearing merriment and laughter in the background.

"I'm in a Franciscan monastery about five kilometers from you," he replied happily.

"You sound like you're at a party," I said.

"No," Alberto chuckled. "The monks here are amazing. They love what we're doing. They gave me a room with a hot shower, and invited me to dinner with them. They told me that Franciscans usually help pilgrims; isn't that great? With all their monasteries in Italy, I think my problems are solved. How about you? Are you well tonight?"

I looked around my simple room, with my clothes scattered on the floor and the loaf of bread and some Parmesan cheese on the table; my dinner. "Oh, I'm fine," I responded casually. "Are we still meeting in the morning?"

"Of course," he laughed. "It's our first day of walking together. I wouldn't miss it."

I hung up the phone, wishing I was with him and wondering if I had too hastily dismissed his approach. As I prepared my backpack that evening, my mobile phone rang. It was a combination telephone and computer that also served as my diary. A distraught Hannah was on the line.

"Alberto needs to call home right away," she declared. "His father been diagnosed with terminal cancer. They don't expect him to live long."

I was stunned, unable to comprehend why such a terrible blow would happen on the eve of our walking together. I didn't know how to reach Alberto, and spent an anxious night trying to figure out how to break this difficult news the following morning.

* * *

I pulled Alberto to a quiet corner of the lobby. "Hannah called last night," I whispered. "Your father is very sick. You need to call home right away."

Alberto dropped his backpack on the floor, took my phone, and strode out the front doors. Through the windows, I saw him pacing up and down, occasionally stopping to look towards the heavens or some invisible point on the ground. His face spoke of the gravity of the situation. When he returned to the lobby, I braced myself for the worst.

"My father has been complaining of stomach pains for the last few weeks and losing weight," he said gravely, sitting beside me. "He went in for a checkup and they found the cancer. It's all over his body. They don't know if he has six days, or six months, to live." I held his hand, telling him how sorry I was. "My mother and brother want me to come home right away," he said. "They say they need me."

The lobby bustled with activity while Alberto and I sat insulated in our private bubble of turbulent emotions.

"Can I look at the map?" He finally asked. I handed it to him. "There's a big town called Terni about fifty kilometers north of here," he said. "We could be there in three days." I agreed it was possible.

Alberto examined the map a while longer, then neatly folded it and absently handed it to me. "I think I'd like to walk to Terni," he calmly announced, "and meditate on whether to return home. If I decide to leave, there are probably buses and trains that I could take from there."

I was surprised by his decision, expecting him to return to his family; but I said nothing. It was already late morning and we had a mountainous fifteen-kilometer day ahead. With backpacks in place, we started out the door. On December 5, 2001, fifteen days since starting this walk, Alberto and I took our first steps together.

We walked at a comfortable pace that Alberto encouraged me to set. Our route wound through the scenic hills and valleys of the Apennine Mountains, their peaks white with snow.

"Did you know that we're on the trails that St. Francis of Assisi used to walk?" Alberto asked, pulling up beside me on a quiet stretch of road. His face lit up when I asked him to tell me more. It was the first spark of light I had seen in him all day.

"He's my favorite saint," he enthused. "He abandoned the comfort of his privileged life to live in simplicity and follow what he believed to be God's calling. He was a mystic who saw God in everything, and who preached that man and all creatures, including the elements, were brothers. He's famous for his song of praise to Brother Sun and Sister Moon."

"How do you know so much about him?" I asked.

"When I was younger," he replied, "I wanted to be a priest. My mother had instilled me a love not so much for the Catholic Church, but for the figures of Mary and Jesus, who she taught me were like my best friends and confidants. For three years, I studied in a seminary in Salamanca, seven hundred kilometers away from my home in Cadiz. Then, I realized it wasn't for me. I was sixteen, and there were too many rules and restrictions, too many contradictions in what they were teaching me; and of course no girls, so I left."

We continued ever upwards, enjoying spectacular sights and brilliant weather. The terrain was challenging, but I was managing it better with a stick that I had found in a field. We rounded yet another uphill bend and stopped to catch our breaths.

"I think that's St. Francis," Alberto exclaimed. I looked at where he was pointing. Framed by the bluest sky and the greenest forest, a cluster of white marble statues sat poised atop a large grey rock. In the center, a figure stood with arms outstretched.

I followed an exuberant Alberto inside the gate. A monk, wearing what I would come to learn as the typical Franciscan attire of open-toed sandals and a brown robe cinched with a rope, came out to greet us. He confirmed that the statue was indeed that of St. Francis and that we were in the monastery of La Foresta, one of the main sanctuaries in the area where the Saint often retreated to pray and meditate. He led us on a tour of the peaceful grounds.

The monastery carried a lovely collection of Tau necklaces. I touched the Tau pendant I wore beside Alberto's eagle pendant, recalling this hand-carved gift from a friend on the Camino and his words that it symbolized brotherhood and service.

"This is the cross of St. Francis," the monk explained. "He traced it on himself before starting any task, painted it on the walls and doors of the places where he stayed, and used it as his signature. It's the defining symbol of Franciscans. We carve these pendants from the olive trees around us."

Alberto examined each Tau closely. "Knowing all this makes me feel even closer to St. Francis," he remarked, choosing one and gently, almost prayerfully, slipping it around his neck. "I feel honored to be wearing his cross," he proclaimed, smiling brilliantly. I returned his smile affectionately, happy to see his enthusiasm return and silently chuckling at the thought that we were beginning to look alike.

A fine mist descended near the end of the day, floating ever so lightly and blanketing the valley below. Perched atop one of the peaks was a quaint village that we were told had a Franciscan monastery. After learning so much about St. Francis, I looked forward to staying at his monasteries, places that I imagined to be infused with his special spirit. After one last hard climb, we arrived at the monastery door tired, hungry, and full of anticipation. A middle-aged monk answered our call and eyed us suspiciously. I tried not to be intimidated.

"*Noi siamo pellegrinos caminato a* Jerusalem for *la pace,*" I said, making the sign of the V with my fingers.

"*Necesitamos techo,*" Alberto added in Spanish, both of us moving our hands back and forth over our heads.

"We have food and *dinero,*" I continued. "*Per favore, ayudare?*"

I bristled under his mistrustful scrutiny, and fought the urge to turn and find a hostel. Alberto returned the monk's gaze directly, smiling gently. I'm not sure what happened in that silent exchange, but the monk opened the door and asked us to follow him. Through dark stone corridors, down a long flight of stairs to another dimly lit corridor we raced, finally stopping in a room filled with beds and blankets. The monk explained that washrooms and showers were down the hall, and then quickly excused himself.

I stood with Alberto in the large, cold room battling mixed emotions. I was grateful to have shelter but disappointed, even angry, at the monk's dismissive treatment. I noticed with disgust the mouse droppings that littered the floor and beds, and pointed them out to Alberto.

"The tourist demands," he reminded me, quoting a common Camino axiom. "The pilgrim gives thanks."

I shot him an impatient glance, grabbed my towel and change of clothing, and headed to the washroom, grateful to find it clean. Over the course of our five thousand kilometer journey, I would come to appreciate the luxury of that night. I showered quickly and came out, anticipating the same dinner invitation that Alberto had received in his monastery experience. I checked my bed carefully for any unwanted rodent gifts and, once satisfied there were none, sat and typed in my diary. Alberto similarly showered and returned to write in his diary.

An hour later, it was clear that no invitation to dinner was forthcoming. I pulled out my chocolate bar and almonds, and laid them on my bed. Alberto added his bread and cheese. We ate our pilgrim meal in silence, as I tried to swallow my disappointment.

"Have I made a mistake following Alberto's path?" I wondered.

4. An Unexpected Blow

Alberto and I sat in the abandoned police residence in Labro, our home for the evening, poring over the map of Mediterranean Europe. We were guests of the surprised but accommodating priest who not only brought us here, but entrusted us with the keys. We had beds, but no heating or running water. I tried to be the grateful pilgrim.

We were trying to estimate the time it would take us to get to Jerusalem. Walking both sides of the Adriatic Sea, and then cutting eastward through Greece and Turkey, then southwards through Syria and Lebanon, we estimated it to be five thousand kilometers. Averaging twenty kilometers a day, we thought we would make it in nine months. However, we reasoned that as our bodies became stronger, we could walk faster and so, averaging thirty kilometers a day, we could arrive in six months. We put away our map, confident in our calculations and ability to do it in that time. One year later, we would realize the futility of trying to plan a walk of this magnitude.

The following day found us rushing to get to Terni. The hurried pace left me with knotted leg muscles and trembling knees. Forced to stop in Marmore, ten kilometers outside Terni, we slept on the tile floor of the games room in the local church hall. We had heating, but ice-cold water flowing out of the taps. It was my second day without showering. I was grateful, but stinking.

I slept poorly, and dragged my weary muscles down the steep switchback roads into Terni. At the first church we found, we were asked to return later in the day, when the priest would be available. We used that time to replenish our food supplies, and to enjoy a lovely picnic in one of the ornate plazas.

Many people walked past us that sunny afternoon. Most ignored us, but I noticed the disdainful glances of others. With our backpacks, slightly soiled clothing, and less than perfectly kempt appearance, it was easy to mistake us for vagabonds. I felt my fear of ridicule rising to the surface, and wanted to scream, "Look, I'm normal. I'm doing this by choice," but there was no way to do so without looking even more foolish in their eyes. I kept quiet, trying to endure the bitterness of knowing that peoples' opinions mattered more than it should.

With the weather becoming increasingly cooler, we decided to seek shelter in the nearby train station. We sat at the café, inhaling too much second-hand smoke, and watched travelers come and go. Two men sat nearby, backpacks and guitar case at their feet. Their clothes were tattered and their appearance disheveled. They were chain-smoking, and I could smell the liquor from our table. They occasionally glanced over, but I averted my gaze. Alberto smiled at them. They greeted him and asked where we were from. I hoped he would give the briefest answer possible, and listened with dismay as he explained our walk. The two men excitedly brought their chairs to our table, eager to hear more. Fearing more than ever that I would be judged as one of them and not knowing how to handle this awkward situation, I leaned back in my chair and folded my arms across my chest.

"We travel from country to country," one of them said, absently petting the dog named Vagabond at his feet. His voice was hoarse and raspy, evidence of his years of heavy smoking and drinking. "I play the guitar and my friend here sells his paintings."

"Nice to meet you," I said, trying to keep the disdain out of my voice, certain that I wasn't pulling it off.

Alberto carried the conversation, speaking about the importance of following your dreams and living your truth. "You know, people look at me and think I'm a failure, a nobody," the guitar player said at one point. "I see them rushing around, all stressed out and worried about their lives, and I know they're not happy. Me, I'm doing exactly what I love to do. I'm on the street with my guitar and my songs. Some days I have money to eat, other days I don't. I always have enough, and never worry about what's going to happen tomorrow. I live in the moment. People call me a vagabond, but I'm a free man." Inhaling deeply on his cigarette, he asked, "So who's the failure?"

That encounter left a deep mark on me. I had sat in judgment of another, believing myself to be somehow superior, and behaved in the same way that, only hours earlier, I had accused others of behaving. I felt ashamed, realizing the depth of my judgments and the work that lay ahead in releasing them.

Alberto left to call his family, and returned a few short minutes later, his face ashen, his eyes bewildered. "My father died last night," he whispered, walking away.

I felt numb, unable to comprehend the magnitude or meaning of what had just happened. We wandered the streets aimlessly. The sun had begun to set and the evening air to turn frigid by the time we finally returned to call on the priest. Before I could even complete our introduction, he was already closing the door.

"Let's go to a hotel, please," I pleaded with Alberto. "It's my treat. We've had an emotional day and need to rest." A nod of the head was all I needed. Passersby pointed us to the nearest hotel where we found a room with two double-beds and the amenities one would expect of a three-star establishment. Alberto dropped his bag on the floor and crumpled onto the bed. I immediately went to shower, and watched with disgust the brown film that washed down the drain after three days without showering. The water from hand-washing my clothes was equally murky.

I walked out to find Alberto as I had left him. I hung my clothes on the radiator to dry, and Alberto eventually stood to shower. I ordered room service, and by the time it arrived, Alberto had come out of the shower looking refreshed, at least physically. We sat down to eat.

"My father was a good man," Alberto remarked gently, picking at his food, "shy, quiet, sensitive. He had great depth even though he said very little. I felt he was trapped in his life, like a bird in a cage, bound by circumstance. Growing up, I didn't understand him and so built an invisible wall between us. I think he believed we deserved a better father, but that wasn't true. I knew how much he loved us by the way he looked at us. As I started to explore my spirituality, I knew I needed to tell my father that I loved and respected him. One day, the words flowed out of me like a river. I told him I loved him and was proud to be his son; that he was a good father; and that I understood him and his choices better now, looking at him through the eyes of an adult."

I looked away, tears filling my eyes.

"My father was speechless," Alberto continued. "He stared at me, his face full of emotion. I hugged him. He held me tightly and we cried for a long time. It was the most intimate and sincere moment I ever shared with my father." Alberto's voice cracked and he stopped speaking. I placed my hand on his shoulder. "I never would have imagined he would be gone three months later," he whispered. "I'm so happy I said those words to him. They liberated us."

I smiled at the tender description of his father, and placed my hand on his shoulder.

"I know it's no coincidence that we spoke that day," he said, squeezing my hand. "My father is walking with me, and is here right now listening to these words. I feel him closer than ever." He smiled at me wistfully. "I've decided to continue to Jerusalem with you." I stared at him in astonishment.

"Are you sure?" I asked hesitantly.

"It's the best tribute I can give my father," he replied. "I know he would want me to follow my dreams."

From the little that I knew about Alberto then, his decision should not have come as the surprise that it did. When we had met on that fateful day in Finisterre, at the end of the world in Spain, I only knew him as a pilgrim, a seeker as I was, someone trying to live a life with meaning and put into practice his spiritual beliefs, although I didn't yet know the depth of them.

He had met Hannah while walking the final stretch of the Camino from Santiago to Finisterre, a section I had decided to skip, preferring to take the bus. I had walked most of the Camino with Hannah and we had become close friends. She was strong, funny, and infinitely kind. We got along famously, the tall blond walking alongside the short dark-haired woman. I was thrilled to see her so happy in Finisterre and to know that she had found love on the Camino.

Alberto had moved to Bonn, Germany soon after their meeting to pursue their burgeoning romance. Their joy was evident when I met them there, on my way to Rome to begin my walk. They spoke of their future and the many dreams they hoped to realize. I glimpsed then the depth of Alberto's spiritual beliefs. He had read many of the same books as I had, and been influenced by the same teachers. I saw that he prized his freedom above all else, the need to continue exploring his spirituality, even while in a relationship. He revealed that it had been difficult for him to break out of the expectations that family and friends had of him, and to remain true to his spiritual path. He had demonstrated that when he left Hannah, and was now doing the same thing again.

5. Messengers

Darkness descended. Eerie shadows started playing in the thick forest that surrounded us, and the wind, stiff and cold, whistled ceaselessly. I shivered. "We never should have listened to that woman," I complained to Alberto. "To these Italians, everything is ten minutes away."

We were now too far away from San Gemine to turn back and so continued ever higher along the sinewy trail that we were assured would lead us to the *ermita*, a supposedly enchanting hermitage with a welcoming priest named *Don*[1] Bernardino. *"This was a crazy idea, chasing after a hermit,"* I thought to myself. *"We should've stayed in the bar."*

We struggled to remain on the narrow, poorly-marked path. The occasional faded sign assured us that we still were. At times we walked on compacted earth; at others, rock outcroppings, fallen branches, and tree trunks. The trail was so steep in some places that when I tried to stop, I began to fall backwards, the weight of my backpack pushing me down the hill. More than once, Alberto had to grab my hand to pull me up because my legs were giving out from under me. I felt terribly frightened, but put on a brave face so as not to worry an already-worried Alberto. I assured him I could make it, even though I wasn't sure I could. Even if we had wanted to camp out, the steep incline now made that impossible.

After what felt like an eternity, the trail finally leveled off. The trees disappeared, revealing a large clearing and what looked like a small medieval fortress in the distance. Its high stone walls guarded several small buildings, one of which housed a glimmering light. We whooped in exhausted exhilaration and hurried as quickly as our weary legs would allow.

We arrived at a gnarled wooden door and rang the rustic hand bell. No one answered. We rang again, this time more forcefully. Still, no one answered. We rang and knocked, yelling *"Buona Sera"*[2] at the top of our lungs; but the howling wind carried our voices away and the door remained firmly closed. We circled the building in search of other doors,

---

[1] A term of respect used to address priests
[2] Good evening

but all to no avail. I leaned my head against the wood door, defeated and hoarse.

From around the corner, several dogs bounded out to us. Each was a different shade of white and, in the darkness, looked like smiling angels. They brushed up against us and reached their heads into our hands. We stroked their backs and began repeating the word "Bernardino", the name of the hermit, hoping they would lead us to him; but they seemed more interested in frolicking with each other than in helping two desperately cold pilgrims.

With dogs in tow, Alberto and I walked around the building once more, now looking for dog entrances. We couldn't find those either.

"You go back to the main door and keep ringing the bell," Alberto suggested. "I'm going to throw some stones at the window of the room with the light on."

"You're going to give whoever is in there a heart attack," I admonished.

"Do you have any better ideas?" he shot back.

I wearily shook my head and sauntered back to my post. After several more bouts of yelling and ringing, the wood door slowly creaked open. I stepped back in surprise. From the darkness, a figure emerged and stood in the doorway. At the same time, Alberto appeared alongside me, grinning broadly.

"*Buona Sera*," the older man said in greeting, smiling in amused curiosity. He was dressed in well-worn Franciscan robes cinched with a rope, and open-toed sandals. His gentle presence and kind eyes put me immediately at ease, but I couldn't help but chuckle at the shock of frizzy hair and the image of Albert Einstein it evoked.

"We are pilgrims," I began, but he interrupted me, gesturing for us to come inside. We followed the presumed Father Bernardino to an inner courtyard while explaining that we were walking to Jerusalem for peace. "*Gerusalemme?*" He exclaimed. "*Benne, benne.*"

We continued through dark corridors until we arrived at a simple wooden door.

"No lights. No water," he explained, entering the room and lighting several candles. "When finish, come eat," motioning with his hands for us to eat.

With our sincerest thanks, Alberto followed Father Bernardino to get water from the well to flush the toilet, while I lit a few more candles and explored our surroundings. In the small kitchen where I stood were an antiquated gas stove, sink, and well-worn cabinets that I saw were stocked with mismatched plates, cups, and cutlery. With candle in hand, I walked into the adjacent room and felt as if I had stepped into a cave. The ceiling was low and domed, the white stone walls marked with tiny niches and crevices that delicately housed the remains of partially melted candles. Rustic chairs, end tables, and several small beds with blankets completed the intimate space.

I lit whatever candles I could find and placed them in the niches. Soft shadows danced along the walls. I felt embraced by a warm, loving energy that defied words. My entire being stilled. Although we had just walked several challenging kilometers, my body felt strangely energized.

I heard Alberto thanking Father Bernardino, and then cleaning up in the washroom. I quickly refreshed my body with wet wipes, imagining how cold mountain water would feel. "That bathroom is pretty primitive too," Alberto joked, coming into the room. "By the way, the water is freezing." I laughed with him, and finished putting on my clean socks.

"Your idea to throw stones at the window was a good one after all," I teased. Alberto chuckled.

"I was going to throw the stones like I told you, but then thought I might break the glass and frighten him even more. Luckily, I found an elevated spot not far from the window and stood there, waving, praying he would see me. He eventually did. I thought he would be terrified but no, he just stared at me with amusement. I put on my best smile and waved again. This time, he smiled back and motioned for me to wait. I'm still amazed at how calm he was."

Dinner was on the table by the time we arrived at our host's home, and we savored every mouthful of the steaming hot food. The intimate space, similar in feeling to our cave, was lined with bookshelves housing volumes with thick, leather binding, and a layer of dust that begged to be blown off. Stacks of opened books and letters had been pushed off to the side of the table to make space for our food.

In addition to Italian, Father Bernardino spoke German, having studied theology there. Alberto's rudimentary German, combined with Italian and sign language, allowed us to explain more fully what we were doing, all to his growing amazement. Despite the difficulty of communication, we understood each other perfectly.

Pointing at our necklaces, he said, "You both wear the Tau. Tau has a long and mystical history." An inexplicable rush of energy coursed through me, and I felt every hair on my body stand on end.

"The Tau is sacred letter," Father Bernardino continued in his mix of languages. "It is a sign of God. All letters are sacred and a sign of God, but the last letter, such as the Hebrew Tau and the Greek Omega, is the most important. Those who carry the Tau are blessed and protected on their journey. They are messengers of God."

He pulled out a Bible from the stack of books on the table, flipped through it and then pointing to a passage, said, "You see here, in Revelations, it speaks about the chosen ones who are servants of God, a force for good in the world. They carry a sign on their forehead. It is God's name, the Tau."

Alberto had commented during our walk that he believed the Universe was using us as instruments to bring whatever message needed to be delivered to the people who crossed our path. I agreed that we would be touching individuals with our message of peace, once we figured out what it was, but I saw it as a by-product of the larger reach that our message would have. I saw people being brought into my life to guide me, but never considered myself as a sign for someone else, or as having anything to offer them. I did not feel special enough to be a chosen one, much less a messenger, and told Alberto so.

"When I say we are messengers," he responded, "I'm not talking about Mony and Alberto's message. We're more like the delivery guys. The message comes from the Universe. The only thing that makes us special is our willingness to do this work."

My sleep that night was deep and restful, and I awakened feeling refreshed, as if the arduous walk had never happened. Alberto commented that he felt surprisingly revitalized as well. We couldn't explain why. After a hearty breakfast, Father Bernardino offered to accompany us back to the main road, and we accepted. Recalling my Lebanese heritage, he stopped to point out the curious presence of a Lebanese cedar that was planted there centuries earlier by Italian sailors returning from that land, adding that the town of San Gemine was named for a beloved Syrian monk who lived there.

With the dogs jumping around us, Father Bernardino led us down a wide, well-marked trail that he said was the main way to the hermitage, and marveled at how we were able to find him walking a path that was long ago abandoned.

Walking alongside him, I couldn't help but feel that something had conspired to bring us to this lone place high in the mountains for a purpose we couldn't divine, but that I was certain was somehow predestined.

At the base of the mountain, Father Bernardino turned to us. With eyes watering and filled with the tenderness of a parent gazing at his children, he said, "I have a weekly meeting in town that I never miss, but for some reason last night, it was unexpectedly cancelled. I see now that it was because we needed to meet."

When he placed his hands on our heads and began to pray in Italian, I felt as if we were receiving a blessing from the highest heavens, not merely for us, but for this path of peace we had chosen to walk.

6. The Message of Peace

The ancient Via Flaminia carried us along the picturesque hills and valleys of the Umbria region, passing through towns such as Acquasparta, Massa Martana, and Bevagna. We were welcomed into every church and monastery where we called, and gratefully accepted whatever was offered, from wooden tables in unheated halls to warm beds with blistering showers. All now formed part of the way of peace. Although I was becoming more comfortable in asking for help, I still battled the feeling that I was taking something I didn't need from people who I sensed assumed we were devout Catholics.

"We're pilgrims walking for peace," Alberto reminded me more than once. "We share the same intentions as the Church: peace, love, brotherhood. We both believe in a loving higher intelligence. I see no conflict there." I wished I could see it that way.

In Massa Martana, full Franciscan hospitality was on display. In addition to private rooms, we were also invited to dinner with the monks. It was our first hot meal in days, and I relished it. The conversation flowed as easily as the food and wine, and I felt my usual reservations melting under their caring attention and enthusiasm for our pilgrimage. Still, I held back, not knowing how they would receive my open spirituality, and not wanting to lie or offend them.

Alberto, however, seemed to have no such reservations and passionately discussed his spiritual beliefs. I listened with interest and learned a great deal, but rarely participated. At one point, Alberto asked about a cross hanging on the wall depicting a hand-painted figure of Jesus surrounded by many drawings that filled up the cross. The style reminded me of the icon paintings of my own Greek Orthodox Church.

"That's the cross of St. Damian," one of the monks replied. "While praying to it, St. Francis received his mission from God to rebuild the church. At first, he thought it was to rebuild the chapel of St. Damian, but later understood it meant to rebuild the Catholic Church of that time. It influenced him greatly, but the Tau is the cross of St. Francis."

"I love that painted cross," Alberto said. "It's the only one I've seen that doesn't show Jesus suffering or dead. He has his arms open wide to the world, embracing it. I think there has been too much focus on his suffering and not enough on his message, a message that he preached and lived. Yes, he died for it, but I believe he wants us to remember him for his life, not his death, and certainly not to spend our lives feeling guilty or unworthy because of what was done to him. He was a courageous man, a revolutionary even, not a poor victim."

I stared at Alberto in horror. I had never heard him express his Christian views; I didn't even know he had any since our discussions usually centered on the spiritual or mystical. We had never delved into religion, and I assumed that he had discarded his Catholic teachings. I didn't have any formal religious training, but I didn't need any to understand that what he was saying was controversial. In the silence that followed, I braced myself for the rebuke that I was certain was coming. To my surprise, most around the table were smiling.

"You sound a great deal like St. Francis," the Superior, the monk in charge, said approvingly. "He too had many views that shook the foundations of the Church of his time. He understood that love, not man-made laws, was Jesus' greatest teaching."

The conversation continued well into the night, leaving me with much to consider. Although I respected all religious views, I wanted to keep religion far from my walk for peace, fearing that any mention of the word God or Jesus would marginalize us and jeopardize the message I was still formulating. I didn't want to be labeled a religious zealot, and hoped that Alberto felt the same way.

* * *

Alberto and I relaxed into a comfortable routine. After an unhurried breakfast, we began walking at around 8:30 AM. We took several short breaks, and stopped before dark. I walked in front so that I could see the road ahead. We decided our route together but I carried the map, feeling a certain security in having it with me. And even though we spoke Italian equally poorly, I led our conversation with the priests, feeling greater confidence in my ability to express myself than in Alberto's, who to me appeared timid. We also reasoned that a woman asking for help would be more likely to receive it than a man.

On the recommendation of Father Bernardino, we stopped at the hotel-monastery in Santa Maria degli Angeli, on the doorsteps of Assisi. We were treated as honored guests and given an apartment with two bedrooms and an eat-in kitchen. After a long hot shower and a pasta dinner that we jointly prepared, Alberto and I sat at the table, updating our diaries.

"So what do you think about carrying a sign for peace?" Alberto asked.

We had spoken about carrying such a sign from the day we met, and had even bought bright yellow, stick-on paper in Rieti to cut out the letters. I wanted to, but hesitated. Partly, it was the emotions of the first few days with Alberto, but perhaps more honestly, the fear of announcing to the world my beliefs about a peace I was still trying to figure out.

"Meeting *Don* Bernardino helped me realize that it was time," Alberto continued. "We are messengers of peace. Every day, hundreds of people see us walking along the side of the road. Just imagine how they can be inspired. Plus, tomorrow, we're walking into Assisi, the City of Peace."

"I agree the timing is good," I replied, "but I don't want to tell people we're messengers. It sounds presumptuous. I mean, who are we? I only know that I want my message to be simple and direct, something that people can connect with. I'm walking to Jerusalem for peace. That's my contribution, but each person can do whatever they feel. I want people to realize they have the power to change their world; that they don't have to do big things or wait for others to do it for them. Any act that comes from the heart creates peace. It begins within."

"I agree," Alberto said. "Outer peace is the natural outcome of inner peace. One thought of peace or act of kindness produces a ripple effect, like dropping a stone in water. I'm walking for peace, not just in Jerusalem but in the world, inner and outer. To me, peace is only a consequence of something much greater; love. It's when you have love that you will have lasting peace. In truth, we are walking for love."

"There is no way I'm going out there with a sign saying that I'm walking for love," I retorted firmly. "Maybe we should put flowers in our hair too. No. This is already hard enough with the word peace."

"I know," Alberto teased. "I'm not ready to carry that message either, especially with flowers in my hair."

"Good," I joked. "Because I was prepared to leave you right here." Then, after a pause, I added, "I want my sign to say that I'm walking to Jerusalem for peace."

"I want mine to say that I'm walking for peace, nothing more," Alberto responded.

"Agreed," he said, and we shook hands.

Alberto now began the pain-staking process of drawing each letter on the yellow paper and cutting it out. He peeled off the paper backing and stuck each letter accordingly onto the plastic rain protectors that covered our backpacks. Two hours later, Alberto stepped back and proudly examined his work. In large, impossible-to-miss letters, my sign said *Camminando verso Gerusalemme per la Pace*, while his said *Camminando per la Pace*.

"How do you feel?" Alberto asked.

"Nervous," I replied. "They're pretty big letters. It's one thing to talk about peace and quite another to be a walking bill-board."

"All we need to do is walk," he affirmed. "We can always take the signs off."

I was opening myself up to the world, and didn't know how I was going to handle criticism. I usually handled it poorly, but hoped that, for this way of peace, I would do so with tolerance, patience and, above all, the peace I was proclaiming.

7. The Path of Peace

The morning traffic to Assisi was heavy and crawled alongside us. I glanced at the occasional car, trying to gauge peoples' reactions to our signs. I saw many looks of confusion, and plenty of double-takes. A few drivers honked in support, and occasionally waved or gave us the thumbs up. Those early shows of support encouraged me to keep carrying the signs, for now.

We wound our way through the maze of narrow, cobble-stone roads that made up this medieval town, searching for a convent that we had been directed to. We were warmly received there and given ample accommodations in what felt like a desolate place. Anticipating the magical in this City of Peace, Alberto and I decided to stroll around and be open to it. The dark clouds, persistent rains, and closed storefronts made our surroundings feel more ominous than magical, but we persisted for several hours before finally concluding it was not to be found there. With little else to do in town, we resolved to leave the next day.

We were surprised to meet another guest the following morning and more so to discover that she spoke English. Our conversation with this American woman moved very quickly into the realm of the personal, where she revealed that she was at a cross-road in her life, trying to determine her next steps. Alberto and I spoke a great deal about our respective lives, the choices we've had to make, and the rewards and fears of following our hearts along this path of peace. She thanked us for our candor, adding that she believed our meeting was providential and that it had helped her.

"We are messengers," Alberto chirped once we had said our goodbyes to her and returned to our room. I didn't answer, preferring to occupy myself with the booklet she had given us detailing all the monasteries in Italy.

"Alberto, there are fifty thousand Liras here," I exclaimed. "That's almost forty dollars."

"I saw it when she gave us the book," Alberto replied.

"Why didn't you say anything?" I accused.

"She obviously didn't want us to see it then," he replied cautiously.

"We don't need the money," I declared without thinking. Alberto gazed at me intently.

"We can use it for emergencies," he suggested.

"How much more am I supposed to concede?" I silently screamed. *"First, calling on the Church for a help I didn't need. Now, accepting money. I've gone from being an independent woman walking for peace to a poor pilgrim seeking refuge. All because of Alberto."*

"OK, you keep it," I said, handing him the bills.

We packed our bags and left the convent in awkward silence, speaking only to agree to visit the tomb of St. Francis before leaving Assisi. We found it under the main Basilica. It took a moment for my eyes to adjust to the dim lighting, but the intimacy of the place immediately embraced me. Few decorations adorned the natural stone walls and, as had occurred at the hermitage with *Don* Bernardino, the low domed ceilings made me feel as if I had stepped into a cave. It seemed the perfect setting for someone who spent so much time in them.

Strangely, a part of me wanted to giggle. I had expected to feel solemn and respectful, and so was surprised by the happiness that swept through me. I felt the humility of St. Francis, a man who seemed to know his place in the Universal order and who lived in harmony with it. Above all, I felt peace.

I pulled out a postcard that I had bought the day before, and that bore the words of the peace prayer of St. Francis. In a voice barely above a whisper, I mouthed the words.

"Lord, make me an instrument of your peace.
Where there is hatred, let me sow love.
Where there is injury, pardon.
Where there is doubt, faith.
Where there is despair, hope.
Where there is darkness, light.
Where there is sadness, joy.

O Divine Master, grant that I may not so much seek
To be consoled, as to console.
To be understood, as to understand.
To be loved, as to love.

28

For it is in giving, that we receive.
It is in pardoning that we are pardoned.
It is in dying that we are born to eternal life."

Tears filled my eyes. I felt the power of those words, inspired words that expressed so beautifully the state of being I longed for; words that, with each breath, swept away confusion and created space for this peace to blossom.

* * *

We took a secondary road out of Assisi, finding the main highway too dangerous for walking. A sign declared that we were now on the Franciscan Path of Peace, the path that St. Francis used to get to Gubbio, site of the legend of the wolf. I was amazed by this coincidence, and as we walked this path, I asked Alberto about this legend.

"It's probably one of the best-known stories involving St. Francis," he explained. "It had been a harsh winter, and Gubbio was being terrorized by a wolf that often attacked the townspeople. St. Francis found the wolf in the forest and told him that he understood that he was hungry, but that it was wrong to attack people, offering to have them feed him on the condition that the wolf agreed to never again attack any animal or human. It is said that when St. Francis held out his hand, the wolf bowed his head and placed his paw in the offered hand. Brother Wolf went on to live in Gubbio among the people. He never harmed a living thing and even protected the town when it needed it. The people grew to love the wolf and deeply mourned him when he died."

"It's a nice story," I remarked.

"I especially love the message it coveys," Alberto added. "Fear saw the wolf as a monster and kept the conflict alive. Love saw him as a brother in need and embraced him. Love is the greatest healer."

I smiled at the almost child-like way Alberto had of explaining things and, at the same time, the profundity of his words.

The trail that day was splendid, leading us along gently-rolling hills and through forests, orchards, and olive groves, all lightly covered with snow. Despite the bone-chilling wind, a magical feeling pervaded the air that made walking almost effortless. It was a marvelous gift that I couldn't help but feel was given us by the saint himself.

We continued the following day past Valfabbrica towards a hermitage that we were told was in the area. The day was long and the road lonely. I began to wonder if we were lost when, once again, we fortuitously came upon the Franciscan Path of Peace. Crunchy leaves replaced hard asphalt, the sounds of nature that of modernity. The setting sun cast a warm glow on the few leaves brave enough to weather the winter cold. I could see my breath and feel the sweat down my back, but was thoroughly enjoying our trek through the woods. We finally saw it; a lovely stone building perched atop a simple plain, with the surrounding hills and fiery vestiges of the setting sun as its backdrop.

We excitedly approached, and knocked on the front door. An austere-looking man dressed in black hooded robes peered suspiciously at us. In the descending darkness, he looked downright menacing. I put on a smile, hoping that my face didn't betray my nervousness, and began to explain our needs.

"Are you Catholics?" he demanded.

"Well, I was baptized in the Greek Orthodox Church," I stammered.

"I was raised in a Catholic family," Alberto responded amiably. "Today, however, I have an open viewpoint and believe that all paths and religions lead to one God."

"Yes, one God, but there is only one Jesus Christ," he retorted indignantly. I shot Alberto a cautionary glance, knowing that in the balance of his answer hung our fate for the night, and whether or not we would be sleeping outside. Alberto smiled indulgently and in a conciliatory tone responded, "Yes, there is."

The priest's gaze barely softened at this response, and I wondered if he even heard that we were walking for peace. He marched past us, indicating for us to follow him, to a beautifully renovated stone building near the hermitage. He opened the front door and turned on the lights. I stood in the rustic, spacious kitchen, marveling at the orderliness and cleanliness of everything that surrounded me, especially the bathroom. We had heating and hot water, and the large bedroom was filled with single beds and blankets.

"There is food in the cupboards," the priest announced formally. "Use what you need."

He walked away before we could say anything, only to return with jars of preserves, bread, cheese, and fruit. I no longer knew what to think of him and invited him to dine with us as a sign of our gratitude.

"I am a hermit," he affirmed, a hint of a smile emerging on his lips. "I eat alone."

"But we've stayed with another hermit, and he ate with us," Alberto persisted gently.

"Really?" he asked. "With whom?"

"*Don* Bernardino," I responded.

"Bah," he choked out, waving his hands dismissively, "he's not a real hermit." I hoped Alberto would stop insisting because I felt no desire to spend more time than necessary with this prickly man.

"By the way," he said, clearly trying to control his emotions and to sound pleasant, "there are some books on the bookshelf that explain how to be a good pilgrim. I encourage you to read them. Good night."

He left once again, leaving us bewildered. Alberto and I poked around curiously, opening cupboards and drawers. In the bedroom closet, we saw clean, fresh-smelling sheets.

"Do you think he would mind us sleeping on the sheets?" Alberto asked.

"I'm sure that's what they're there for," I replied, placing a set on the bed. "He didn't say we couldn't."

We ate well that night and, under the warm soft sheets and blankets, slept peacefully. In the morning, we made the beds, packed our clothes, and went to say our goodbyes. We found the monk in front of the church, in a seemingly pleasant mood, and thanked him for his hospitality.

"Did you sleep in your sleeping bags?" he asked.

We explained that we had showered the night before and left the used sheets folded on a chair. He shook his head angrily, his pursed lips and hard face showing his displeasure. He rushed to the gate, opened it and stood aside like a sentry. I walked past him, grumbling a "thank you." Alberto stopped in front of him and held out his hand.

"Thank you again for your hospitality," Alberto said with more warmth and humanity than I could imagine possible muster at that moment.

It was barely perceptible, but the hermit's face softened. He returned Alberto's gaze and momentarily held it. His lips parted in a faint smile, and he reached for Alberto's hand. "You are welcome," he replied gently.

"I'm amazed at how nicely you treated him," I remarked, once out of earshot.

"I've known people like him," Alberto replied pensively, "who are trapped in their ideas of right and wrong, of how things should be. They often turned out to be wonderful human beings once I got to know them, and have taught me not to judge so quickly what I see on the surface. It's not a lesson I've mastered, but I feel more compassion than anger towards them."

Intellectually, of course, I agreed with him but was finding it difficult not to have expectations of priests because, to me, their calling carried an obligation to help. I had judged this one and dismissed him when he didn't live up to my expectations, in the same way that he had dismissed us when we weren't the perfect pilgrims of his ideals. I admired Alberto for having the courage at that moment to seek that man's humanity, to connect with his heart. Just as St. Francis did with the wolf. On the Franciscan Path of Peace to Gubbio that day, I renewed my resolve to see beyond appearances and act from that place of love.

8. Christmas Angels

We spent an uneventful evening in Gubbio, on the floor of the church hall, and pushed ever deeper into the Apennine Mountains. Bitter cold, wind and snow became our steady companions, along with increasingly more challenging climbs. I wore all my layers. A few days earlier, Alberto and I had shipped some of our camping supplies home, but kept Alberto's two-person tent in case of an emergency. With our lighter backpacks and stronger bodies, we climbed with greater ease.

We pressed on past Scheggia and towards Cantiano, always seeming to find the Via Flaminia, the ancient pilgrim's road. I sometimes wondered if we were walking it, or it was walking us, secretly conspiring to bring us to where we needed to be, not where we wanted to go. In Cantiano, we awaited the priest's arrival at the church. As had become our custom, we left our backpacks near the entrance with the signs facing out, so that people could read the message.

Excited giggles rang throughout the church as a group of adolescent children approached, asking if we were the ones walking to Jerusalem. We answered that we were.

"How many kilometers a day do you walk? What do you eat? Where do you sleep? Don't you get tired? You must be so strong!" Their squeals of delight grew with every answer and reverberated off the stone walls.

A girl of about ten, with shoulder-length hair and saucer-like brown eyes, inched closer. I was drawn to her eyes. "Are you Christians?" she whispered, gazing at me intently, then at Alberto.

My mind raced but could not find a response that would not disappoint the expectant eyes staring back at me. I looked at Alberto, and saw his face reflect the same struggle. After what seemed an eternal silence, Alberto smiled affectionately at the girl and said, "Yes, we are."

"I knew it," she enthused.

The priest finally arrived and gently shooed away the gleeful mob. We followed our friendly host to our lodgings for the evening. As we settled into the sparse room, I asked Alberto why he told the girl we were Christians.

"She was looking at me so trustingly and with so much faith," he replied, "that I couldn't say no. How do I tell her that peace—that love—transcends all religions? That in some way I feel Christian, but also

Buddhist, Muslim, and Jewish because we all share the same intentions for peace and believe in a Higher Intelligence. I saw it in your face too. You didn't want to disappoint her either."

"I just didn't know what to say," I exhaled in frustration.

We rolled out our sleeping bags on top of the cots and turned the heater on full-force on this especially cold night. I crawled into my sleeping bag with all my clothes on including hat, scarf and double socks. Alberto did the same in the cot beside me.

"Are we lying if we say we're Christian?" he mused. "What does it mean to be Christian anyway? If it's to admire Jesus as a teacher and to connect with his message, then I can't say I'm lying."

"But you don't follow his teachings exclusively," I clarified. "You've also read other spiritual texts and agree with some of their beliefs too. Technically, we can say we're Christians because we're baptized, but it's not the whole truth. I'm trying so hard not to be labeled, and now even children are doing it."

"But we're not introducing ourselves as Christians or Catholics," Alberto replied.

"I know, but I feel they're assuming we are," I said. "If we're going to keep asking the Church for help, then we need to find a way to clarify all this."

"Introducing ourselves as non-Christians is no closer to the truth either," Alberto responded. "That little girl was trying to see that we weren't different from her, and she did it in the only way she knew how. How would it have helped her if I said that I am a free spiritual thinker?" I didn't answer. Inhaling deeply, Alberto added,

"I don't have a formula, Mony. I'm trying to do the best I can in every moment, to listen to my heart because that's where I believe wisdom resides."

* * *

The streets glowed with colorful Christmas lights. Carols rang out from around every corner, the familiar music now put to Italian lyrics. It was all so beautiful, and made me miss my family and friends even more. I had always found a way to get home for Christmas no matter where I was, but this year I wouldn't. I imagined my Mom baking up a storm weeks in advance, and my Dad preparing all my favorite Lebanese dishes. I imagined my sisters and brother gathered at home, having drinks, and opening gifts at midnight, a left-over tradition from our childhood when we couldn't wait for Christmas morning.

I saw that Alberto too was melancholy, his father undoubtedly on his mind. We didn't speak much during this time, but occasionally reassured each other that we were doing the right thing in continuing to walk. As if sensing our loneliness and need, the Universe kept bringing people into our path to lift our spirits and remind us that we were not alone.

Goodwill accompanied us wherever we went. People invited us into cafés for a warm drink or to offer words of encouragement. Some even gave us wine and *panettone*, an Italian Christmas cake, as gifts. Something had clicked, and made those magical days of walking unforgettable.

We pressed on past Acqualagna and Urbino, and were making good time to spend Christmas Eve in the village of San Salvatore; but for some reason that day, our map did not match the road signs and we ended up lost in the mountains for several hours before finally finding the main road again. My feet and shins ached terribly, so we decided to stop in the nearest town, Coriano.

We were surprised to find the priest's office filled with people. Everyone greeted us politely, but curiosity was etched all over their faces. The crowd slowly thinned, leaving only a middle-aged couple who smiled warmly at us. We returned their smiles and greeted them, but the exchange ended there. The priest re-emerged and asked how he could help us. We stated our needs. The priest apologized that he could only offer a cold room in the church hall but that we were welcome to use it. We accepted.

The smiling couple stood and eagerly began speaking with the priest. It was rapid-fire Italian and I had a difficult time understanding them, but it clearly pertained to us because they kept looking over at us. The priest finally said, "*Benne, benne,*" before leading them into his office and closing the door. When they came out again, the young couple asked us to follow them.

"Please, we would like you to stay in our home this Christmas Eve," the woman said.

I quickly controlled the tears that threatened to spill over and thanked them. "*What is wrong with me?*" I thought. "*I need to get a grip on my emotions or I won't make it to Jerusalem.*"

Our generous hosts, named Seraphino and Loretta, drove us the short distance to their home. "This is an apartment that we normally rent in the summer," Seraphino explained upon our arrival, leading us to a side door, while Loretta entered the main house.

In the darkness, we stood in an unfurnished living room anchored by a fireplace. I saw light switches, but no fixtures. A door led to a small kitchenette and another door led to a hallway that I imagined had more rooms.

"I am sorry there is no heat or hot water," Seraphino apologized, "but I will bring you some wood for the fireplace. I will also bring in a light. We can move the beds in here so you can keep warm, and you can wash up in our home."

Seraphino and Alberto left to bring in the firewood. I had been holding in my tears since meeting them, and now I finally had a few moments alone. Overwhelmed on all levels, I dropped to my knees and began to weep.

"*Dear God, thank you. Thank you for leading us to these beautiful people. Thank you for opening their hearts and allowing their kindness to shine upon two strangers on this cold Christmas Eve. Thank you, thank you, thank you.*"

I heard the men coming up the stairs and quickly stood and wiped my tears. Seraphino handed me some candles to light, and then busied himself with starting a fire. Alberto hooked up a small lamp and helped Seraphino bring in two cots from another room. By the time the preparations were finished, we had a comfortable, warm, and inviting space.

"Dinner is ready," Seraphino said. "Please join us."

I silently followed the men, hoping I could hold it together for the evening. We brought a bottle of wine and *panettone* that had been given us, and soon we were sitting at a cozy kitchen table, filled with delicious foods and aromas, part of a family, hearing words that we would grow to love during our time in Italy, "*mangea, mangea,*" meaning "eat, eat."

I did manage to control my emotions that evening, but the love and caring that we received that magical night has remained with me to this day. I will forever remember Loretta and Seraphino, our Christmas angels.

9. Extra Ordinary People

Christmas Day finally found us in San Salvatore, a short ten kilometers from Coriano, accompanied by the same good cheer that had marked this holiday. Even more drivers stopped their cars to greet us. Housewives and children came out of their homes to wish us a safe journey, many offering us a hot drink. I floated into town, half expecting a welcome parade. A kind-looking man informed us that the priest had already left, so we explained our needs to him.

"Oh, you must go to San Lorenzo," he enthused. "There is a wonderful priest there called *Don* Giovanni. I'm sure he will help you."

We examined our map. San Lorenzo was on the way to Rimini, and only about two kilometers from where we were. We had not even considered it, thinking it a tiny village and unlikely to even have a church. We decided to go there.

The sun was brilliant, its warm rays inviting us to slow down. I did, trailing behind Alberto, enjoying the act of walking without rushing to arrive. The country lane snaked among fields long ago harvested, and eventually deposited us at the church steps. There, we learned that Father Giovanni would return later that evening, and were encouraged to wait at a nearby bar. Spotting phone booths, we decided to call our families.

"Hi, Mo," my mother squealed. "It's so nice to hear your voice. Where are you now?"

I updated her on our whereabouts and assured her that I was safe, healthy, and eating well; her main concerns. I elaborated on the many kindnesses that had been visited upon us, and conveniently ignored the more difficult experiences. I didn't want to make her more worried than I knew she already was.

"I've told some people about your walk, is that all right?" She asked.

"Of course," I laughed.

"Well," she continued hesitantly, "some people think you're in a religious cult and have been brain-washed into doing this."

"I'm not part of any religious cult," I interjected in irritation. "If people want to know my reasons, just tell them I'm trying to do something positive for peace."

"I'm trying to understand, truly," she answered. "It's all just so different than what you were doing before. Just take care of yourself, OK? I love you."

My father now came on the line, expressing the same concerns as my mother, while I tried to equally reassure him.

"Why don't you come home for the holidays?" he asked. "It would be like taking a vacation from your walk." I heard the worry behind the plea and understood his desire to have me safely at home. I didn't like to see my parents suffering, but I knew I wasn't going back.

"I can't," I replied earnestly. "I need to do this right now." We spoke a little more and I hung up feeling sad. At our table, I found a despondent Alberto. He asked about my parents.

"They're happy I'm walking with a man," I responded, "which is very funny considering how traditional they are." Alberto chuckled.

"Hannah's happy that we're having such great experiences," he said, "but feels lonely. My mother, as you can imagine, is still in shock, but surprisingly understands why I'm walking, and has asked me to pray for my father."

With our drinks finished and the sun firmly set, we agreed that it was time to call on Father Giovanni. I now worried that he wouldn't even open the door at night, and was more than surprised when he immediately invited us inside. A slightly rotund, middle-aged man, Father Giovanni radiated joy and peace. He listened with amusement to our story and shook his head in wonder, as he led us to a room filled with bunk beds and blankets.

"There's hot water for showering," he proclaimed. "There's food in the kitchen. Help yourself to whatever is there. I have to attend to some matters but will join you shortly."

The kitchen cabinets were overflowing with pastas and canned goods. We nibbled on crusty bread, flavorful cheeses, zesty olives and irresistible home-made treats. After freshening up, we met again in the kitchen and, accompanied by a lovely wine, unhurriedly prepared an abundant hot pasta meal.

"If it's all right with you, I'd like to say a small prayer of thanks before we eat," Alberto said. I couldn't think of a more appropriate time to give thanks, and immediately said, "Yes," closing my eyes. "Thank you for this food and for all the abundance that we are receiving," Alberto spoke softly. "May the spirit that has filled this table also fill the hearts of all people. Amen."

"Amen," I affirmed.

"When I was a child," Alberto said, biting into his food, "I celebrated on this day, like all Christians, the birth of Jesus Christ who I was taught was our savior. That was why I wanted to be in San Salvatore today; the name means *holy savior*. It's funny that we are in San Lorenzo because I was also taught that Lorenzo is the name of the sun, which means that we're in the *holy sun*, which to me also symbolizes God. I believe we are all rays of that Sun, and that the light that shines inside each and every one of us is the Christ light. Some also call it the Christ, consciousness, or the Buddha or Krishna consciousness; but to me it is all God's love. I feel good remembering that this light is also within me, and so celebrate that as much as I do the birth of Jesus."

The spirituality books I had read used words such as inner being, divine spark, or higher self to describe our essence; but I had never heard these ideas applied to Christianity, much less to the figure of Jesus who, to me, always seemed such a removed and untouchable figure. The way Alberto described Jesus, however, made him seem more interestingly human. I mentioned this to him.

"I think that's what offends some Christians," Alberto said. "They think I'm making Jesus less, merely human; but I'm not. I'm raising us, humanity, making us also divine. Jesus himself taught that we too are like him."

Father Giovanni appeared as we finished cleaning up, and invited us to join him in his study for a drink. What struck me most about that evening was the matter-of-fact way in which he spoke about his many projects, especially ones that promoted the integration of immigrants into his small community. Books on Buddhism, Islam, and other spiritual teachings sat alongside more traditional Christian titles. He explained that he preferred seeking what unites the religions rather than what separates them and that, ultimately, the peace we were seeking in the world began within the heart of each human being. I agreed wholeheartedly with this man of peace.

Father Giovanni then put on a video of the town's Christmas production. Expecting a cute children's play set on some small stage in town, I was amazed to see the entire town transformed into a scene from ancient Palestine with period costumes, Arab lettering on shop windows, ironsmiths making swords, women weaving wool, beggars in the street, and pigs roasting on an open spit. Naturally, the main attractions were Joseph and Mary. Cradling a newborn baby in her arms, Mary rode through town on a mule while Joseph asked door to door for a place to sleep.

"That's like us every day," I joked, "only without the mule."

The entire evening was unforgettable, and made me appreciate the tremendous man sitting with us. He was one of the many people we had met along this journey, people working quietly but tirelessly for peace in their own communities, each in their own way trying to make the world a better place. They were the people who took a moment to offer us a word of encouragement, who invited us for a hot drink or warm meal, and who even opened their homes to us.

They were ordinary people who had chosen to live the way of peace but who didn't announce it on their backpacks. No one outside their immediate circle knew about them. Their kindness or generosity didn't make the evening news; but their simple acts of humanity were weaving the fabric of peace in our world. I resolved that Christmas Day to somehow shine a light on these extraordinary ordinary people, so that all may draw inspiration and courage from them and witness the dream of peace one day becoming reality.

* * *

The following day, we descended from the mountains and walked into Rimini, a large city on the Adriatic coast. I was looking forward to walking near the water, but in the crush of people and far from the protection of small towns, I felt exposed and vulnerable. I saw peoples' hard stares and nervous glances, and felt misunderstood. I heard their chuckles and laughter, and felt myself shrinking in response. I desperately wanted to disappear, to run away from their judgments of me. Alberto, however, didn't seem to care and was annoyingly happy beside me.

"Look at the beauty around us," he proclaimed happily, his hand sweeping the horizon. "We're finally beside this amazing sea and walking on flat ground for a change. We even have a sidewalk. There are more cafés, shops, churches, and places to rest."

"And people," I added impatiently.

"But, Mony, that's a good thing," he continued, unaffected by my mood. "Just think of how many people are seeing our signs. Who knows how the message is affecting them. Maybe it's making them think about peace or wonder why we're doing this. So what if some of them are laughing at us? I'm sure the majority support what we're doing, even if they don't say anything. We are touching people, whether you think so or not."

Our path led us past a high school, where a group of young people sat at the front steps. I heard their jokes and snickers as we walked by.

"You see," I raged at Alberto, pointing at them. "Nobody in this big city cares about what we're doing. They think we're a joke. That's it. Tomorrow, we go back to the mountains."

I didn't care about Alberto, the message of peace or anything else connected with this walk. I simply wanted that infernal day to end. I turned inwards then, aware only of my own feelings of inadequacy.

My steps led me away from the bustle of the city to the sea walk, where the soothing sounds of waves lapping the shore should have soothed me, but they didn't. I heard Alberto calling my name, and turned to see him walking down some steps to the sand.

"This reminds me of home," he enthused, inhaling deeply. "The sand is hard and great for walking. Come on, let's go closer to the water," he cajoled, holding out his hand.

Secretly, I wanted to feel good and draw from his positive energy, but I couldn't get myself out of my own funk to do it.

I had just taken my first steps onto the sand when I suddenly heard the sound of a car screeching to a stop. Alberto and I turned around in alarm, and saw a car half in the sand, half on the sea walk. We rushed over, fearing that something had happened to the occupants but, to our surprise, found the young driver smiling exuberantly and motioning for us to come closer. When we arrived, we saw him pulling money out of his wallet. With child-like enthusiasm, the man held the bills out the window in offering.

"No, no, thank you," I said quickly. "It's not necessary."

"We appreciate it very much," Alberto remarked softly, "but we don't need it. Thank you, my friend." The man gazed at us for several moments, incredulity etched on his face. Then, without warning, tears welled up in his eyes and began rolling down his cheeks. I began to weep.

"What's your name?" I choked out.

"Niko," he spluttered.

"Thank you, Nikolas," I said, bending over to kiss his cheek. "Merry Christmas." I stepped back. Alberto reached into the car, his eyes also moist with tears, and took Niko's hands in his.

"It's nice to meet you," he whispered.

Niko nodded, clasping Alberto's hand. I walked away, overwhelmed with emotion. I glanced back one last time and saw Niko still in his car, his eyes following our steps, contemplating us with wonder and disbelief.

"Never underestimate the power of this path you have chosen," a voice resounded in my mind.

Dark clouds started rolling in and soon a light rain began to descend. Alberto and I hurried to the first church we could find. It was large and dimly lit, the only lights coming from the various nativity displays. I walked around aimlessly, not really paying attention to the décor, still caught up in the emotion of Niko. Alberto went to look at some displays at the other side of the church.

An older woman entered the church and greeted me. I returned her greeting and turned to look at the nativity scene, pretending to be admiring it, not wanting company. When I looked up again, she was standing beside me.

With her grey hair and black dress, she reminded me of the stereotypical Italian grandmothers so often portrayed in movies. Her eyes bore gently but firmly into mine, drawing me closer, even though I wanted to turn away.

"What are you doing here?" she asked in a friendly tone.

"We're walking to Jerusalem for peace," I whispered, unable to break her gaze. Her eyes shone with love and tenderness. With both hands, she reached up and cupped my face. She brought it closer, and then brushed her lips against each cheek with the softest kiss.

"What you are doing is very good," she said, stroking my cheeks, her loving eyes never leaving mine. "Do not fear. The Holy Mother and Father bless you on your journey."

Still emotionally raw from the meeting with Niko less than half an hour earlier, I once again felt my tears spilling down my face. She gently wiped them away with her silky touch, and then embraced me. I wept in her arms, enveloped in the love of this complete stranger.

Alberto came towards me. I pulled away from this woman and introduced him. With similar love and tenderness, she cupped Alberto's face in her hands and kissed his cheeks.

"Our Holy Mother is always with you," I heard her say, gently stroking his cheeks. "You are protected."

Alberto's eyes watered, and he nodded silently at her. With a final, "God bless you," she kissed us one last time before disappearing out the church door.

That unforgettable day, the entire Universe orchestrated events to lift me out of my despair. I would still have many moments when I would question the wisdom of my decision to walk and if we were making any difference but, on that day, I had no doubt of the power of our message, its messengers, and the invisible force that was moving them.

10. Finding Light

"I think we should consider accepting the money that people are offering us," Alberto said.

We were walking along the touristy Adriatic coast, enjoying lovely sea views and flat roads. The emotions of Rimini were behind me and I was once again at peace with myself and the world...until now.

"Oh?" I replied evasively.

"It's obvious that people want to support our walk," he added. "Some have been doing it by inviting us for drinks or opening their homes to us. But some, like Niko or that woman in Assisi, want to do so by giving us money. I think it makes them feel good knowing that they're contributing to our walk, and to peace."

"I'm not comfortable with the idea," I responded. "Besides, I don't think they're contributing to peace, but to people who they think need money. I don't need charity."

"Money is just another form of help, not charity," Alberto insisted, a slight edge in his tone.

"To me it is different," I retorted, feeling agitated. "I don't need the money," I added emphatically.

"You're being closed and proud," Alberto shot back. "What if more people want to join us? Would you refuse them if they couldn't pay their way, or were you thinking of paying everyone's way?"

"I think you're taking advantage of the situation because you have no money," I accused, regretting the words as soon as they left my mouth. Alberto tensed. I stormed ahead, almost slipping several times on the icy road, but not daring to stop. An issue that I had hoped was a minor irritation had now become a major point of contention, and I didn't know how to deal with it.

I grew up in a middle-class family that was financially comfortable but that had no luxuries. I came into wealth during the boom years of the software industry and, although I was grateful for it, it wasn't something I was attached to. I enjoyed the material gifts that money offered me and generously shared it with family and friends. It gave me the freedom to travel freely and pursue my personal interests, but I never obsessed about it.

I also knew that money gave me power and, in the circle of friends that I kept in those days, had seen that power wielded, and not always for good. I witnessed the arrogance and entitlement that went with money, and was cognizant of how easy it was to fall into that trap, to lose my humanity and think myself superior to those who had less.

Even though Alberto and I disagreed on some elements of our walk, I wanted to maintain some balance of power between us. I didn't want to make him feel bad for having less, but I didn't want to feel bad for having more. The Universe had thrown us together for a reason and, although I seriously questioned its wisdom, I had to believe it was for the good of both of us. On a quiet stretch of sidewalk, I opened up to Alberto regarding my beliefs.

"I understand what you're saying but I don't think you're being fair," Alberto answered. "When I started this walk, I knew it was going to be difficult for me to get to Jerusalem with the little money I had, but I didn't want my fears to stop me. I knew the Universe was sending me on this journey and so left it in its hands to solve my money problems, trusting that I would receive what I needed when I needed it. I believe this is God's way of helping me, through people contributing to our walk. I want to receive the money graciously, as a gift that is helping me in this way of peace. I don't want to receive charity either."

I promised to try, and to be open to each situation. I only hoped I could follow through when the situation presented itself again.

* * *

The coastline was deserted. Hotels, restaurants, and cafés, all catering to summer tourists, now had their doors closed to us. Even the churches were closed. Much to my distress, we learned that priests in these areas often lived in one town but served several at once. The few people we met were usually tourists and had no idea where any priest lived.

We continued northwards, passing Ravenna, towards a village that was our destination that day. It was New Year's Eve, and I secretly, expectantly, awaited a night as special as the one we had celebrated with Seraphino and his family on Christmas Eve.

We waited well into the evening for the priest who we were assured would help us; but he turned us away. With no other shelter in town, we began our slow march towards the next town seven kilometers away.

"We'll be fine," Alberto reassured me. "This just means we're meant to be someplace else." But I heard the quiver in his voice.

The full moon was triple its normal size and glowed like a night-time sun, casting the only visible light in the darkness that enshrouded us. We eventually reached a main road where now the headlights of rushing cars lit the way. The negligible shoulder was covered with a thick layer of ice and snow, making a normally difficult walk treacherous. With the bitter cold, our flashlights began to fade, and so we blended into the night, a hazard to ourselves and motorists. For the first time during our walk, I seriously feared for our safety. Ninety harrowing minutes later, we finally veered off into town.

In the distance, a large star ornament shone brilliantly, its hopeful light beckoning us. It led us a beautifully decorated church and the priest's house nearby. A large, robust priest with graying hair answered our call, and smiled paternally. Hope surged within my heart as I listened to Alberto explaining our needs and watched the priest nod in understanding.

"This is not a hotel," he responded, the smile never leaving his face. "I cannot help you."

I stared at the ground and inhaled deeply. *"Don't cry, don't cry,"* I repeated to myself. *"Don't give him that satisfaction."*

"We are pilgrims walking for peace," Alberto continued in a soothing tone. "We have been received in monasteries, churches, and people's homes. We don't need beds. We can sleep on the floor in the hallway. Please." The door began to close. "Can you at least tell me where we can find a place to sleep?" Alberto persisted.

"All hostels are closed for the holidays. I'm sorry," he replied, firmly shutting the door.

"Please *Padre*," Alberto pleaded, his voice barely above a whisper. "We can't walk anymore. It's late, and we're so cold."

I couldn't bear to hear Alberto beg and walked away, tears of anger and hurt streaming down my face. I dropped on a park bench and wept. Alberto slumped beside me and placed his arm around my shoulder, whispering distracted words of comfort. Only his eyes betrayed bewilderment and confusion.

A moped weaved down the road and braked in front of us. Its young driver grinned at us happily. I could smell the liquor on his breath. "Do you have a light?" he slurred, waving a cigarette.

"No, I don't have a light," I replied weakly.

Alberto pulled out his lighter and offered it to the man, telling him it was a Christmas gift. The surprised man shyly pushed it away, but then gushed at Alberto with gratitude before finally driving away.

"That's the only lighter we have," I said, despondent.

"Don't worry," Alberto replied. "It will come back to us in another way."

"What are you talking about?" I asked.

"He asked for light, so I offered it to him," he said resignedly. "It was a symbolic act. Besides, when you give from the heart, it comes back double."

"*It's late*," I mentally lamented. "*I'm freezing. We don't have a place to sleep. I'm in no mood for esoterics.*"

We waited for some miracle to happen, for all the forces in the Universe to work their magic; but in the end, no one showed up to rescue us. No sign appeared to show the way. No magic. We needed to make a decision. At 10:30 PM, we began our slow march to the next town eight kilometers away.

The highway was less busy, but without flashlights or reflective clothing, we must have appeared like ghosts to passing motorists. With each car, we stopped walking and stood as close to the edge of the shoulder as possible without falling into the ditch that separated the road from the adjacent fields. Having eaten nothing but *panettone* that morning, I began to feel weak and disoriented. My eyes began to close and, more than once, I weaved onto the road.

Alberto occasionally stopped to ask how I was doing, the worry clearly etched on his face, but I couldn't hide my pain. He suggested looking for a place to camp, but surrounded by open, ice-covered farm fields, it was clear that our pegs wouldn't break through the frozen ground and that our tent would be a flimsy barrier against the howling wind.

An hour passed. On the other side of the road, a cluster of buildings set back about two hundred meters appeared. "Let's go there," I declared.

We ran across the road and walked around the dark structures, our feet crunching through the ice. We tried some of the doors but they were locked. Alongside one building was a long open corridor, so we walked into it. To one side was a door opening, but no door, leading into a dark space. We hesitantly stepped inside, and found ourselves standing on dry compacted earth in an area measuring no more than thirty by ten meters, surrounded by tall brick walls. Two of the opposing walls had large window openings, set high, but no windows. The wind whistled through them but it wasn't nearly as cold as it was outside.

"Look what I found," Alberto called out. Against the wall were several boxes of hay, two oversized towels, a wooden ramp, and a small trough for feeding animals. "We are in a manger," he exclaimed, balancing the trough in his hands. It looked like a crib.

Every hair on my body stood on end, and not only from the cold. I walked around the manger, speechless with wonder and gratitude. I knew there was a deeper symbolism and meaning to this night, but I was too exhausted to contemplate it. Overwhelmed with hunger, we devoured the little cheese and bread that we had and drank the bottle of wine that had been given to us on the road earlier that day. Our water was frozen in our bottles.

To make a bed, we pushed the wide ramp against the wall, sprinkled it with hay, and placed the towels on top. We rolled out our foam mats and sleeping bags, slipped into them, and then covered ourselves with the two plastic pieces of Alberto's tent.

"Comfortable?" Alberto asked with a twinge of laughter.

"No," I laughed, "but eternally grateful."

"Amen," he whispered. "Happy New Year."

"Happy New Year," I responded solemnly.

Weeks later, we would learn that all priests had recently received strict orders from their Bishops not to admit anyone into their homes. We never learned why. It made me understand those who had rejected us better, and appreciate those who received us even more.

These experiences would remind me that refusal to offer lodging did not imply rejection of me or my ideas, and that I needed to be more confident in my path and my choices. This would be an ongoing lesson and form an integral part of my inner journey towards peace.

* * *

We walked the hazardous road into Alfonsine the following morning, our attention fully on avoiding the innumerable trucks that seemed intent on pushing us into the ditch. Near the city limits, I noticed a man about my age standing on the steps of a bar watching our approach and smiling broadly.

"Please, come inside," he enthused when we arrived, holding the door open. "I saw your signs when I drove by this morning and hoped to meet you."

I followed him, trying to control my rollercoaster emotions. The slightest act of kindness seemed to trigger my tears. "You must be cold and tired," the man fussed, pulling out a chair for me to sit. "Here, let me help you with your bag," he continued kindly, slipping it off my shoulders. "Oh, it's pretty heavy," he chuckled.

Over the hottest coffee and most delicious cookies, I relaxed into our conversation with the owner of this bar. He commended us on trying to make the world a better place, when many others were not. We shared stories of the many ordinary people who were doing just that, and added him to the list. The caring with which we were received that morning almost completely obliterated the events of the previous evening.

As we stood to leave, he reached behind the bar and handed each of us a lighter advertising the name of his establishment. "A gift for the way, so you won't forget me," he said.

I stared at the lighter, and then held Alberto's knowing gaze, recalling with amazement the drunkard on the moped the night before and words that now seemed prophetic; when you give from the heart, Life gives back double.

We continued into town, where Alberto noted the numerous churches and I, the various open hostels. No matter what happened, this night we would have shelter.

At the first church we stopped at, two young men jovially greeted us and asked about our signs. With an infectious smile and boundless energy, the one named Nino explained that he was a church volunteer and had the key to the church hall. The calm other was Lucio. They showed us to a classroom and brought in mattresses and blankets, confidently assuring us that the priest would allow us to stay. I did not unpack my bag.

Our new friends were easy to speak and laugh with. I marveled at our Italian, a language we were quickly becoming comfortable with. We spoke openly about our spirituality and all confessed that we believed in angels.

"Angels appear in many forms," Lucio asserted, "not just with wings and flowing white robes. The Archangel Rafael, for example, appeared to a pilgrim as an ordinary man. He accompanied him and helped him on his journey, but the pilgrim never knew he was an angel."

I recalled an incident along the Camino where a woman I had befriended offered to read my tarot cards. What stayed with me was her confident assertion that I would be accompanied on my walk to Jerusalem by an angel. I naturally assumed she meant from the spiritual realms, but now considered that this angel could also take human form.

"With your green eyes and light brown hair, you even look like one,"Lucio winked at Alberto, and soon left with Nino to attend to various matters, promising to return.

I sat with Alberto on the church steps, enjoying the remnants of the late afternoon's warm sunshine.

"Did I ever tell you that I worked as a claims adjustor in a large insurance firm?" Alberto remarked. Looking at him now, with his easy-going manner and unassuming presence, it was hard for me to believe that, and told him so. "Oh yes. I even wore a suit and tie," he joked. "It wasn't my dream, of course, but I did what I thought was expected of me. I wanted to be an artist, and even tried to dedicate time to it, but the demands of my job wouldn't allow me. So I buried my dream in order to be the responsible adult my family and wife at the time expected me to be."

"My family wanted me to be a doctor," I revealed, "and were disappointed when I pursued a business career. Unlike you, I had no impossible dreams, only practical ones; to climb the corporate ladder, get married, and own a nice home in the suburbs. Now, for the first time in my life, I'm pursuing a dream."

"I think I found my dream the first time I walked the Camino," Alberto said. "I was going through a profound spiritual change then, reading books that were opening my mind and my heart to new ways of being and living. Like you, I saw that I was a spiritual being with a divine purpose, and that I was the creator of my life, not its victim. I became vegetarian and started practicing yoga, like you. My wife and family thought I had joined a cult. I couldn't make them understand that I was trying to live my new principles. When I quit my job, it was too much for my wife, and eventually we separated."

"What happened on that Camino?" I asked.

"I could speak my truth, and no one thought I was crazy," he chuckled. "I saw how sharing my beliefs helped people gain a different perspective on their problems. I felt so happy doing it, and realized I wanted to dedicate my life to that purpose. My art would also become a way for me to express these truths, this wisdom that was emerging within me. On a night that I will never forget, I fervently asked the Universe to help me fulfill that wish. At that moment, I saw a shooting star and knew that my prayer had been heard."

It was the first time we had spoken so openly about our lives, and I felt a closeness to him that I hadn't felt since we met.

"There's one more thing," Alberto added, "but I don't know how you're going to react." Intrigued, I asked him to go on. "That same night, I promised to be an angel, doing only good in the world. I could think of nothing more wonderful than traveling from place to place, guided by Life, and helping people along the way; like Michael Landon in *Highway to Heaven*. I never would have imagined having that wish fulfilled in this way with you, but I'm so glad that it has."

I wasn't sure what was greater in that moment, my surprise at his confession or my horror that he could possibly be the angel that the tarot reader saw. I could understand, even accept, his earlier assertion that we were instruments of God brought into peoples' paths to help them, but the idea of being an angel just seemed too much, and I thought it pretentious that Alberto considered himself one.

11. Fame

"I saw your signs and would like to ask you a few questions," the young man enthused, pulling out a pen and writing pad. "I'm a journalist."

We were on the road somewhere north of Alfonsine, and this man had stopped his car and approached us. I was accustomed to speaking with the media from my marketing life and normally felt confident evangelizing the benefits of Microsoft software; but here, before the opportunity to broadly communicate our message of peace, my confidence wavered. The questions were easy to answer, focusing on the physical aspects of our journey such as the number of days we had been walking, kilometers per day, where we slept and our anticipated route. When he asked why we were walking, my stomach clenched.

"I am walking to Jerusalem for peace," I replied slowly. "I want people to know that peace is a choice. It is something we create, and that begins within each of us. We can all do something for peace." The journalist scribbled down my words, and then looked at Alberto.

"I am walking for peace, but not only in Jerusalem," Alberto said. "To me, this is a pilgrimage, a spiritual journey." I cringed.

The journalist scribbled with a smile. We agreed to his request to take some pictures. With our backpacks at our feet and the sign facing outwards, Alberto and I stood side by side for our first official photograph together.

I was becoming accustomed to hearing Alberto speak openly about his beliefs to priests, but now, hearing him utter the words "pilgrimage" and "spirituality" to the journalist, I felt concerned. I considered my spirituality a private matter, and did not feel comfortable sharing it with others unless they expressed an interest first. On more than one occasion, among ordinary people we met in bars or on the street, I had seen how Alberto's use of the word "God", or anything related to religion or spirituality, made some uncomfortable. I didn't want to alienate them. Independent of their spiritual beliefs, I wanted all people, not simply those we met in churches or monasteries, to embrace the message of peace through personal empowerment and choice.

I also saw my future life work being for peace in the Middle East, and feared that too much focus on the spiritual aspects of our walk would distract people from the message. To me, whether one believed in God, Allah, the Universe, the Creator, or nothing at all, was irrelevant so long as one's actions demonstrated the universal beliefs of peace and brotherhood. Especially with the media, I wanted our message to be straight-forward, and for me, that meant God-free.

A brief article did appear in the following day's paper, along with a large picture of us. I was pleasantly surprised to learn that my name was Monica, even though I had spelled it for the journalist, and that I was twenty-five years old and Alberto twenty-three. We had somehow lost a decade in the translation. We had a good laugh at our first brush with fame, and kept a copy of the article.

* * *

"We've been driving up and down the road hoping to see you," the woman exclaimed, shaking our hands. "My husband and I read the newspaper article, and want to congratulate you." The couple fussed over us, asking if they could bring us something to eat or drink, wanting to know how they could help us.

"Your stopping here helps in more ways than you can imagine," I said.

The woman reached inside her purse and pulled out her wallet. I instinctively said no and heard Alberto do the same. She waved away our objections, pulled out several bills, and pressed them into my rejecting hands.

"Please," she pleaded. "I know you don't need the money but we want to help. Enjoy a good meal on us."

I contemplated her in silence; at the joy that illuminated her face, and felt the fight leave me. I took the money from her hands and thanked her. She smiled brilliantly. Alberto gazed at me proudly. I handed him the bills.

Perhaps I had been too harsh in my judgments of what was acceptable help for our walk. It wasn't simply about receiving money, but receiving in all its forms. I never wanted to burden anyone or feel indebted to them. I preferred to give, to control, believing that it made me independent and free. I realized then that it imprisoned me in a cage of judgments, and protected a fragile sense of self-worth. I gave—love, friendship, kindness—believing that I was somehow stronger than others, with infinite reserves to share. I made light of loving words and gestures, keeping myself forever sealed in my cage, safe from hurt and disappointment. I wasn't sure where these feelings stemmed from, but I couldn't deny their truth. With these revelations, my healing journey suddenly seemed very far indeed.

Moments later, an elderly gentleman standing at the edge of his driveway waved us over and congratulated us on our walk. He reached into his pocket and pressed some bills into my hand. I began to resist.

"Why not?" he asked, puzzled, and then closed my hand over the money. "Take it. I want to contribute to what you're doing. I want to contribute to peace. It's not much, but I offer it sincerely and with great pleasure."

It was impossible to ignore the repeated hits on the head that the Universe was dealing me that day. My heart finally opened and, on all levels, graciously accepted his gift. "Thank you," I said.

12. Touched by an Angel

I dragged my feet into Lugo, wanting this day to end. My period had started, sapping the precious reserves I needed for walking. Being turned away at two consecutive churches did not help my irritability. I was so inward-looking that I brushed off a man who I thought was a curious on-looker, but who Alberto later explained may have been trying to help us, which only exacerbated my feelings of remorse.

Across the street, a car screeched to a halt, and a young man excitedly bounded up to us, followed by a much calmer woman.

"I saw you walking and had to stop," he exclaimed. "Where are you from? Where are you staying? Have you had dinner?"

"We were just searching for a shelter that..." I began.

"No, no, no," he interjected, "you can't do that. You must stay with me. Please, I insist."

The man named Giordano was of average height with an athletic build and fair features. Unbridled enthusiasm flowed through him, and infected me. His rapid-fire Italian and gesticulating body movements made me smile, and reminded me of the Energizer bunny. His friend Gabriella, a short, slim woman whose dark eyes seemed to melt with sweetness, chuckled at his antics. I couldn't help but relax, and accepted their invitation.

We squeezed into Giordano's small car for the high-speed drive to his apartment. The movie and football posters confirmed that we were in a bachelor's apartment. Giordano offered us his bedroom and large bed, which we hastily declined, clarifying that we were friends and that the sofas were comfortable enough. He shrugged his shoulders, and then proceeded to open his closet and offer us whatever he could see: t-shirts, socks, underwear, jackets. We accepted the towels.

We came out of our showers to find a pasta dinner awaiting us. We contributed our bread and cheese which, added to the wine, made for a copious feast among our new friends.

"So why are you in Lugo?" Giordano asked at one point.

"Didn't you see our signs?" I responded.

"No," he replied. "I just saw two backpackers. I've backpacked all over the world and always appreciated it when someone invited me to their home or made the effort to help me."

I had assumed that Giordano had stopped because he had seen the newspaper article about us; the fact that he had stopped to help two ordinary people made me appreciate him even more.

The following morning, Giordano came out of his room, announcing, "Here, take my keys. I'm in Rome all day for a football game."

With this most unexpected gift, we were in Lugo another day. I washed my clothes, and cleaned out and re-packed my backpack. Alberto and I briefly strolled around town, but most shops were closed for *Befana*, the Feast of the Epiphany, and the day that children received their Christmas gifts. We returned to the house, each lounging on a sofa, and wrote in our diaries.

"I had a dream about my father last night," Alberto said, looking up. I asked him to tell me more. "It was more than a dream," he elaborated. "It felt real. I saw a big place with no boundaries or walls, only white light as far as the eye could see. There were many people there, all dressed in long white robes. I had a feeling they were all wise people, and were meeting to discuss some important projects concerning humanity. Then, one of them turned around and looked at me. It was my father. He looked young and healthy, his face radiant. He smiled at me with so much love. My heart swelled. He was proud of me, of this pilgrimage, at how I was handling people and situations along the way. It reinforced what I already believed to be my life purpose, to share what I have learned, and to offer that gift to the world."

I was touched at the way that Alberto's father was communicating with him, but still couldn't help but feel it presumptuous of Alberto to think of his life purpose in such a grand way. Working for peace was one thing, but to share what he had learned? Who was he? What made him think he was so special? He wasn't perfect. He had things to learn. He could be wrong. Whether he labeled himself a messenger or an angel, to me it was all too dangerously close to arrogance.

A knock on the door heralded the arrival of Gabriella, balancing three pizzas in hand. It was our first time alone with her, and I looked forward to knowing her. We learned she was a divorced, single mother of two teenage children, and that she worked as an aide in a nursing home. She was intrigued by our journey and asked about every detail, every person, every lesson. I felt at ease with her, and spoke openly about my life and experiences.

"I love what I do," she said at one point. "I feel good helping my patients. I see that they appreciate it, but suffer terribly when they pass on. I grieve their loss as my own, and have a hard time emotionally letting go of them."

"A few years ago," Alberto said, "my best friend Javi died in a construction accident. In one week, I went from laughing and joking with him, to watching him lie in a coma, and then, finally dying. I didn't understand. He was so young. He did all the things he was supposed to do; he worked hard in a full-time job, he was saving up to buy an apartment and to marry. He didn't have impossible dreams, he didn't take huge risks, yet there he was, dead, at only twenty four. His death shook me to my foundations. I realized that I too could die at any moment, never having tried to live my dreams; and all because of fear and insecurity. I resolved then and there never to allow them to stop me, and to follow my biggest dreams."

Gabriella and I leaned in, attentive to his words. I was learning a great deal about my walking partner that night.

"I have felt Javi's presence around me many times," Alberto continued. "I also feel my father's presence. Since their passing, they have spoken with me through signs, coincidences, and especially dreams. I know they're in a good place. Just as I'm sure your patients are, and that they're smiling down on you right now."

"I never thought of it that way," Gabriella said, wiping away her tears.

Alberto had opened a door that Gabriella seemed keen to explore, and by the time she left, her mood was appreciatively brighter. So was mine. It had nothing to do with peace in Jerusalem, or so I believed then, but I felt good helping her and gratified to know our words had brought peace to one person.

* * *

The following day's walk into Giovecca was uneventful, but the previous evening's conversation kept replaying itself in my mind. I could see what Alberto was saying about being messengers, but I still had so many questions about this peace I was walking for. I didn't have his certainty, and until I did, preferred to be a walking billboard and allow the message to reach whoever it needed to without my personal involvement.

On the other side of the busy road, an older woman stood at the edge of her driveway, motioning for us to stop. We ran across.

"I've been waiting for you to pass by," she enthused. "I drove by you many times this week, and hoped to meet you." We introduced ourselves to the woman named Mercedes, who insisted we eat something. With the afternoon still young, we accepted and followed her inside her home.

As I stepped into the family room, I heard someone call out, "Monica, Monica." I had become accustomed to being called that, and so looked around, but didn't see anyone. I realized then that the television was on, and that the program *Touched by an Angel* was playing. The moment I walked in, someone was calling out the name of the angel named Monica. An electric jolt ran through my body. Alberto couldn't contain his surprise.

Holding my hand, Mercedes led me to the table and sat beside me, offering me cookies and juice, while Alberto chatted with her grown children.

"My husband died a short while ago," she confided, her voice filled with pain. "I can't believe he's gone, that I'm here all alone. I don't know how to move on. I don't know how to get the sadness out of my heart. The stress has been so bad that I have developed eczema on my hands." She held out her hands, encased in with white gloves. "People are afraid to touch me because they think I'm contagious," she said, her voice trembling, her eyes searching mine for understanding. "I wear these gloves all the time so I won't scare them."

As if to prove her point, or perhaps to share her pain, she took off her gloves and showed me her hands. They were dry and flaky, and looked red and irritated in some parts. Having suffered with eczema myself, I understood her feelings of rejection and isolation. I never wanted to scare people either, and so hid my hands like Mercedes. I gingerly held her hands in mine, caressing them, feeling the hardness of the skin beneath my fingertips. I smiled softly at her, happy to share the only gift I could offer her at that moment, my unconditional acceptance. Tears streamed down her face. I gave her hands a gentle squeeze and slowly released them.

"He's in a beautiful place now, surrounded by light," I said. "I'm sure he prefers to see you happy and enjoying life, not grieving."

A radiant smile illuminated Mercedes's face. Sitting close to me, she lovingly and tenderly caressed my hair, my face, my arms. I felt awkward, but did not want to hurt her feelings or reject her in any way, and so I sat beside her and allowed her to draw whatever she felt she needed from me.

"If you would like, we can bring a photo of your husband to Jerusalem with us," I offered.

The family excitedly accepted and, after a lengthy search, settled on one and wrote a note on the back. I promised to find him a special place in Jerusalem. Mercedes would not allow us to leave without stuffing fruit into my backpack, and bills into my hands. We finally left, the vision of this lovely woman standing in her driveway waving, waiting for us to disappear, forever etched in my mind.

"Did you see what happened back there?" Alberto exclaimed.

"I don't know what it was exactly," I replied evasively, "but something did happen, yes."

"The way that Mercedes was looking at you and touching you..." he enthused, "she was seeing you as an angel, like the angel Monica from that television program. It's also no coincidence that as soon as we walked in, your name was being called out."

"I'm no angel," I replied in irritation. "You've been witness to my less than angelic behavior."

"I know," Alberto teased, but then more seriously added, "Forget for a moment the idea you have in your head about what an angel is. I'm not talking about flowing white robes and feathered wings. For me, an angel is someone who uses his life as an instrument of love and peace in the world."

"Alberto, an angel is perfect," I pronounced. "Neither you nor I are perfect."

"We all have our weaknesses, Mony," Alberto countered, undeterred, "but that doesn't make you any less of an angel. Your pure intention now is to be of service to mankind, to help others. That's what angels do." He firmly placed his hand on my shoulder and turned me to face him. "You are an angel too, believe me," he said gently. "I think this is what the Universe was trying to tell you today. It's not your perfection that makes you an angel, Mony, it's your intention."

I walked away, not wanting to hear any more, feeling confused. Alberto was challenging me in ways I didn't like, asking me to see myself in ways I never would have dreamed. I couldn't deny that something important had happened that day, that the Universe was trying to tell me something; but I wasn't prepared to embrace the vision that he was suggesting. Being a peace-maker was something digestible, even attainable. I could even handle being a messenger, but Alberto's assertions seemed too impossible, no matter how beautifully he couched the words.

13. The Fighting Pacifists

We moved northwards, Padua in sight, passing towns such as Portomaggiore, Ro, and Rovigo. One evening, entering our destination for the day, a handsome, well-dressed man stopped to ask about our signs. The man named Carlo explained that there was no priest in town but eagerly offered to find us accommodations. He did—in the men's change room of a soccer stadium—and then invited us to a drink.

In a voice loud enough for everyone to hear, Carlo asked about the purpose of our walk. Conversation in the crowded bar ceased, and people gathered to listen. We spoke about our lives and shared stories of the way, all to the admiration of those gathered. However, what most seemed to fascinate them was the fact that Alberto and I were only friends.

"*Amici*[3]," I repeatedly laughed, assuring the scoffing patrons that there was absolutely no romantic relationship between us.

"Are you kidding me?" Carlo exclaimed. "You are an attractive woman with an attractive man. There is no way you will not end up together, of that I am sure."

"There's no way that will ever happen, of that I am sure," I reiterated, to the continued laughter and amusement of everyone in the bar.

* * *

Carlo had promised that we would appear in the following day's newspaper, but when no journalist appeared for an interview, we assumed he couldn't make it happen. Still, at the first bar we found the following morning, we searched the local newspaper for a possible article and were surprised to find a short paragraph describing how the opposition political party had welcomed and hosted two pacifists. The commentary was brief, promoting the party's efforts, but saying nothing about our walk. Worse still was a picture of a party representative accompanying the article.

I was livid. Never had I considered the possibility of anyone using our walk for their personal gain. I walked that day with a growing

---

[3] Friends

sense of mistrust, thinking of ways to control the message, and feeling more determined than ever to safeguard it.

"I've been receiving signs about the importance of speaking with ordinary people about our message," Alberto commented during one of our breaks at a roadside bar.

Still reeling from the skewed newspaper article, I now shuddered at the thought of Alberto out among the people spreading the good word. I needed to find a way to bring him around to my point of view, to make him see that caution was the prudent choice, without triggering an argument.

"I saw that you didn't use the word pilgrim or speak about your spirituality with Carlo," I said casually. "I thought it worked very well, didn't you?" Alberto faced me, his gaze hard and cold.

"I know what you're trying to do, but it's not going to work," he charged. "I can't believe what a hypocrite you are. You wear different masks for different people. You're afraid to talk about what's really happening, about the miracles and magic; and it has everything to do with God, the Universe or whatever you want to call it." My mind raced for words to say.

"When someone asks about my experiences, I will tell them," I replied tersely. "I don't need to push my ideas on people."

"What we are living is important and I will speak about it however, and to whomever, I please," he retorted.

"You're preaching," I shot back. "What's important to you may not be important to others." Alberto's hard eyes bored into mine. His jaw was firm and his face just as flushed as mine.

"I want to speak my mind," he said, "but you stop me every time. You want to control everything, what we say, how we say it. It's not what I want."

"I think you're being too pushy and should keep your ideas to yourself," I accused.

"It's better than being a fraud," he accused, "and hiding who you are. I'm proud to be a pilgrim. I'm being authentic when I speak about my spiritual experiences. I think people want to have meaningful discussions that go beyond how many kilometers a day we're walking and, even if they don't, so what? It's no reason to stop having them. I will speak my truth."

"You're so presumptuous to think that you know what's good for other people," I scoffed.

"Aren't you doing the same thing by hiding our real experiences?" he asked, and then exhaled in frustration. "For so many years, I hid what I believed for fear of being rejected or misunderstood, and I do not intend to go back to that again. I refuse to fall into the trap of worrying about what people will think. I'm not inside their heads. I can't predict what they're going to think."

Alberto was demonstrating a backbone I never realized he had, and I felt momentarily off-balance. He was always so sweet, almost innocent, in the way he saw the world and spoke about love that I considered him weak and naïve, and myself strong and worldly.

"You witness the same miracles I do," Alberto continued passionately. "You feel the same way I do. We speak about it all the time. How can you deny it? You can say what you want, but don't even think about trying to manipulate my words or my purpose. You still think this is your way; that I'm your follower and must obey your commands, but you are mistaken. You are not my boss. This is the way of peace, and my way is just as important as yours. There is a higher wisdom that is guiding us here, and I will only submit to it." I stared icily at him, and finally uttered the only words that I could muster at the moment.

"Maybe we need to walk our separate ways," I declared, my voice sounding hard, but betraying the lump in my throat. "I don't have the energy for you and this walk. I'm going to Jerusalem. I really don't care where you go."

"Don't worry," he replied coolly. "I've thought the same thing."

I didn't want Alberto to see how badly his words had affected me, how much he had hurt me. I threw on my backpack and stormed away, fighting cross-currents of emotions. I was angry at his personal accusations, but sad at the thought of us separating, even though I suggested it. I had felt liberated by the idea of walking alone, but when he expressed the same desire, I felt he was betraying me and the way of peace.

I forged ahead, the combined weight of my backpack, our argument, and my turbulent emotions weighing down each step. I wanted to be invisible, to disappear to a place with no noise, no message, and no Alberto; only peace. A large tree in a nearby field invitingly offered its shade, its refuge. I wearily slumped against it. My head sank between my shoulders, and I closed my eyes. *"It would be so much easier for me to go it alone."*

I heard Alberto sit beside me. The moments passed and where earlier tension reigned, now a resigned silence prevailed. "I didn't mean to hurt your feelings," Alberto whispered. "I'm sorry." I nodded in response. "Here we are walking for peace and we're ready to strangle each other," he chuckled. "It's pretty funny, don't you think?" I smiled faintly at the image of fighting peace pilgrims.

"I believe that the Universe wants us to keep walking together," Alberto continued softly. "How can we create peace in the world if we can't even create it between us? I think we'd be losing an important opportunity to do that if we separate." I glanced at him sorrowfully.

"I agree that the way of peace is better served with us together," I finally admitted, "although at times I question the wisdom of the Universe."

"Tell me about it," Alberto quipped, then gazed at me intently. "Mony, I need you to trust me."

"I'm not trying to control you, Alberto," I replied earnestly. "Of course you have the right to speak your mind. I just feel more nervous around journalists, that's all; especially after our experience with Carlo."

"How about you say what you want," Alberto suggested, "and leave me to say what I want. We will make it perfectly clear to the journalists that we have differing opinions."

I saw my walk slipping away from me, and felt helpless to stop it. With every compromise I made, I whittled away a little more my vision of this walk and risked a future I dreamed. Yes, I believed in the spiritual journey; but to me it was private and secondary to the message of peace, while to Alberto it was public and primary.

I was being challenged to trust Alberto, to believe that his words, his truth, would not hinder my way. At a level I wasn't yet prepared to confront, I was being invited to be authentic in every sense; to have my words reflect my spirituality, and my actions be its testament. I had taken some tentative steps, but wasn't ready to make the leap.

14. Captains and Sailors

We raced through Padua the following day, trying to arrive in time to an inter-faith peace march we had heard about a few days earlier. We arrived at sunset, tired and sweaty from having walked thirty-five kilometers, just as organizers were ushering the crowds into a large auditorium.

Our signs generated a buzz of excitement, and soon, event organizers came out to greet us. They led us to front row seats, and then hurried to the podium to speak with several people seated there, some of whom wore the traditional garb of their religion. They nodded in our direction. I felt my heart beating with excitement.

The event began with the leaders of various religious communities and peace organizations emphasizing the need for tolerance and understanding. We were welcomed and introduced as examples of people working for peace. When the speeches ended, photographers and journalists descended upon us, peppering us with questions. Well-wishers reached out to us, shaking our hands, patting our backs, kissing our cheeks. My tears, consequence of my shaken confidence and recent arguments with Alberto, mixed with theirs, so filled with love. I melted into their embrace and took from them the emotional strength I so desperately needed at that moment.

The march started, and so we joined the masses spilling out onto the streets. We were given white candles the size of baseball bats, and added our lights to the sea of flickering lights that lit up the night. A priest sauntered alongside us.

"I just want to congratulate you," he enthused in English. "I'm sure it's been a long day for you. You must be tired. Do you have a place to sleep tonight?" When we replied no, he asked us to follow him. In a scene that was surely comical, we trotted behind him, our heavy backpacks swaying from side to side, trying to keep him in sight while balancing our burning candles. He stopped to speak with a woman, and then disappeared into the crowd. The woman came towards us, the light of her candle illuminating a lovely face and brown eyes that sparkled with kindness.

"My name is Luciana," she said, ushering us to her car. "You will be sleeping in my home tonight."

Luciana was a generous host, doting on us as if we were her own children. We slept on comfortable sofas under cozy blankets that I was reluctant to crawl out of. The smell of freshly-brewed coffee the following morning hinted at the breakfast that awaited us. Luciana brought in *Il Gazzettino di Padua* and showed us the article that highlighted us at the peace march. She even took our clothes to machine-wash them, a luxury we had not enjoyed in almost two months. The smell of detergent was headier at that moment than that of the finest perfume.

The unhurried pace of the morning flowed into lunch, where we were joined by Father Sergio, a priest friend of Luciana's. As all-embracing as Luciana, Father Sergio wanted nothing more than to hear about our experiences, especially the magical coincidences which he termed providence, elaborating that we were in the land of St. Anthony, the saint of providence. We accepted his request to speak to his youth group, and jumped at his invitation to tour Padua. The clearly pleased Father Sergio showed us the many sites of this magnificent city, and ended our day with a visit to the Basilica of St. Anthony, which housed the saint's remains.

"St. Anthony was the most famous disciple of St. Francis," Father Sergio whispered, "and a great preacher." He showed us to a container that purportedly held the saint's tongue, saying, "When his body was exhumed thirty years after his death, the tongue still glistened, which people took as a sign of his gift to inspire and teach others."

I hoped Alberto wasn't taking that as a sign to speak his mind even more freely.

We continued around the Basilica, enjoying its many treasures, and stopped to admire a drawing of an eagle. I had seen similar drawings in other churches, usually accompanied by a bull, a lion, and an angel, and asked Father Sergio what they meant.

"They represent the evangelists," he explained. "The lion is St. Mark. The bull is St. Luke. The angel is St. Matthew, and the eagle is St. John. The gospel of St. John is considered one of the most mystical and beautiful depictions of the life and teachings of Jesus."

I wondered if there was a connection there for me, a message from my totem to explore the teachings of St. John. More than once, I had tried reading the Bible, searching for such mysticism, but eventually put it away, finding its judgmental and wrathful depictions of God, especially in The Old Testament, demoralizing and inconsistent with my beliefs. The New Testament left me similarly uninspired, and I finally concluded that, for me, the mystical was not to be found in the Bible or the Christian faith.

* * *

The church hall filled quickly with eager young faces wanting to hear about our pilgrimage; but unlike the people we usually met, these were fellow pilgrims. They too had walked the Camino, and so understood the language of pilgrims, the stories of magic that needed no explanation or justification, and the feeling of being guided and protected by invisible forces. There were no cries of incredulity when we spoke, merely acknowledgement among equals of events wholly natural.

A young man pulled out a guitar and started strumming the music to Simon and Garfunkel's *The Sound of Silence*. The group stood and, holding hands began singing this version of *Our Father* in Italian. Alberto sang the words in Spanish.

It was at that moment, standing in the far corner of the long table, that I felt most distant from the group. My walk had been taken over by the religiosity I had so desperately fought to keep out. I felt guilty for my feelings, for I was among genuine, kind-hearted, and kind-spirited people, and I should have had the spiritual maturity to embrace their beliefs.

"*Chanting and singing religious songs are not what this walk is about for me,*" my mind silently rebelled, as my lips mouthed the words in English.

"Hey, we know one song in Spanish," declared the man playing the guitar, strumming the tune to Ritchie Valens's *La Bamba*. Alberto cheerily sang the words in Spanish to the delighted group. At the chorus, he turned to me with a mischievous grin and sang, "*Yo no soy marinero, soy capitán, soy capitán.*[4]" Only I picked up the veiled reference about his role to what I still considered to be my walk.

---

[4] I'm not a sailor, I'm a captain, I'm a captain.

Perhaps providence had brought us to these fellow pilgrims. In time, I would come to appreciate that my rigid ideas of how this walk should be, and my insistence that it transcend religions, in fact excluded religions. In this case, being labeled a Catholic, combined with my preconceived notions of what that meant, frightened me and blinded me to the great love that is also a fundamental part of that faith.

I am forever thankful to Father Sergio, Luciana, and our friends in Padua for sharing their love so openly with a pilgrim who was learning to receive it without condition or prejudice.

15. Crossing Over

Two days had passed since Padua, and we were on the outskirts of Venice walking through a heavily industrialized area. Noise, pollution, and the smell of exhaust fumes made the day's walk especially odious.

"Have you ever heard of Caronte?" Alberto asked.

"No. What is it?" I replied.

"Caronte is a character from Greek mythology," he explained. "He's the boatman who carries the souls of the dead to the other world. I've been receiving signs connecting his name with Venice, with death and crossing over." Alberto paused before adding, "Maybe something important is going to happen here."

"Unless Venice plans to sink entirely while we're there, I don't want to know about it," I replied dryly.

My mood lifted considerably when I saw the long bridge that led to the city. We crossed it quickly, our destination the centrally-located St. Mark's Basilica. Alberto was lagging behind, and I was about to become irritated when the look of amazement on his face stopped me. I slowed my pace and for those brief moments saw through his eyes the reason for that awe. Canals wound through the city like streets. Romantic, arched foot-bridges neatly connected neighbors across the watery divide. Boats rocked gently in front of candy-colored houses, an odd yet natural resemblance to cars parked in their driveway. An accordion tune floated across the air, completing this unforgettable scene.

"It's always been my dream to come here," Alberto sighed dreamily.

I slowed my pace and strolled with Alberto past the pink-colored Ducale Palace, the ancient seat of government, to St. Mark's Plaza, the square in front of the Basilica famous for the thousands of pigeons that used it as their playground. With the sun setting, we entered the Basilica in search of shelter. The soft lighting added a touch of mystery and holiness to this sacred site, location of the tomb of St. Mark. An attendant listened to our needs and advised us to go to the Church of the Holy Savior, assuring us that the priest there, Father Natalino, would attend to our needs.

He instructed us to go right, but in the maze of narrow streets in which we found ourselves, we weren't sure what direction we were going. We kept the Basilica's dome as our guide. Even in the dark, it was impossible not to be captivated by this city. Despite being January, the night air was filled with the perfume of flowers, intoxicating and heady, that seemed to transport me to another time and place, hinting at something vaguely familiar.

My wandering eyes casually hit upon the name of the street we were walking; *Calle Del Pelegrin,* the Pilgrim's Street. We were excited by the sign and felt a sense of expectancy, or destiny, that we couldn't quite pinpoint. The Pilgrim's Street eventually led us to a majestic church that looked distinctly out of place among the ordinary homes of this quaint neighborhood. Passersby confirmed that this was indeed the church we were looking for. We climbed the wide marble steps and pushed open the antique wooden door.

The priest was at the altar speaking with some people, and motioned for us to wait. Impressive paintings dotted the walls while intricate mosaic tiles converted the floor into a shining masterpiece. Despite its grandeur, there was a light feeling here, and I enjoyed walking around. The priest approached and introduced himself as Father Natalino. His manner was relaxed, and his gaze curious but inviting.

"You two remind me of a painting I have here," he said, leading us towards the back of the church. "I felt it as soon as you walked in with your backpacks and sticks." He stopped in front of a large painting depicting Jesus in the center of a dinner table flanked by four men. Two of the men had bags and sticks at their feet.

"This painting is called *Supper at Emmaus,*" he explained. "After Jesus died, two of his disciples left in anguish towards Emmaus, a town outside Jerusalem. On their way, they were befriended by a pilgrim who accompanied them. They didn't recognize that it was Jesus until he broke the bread at dinner."

I wasn't sure what he was trying to tell us, but I appreciated his warm welcome and genuine interest. Our accommodations in the games room of the church hall were comfortable. As I hung my clothes to dry, Father Natalino walked in. His eyes roamed his transformed games room: sleeping bags sprawled on the floor atop some cardboard boxes; socks and underwear dangling on the heater; cheese, bread, margarine, juice, and a half-finished bag of cookies on the pool table. He smiled in appreciation at what was a typical day in a pilgrim's life.

"I was just thinking that your walk into Venice must have been very difficult with all the noise and traffic," he said. "I know a route out of the city that's much more tranquil. It means having to take a ferry, but I think you will enjoy it."

I pulled out our map and saw that there was a short crossing from Venice to Porto Sabbioni. I had never even considered that as a possibility. Alberto's earlier comments about Caronte came back to me. I was now more curious than ever to make that crossing.

* * *

Early the next day, we stood on the church steps, saying our goodbyes to our host. Once again, he contemplated us in silence.

"You know, Venice has a long history with pilgrims," he finally said. "Pilgrims of old used to come here to take ships to Istanbul, and then continue from there on foot to Jerusalem. If there was a war or for some reason they couldn't leave, they would stay and work until the next opportunity. Many never left Venice. Of those who did, the majority never returned to their original homes. A pilgrimage was a major commitment, a demonstration of perseverance and faith. Those who returned were forever changed and often found it difficult readapting to their old lives."

I could easily relate to what he was saying. I could not imagine going back to my old life.

"Pilgrims like you stood here," he went on, "on these very steps, before walking down the very streets that you are about to walk, to attend a special pilgrim's mass in the Basilica, and to be blessed before walking the short distance to the port. The two columns just past the Plaza and Palace are the remnants of that port. They marked the entry to Venice, and it was where families said their final good-byes before pilgrims boarded their ships to Istanbul."

Gently resting his hands on our heads, the priest said a small prayer, ending with, "May God bless you on your journey of peace," and making the sign of the cross on our foreheads.

We walked the Pilgrim Street slowly, deliberately, absorbing all these coincidences, and continued past St. Mark's Plaza with the intention of walking through the columns of the old port and ceremonially boarding our awaiting ferry.

"Hello, hello," a man's voice yelled out excitedly. He was rushing towards us, waving his hands and gesturing for us to stop.

"When I saw your signs, I couldn't believe it," he said breathlessly, grasping my hands in his. "I'm a television producer and am here with some children who have just returned from Jerusalem. Please, can you speak with them? I know they will be thrilled to meet you."

A group of about thirty children, all under the age of fifteen, swarmed us and started firing the usual questions. They squealed in excitement, pointing incredulously at our signs. A young girl reached into her bag and handed me a book. On the front cover were three cartoon fish in a row, each holding a paintbrush while walking along a rainbow bridge that extended to infinity. The fish in front wore the *kaffiyeh* (the Palestinian black and white scarf), the fish at the end other wore a *yarmulke* (the Jewish cap), and the fish in the middle a yellow baseball cap. Above their heads was the title *We Give a Boost to Peace with Six Hands* in four languages: Hebrew, Arabic, Italian, and English.

"The idea originated in Italy," the producer explained. "Italian school children started a drawing which was delivered to a Palestinian school, where those children added to it, and finally to Israeli children who completed it. The parents also added their drawings. The process took many months, but the drawings were finally completed. At the end, they were all displayed at a cultural center in Jerusalem, and the children invited to see their handiwork. You cannot imagine the sight. Five hundred excited Israeli and Palestinian children, each searching curiously for their picture and squealing with joy and delight at finding it and their partners who created it. I cannot describe with words the energy that filled the center. There were no barriers, no differing religions, cultures, ideologies. There were only children, playing, singing, dancing. These children are our messengers of peace, creating with their hands and hearts what the adults are failing to do."

I wanted to know more, to speak with the children, but our ferry was leaving and they needed to continue their tour. We reluctantly said our goodbyes and walked towards the port, their cries of *Ciao, Bon Viaggio*, and *Pace* ringing in the Plaza. My heart swelled. They waved and blew kisses until we boarded our ferry, putting the finishing touch on this unforgettable day and the ancient circle we had just completed.

The ferry pulled away, ever so slowly placing distance between us and Venice, until its shore disappeared. I leafed through the book, this treasure of hope I was offered, and finally surrendered to my tears. Most drawings depicted Israeli and Palestinian children holding hands and wearing each other's headdress. Many showed doves flying with olive branches in blue skies, while others showed the various symbols of their religions and flags intertwined and united. Their simplicity and innocence was moving, their bright colors full of joy and hope; a permanent testament to peace amid the killing and bloodshed.

The old world that had so defined me and my ideas was disappearing. Just as Caronte carried spirits to a new world, I too was being carried to a new land with an expanded vision of myself, one grounded in openness, trust, authenticity. I was only now beginning to see the importance of these values in creating peace within and without. The new world, like the new self that was unfolding, was full of unknowns but, as an innocent child, filled with promise and dreams.

The ferry maneuvered into the port of Sabbioni. I took one last look behind and said a silent goodbye, stepping onto the new shore.

16. The Anchor

We followed the pine-tree-lined road through beach towns and villages that were abandoned for the winter. We were hosted our first night in the hall of a local church, and continued the following morning along the coastline of the Gulf of Venice. My left foot ached terribly that day with a searing pain that extended from my arch to my shins. I managed to hobble about fifteen kilometers to the nearest town and dropped at the church steps to await the priest, who arrived shortly after.

A robust man of about sixty, Father Claudio emanated enthusiasm and goodwill. He was fascinated by our walk and immediately responded to our need for lodging. Placing his arms around our shoulders, he led us to a nearby building, all the while peppering us with questions and delighting in our responses. In the fully-furnished apartment that would be our home that night, he turned on the heating and hot water, and then handed us the keys. I finally put down my backpack and sat on the sofa, wincing in pain. Father Claudio looked at me with concern as I explained about the pain in my foot.

"Well then, you must rest an extra day," he commanded jovially. "You have a long journey ahead of you. I have some things to do now, but please join me for dinner." He left us with directions to his home.

We went about our daily arrival ritual. Refreshed after my shower, I attempted to massage my feet but they were too painful to touch, so I lay back on the sofa, closed my eyes, and elevated my feet, enjoying this rare creature comfort for a pilgrim.

"Would you like to go to mass?" I heard Alberto ask. It was the last thing on my mind, but I knew that Father Claudio would appreciate seeing us there, and so as a gesture of thanks, I agreed to go. The priest beamed when he saw us. I was glad of my decision.

The church was by far the simplest we had seen on our travels, looking like a retail space that someone had rented and decided to decorate as a church. The simple altar was adorned with fresh flowers and presided over ten rows of pews with just as many parishioners. I noted a statue that Alberto whispered was St. Leopold, the saint of confessions, but the large black anchor near the altar was not a sight we saw every day.

At the point in the mass where parishioners look to their nearest neighbor and offer words of peace, each one came up to us and shook our hands, warmly welcoming us and repeating the words, "Peace be with you." It was the first time we had ever been so warmly welcomed in a church, and it touched me greatly. We returned their greeting with equal sincerity. Mass ended and parishioners began filing out, again shaking our hands. We said our goodbyes to Father Claudio, agreeing to meet at his home in thirty minutes.

I used that time to call a journalist named Anna who had stopped us on our way into town that morning. Unable to grant her an interview at that moment, we had exchanged phone numbers and now made plans to meet the following day.

Our host received us into his home with the same warmth and hospitality we had come to expect from him. Delicious aromas filled the air, compliments of his housekeeper. He led me by the hand to the sofa, sat me down, brought a footstool, and raised my foot. "Don't move," he gently commanded.

"I'm feeling better, really," I stammered, surprised by the gesture.

"No," he replied firmly, heading to the kitchen. "You must rest and soak your feet."

My eyes begged Alberto's to stop this priest, but he smiled in amusement, folded his arms across his chest, and shook his head. *Don* Claudio reappeared, balancing a pail filled with saltwater. He reached for my left foot and gently placed it in the warm water, taking care not to touch the arch area. He pulled out some ointment and reached for my right foot. Ignoring my protests that I was fine, he began to massage my foot. It felt undeniably fantastic, but I couldn't enjoy it because it was being given by a priest, a man old enough to be my father. He placed my right foot into the water and repeated the massage with the left foot, then replaced it in the water, again commanding me not to move.

"Like Jesus washing the feet of his disciples," Alberto teased. I shot him a "help me" glance. He shook his head.

The not-to-be-deterred priest lifted my feet and tenderly dried them. His assistant entered with a pair of wooly slippers, explaining that this extra pair of hers was now mine, similarly ignoring my pleas that I have sandals. Father Claudio slid the slippers on my feet, helped me stand up, and then held my elbow all the way to my seat at the dinner table. My own parents could not have treated me with more love. Their attention left me speechless, and I was one who was never at a loss for words.

Our meal was copious and delicious, the conversation lively and engaging. Father Claudio said he was thinking of walking the Camino, and eagerly lapped up the stories of our experiences. Time passed too quickly, and when we finally said our goodnights, it was with the twinge of sadness one feels at having to leave good friends.

"I'm thinking of taking communion tomorrow," Alberto announced, back in our room. I asked him why, when he didn't believe in the rituals of the Church. "For me, it's more of a symbolic act, a way of acknowledging God's presence in my life and giving thanks for it. The only problem is that I have to confess, but I don't believe in sin. Sin reinforces a God of fear, one that condemns those who don't follow his rules. And that's not the God of my experience."

My only reference to Alberto's dilemma was my own Greek Orthodox Church. When praying *Our Father*, instead of asking to be forgiven for our sins, in Arabic we ask to be forgiven for our mistakes. This interpretation always seemed to me more loving, recognition that we are human. I was astonished that I could even recall this prayer, a surprise remnant from my childhood in Lebanon. Alberto immediately agreed with my observation.

"God knows we're all doing the best we can in every moment," he concurred. "God knows our limited understanding. To even ask for forgiveness is to consider the possibility that there's something in me that God's not happy with; and that, for me, is not God. We don't have his wisdom or awareness, so of course we're going to make mistakes. If God wanted us perfect, he would have made us perfect. So how can he be angry at his own creation?"

Our conversation continued, but did not resolve whether or not Alberto would take communion.

* * *

The following morning, we met the journalists. "I'm so happy you called," Anna exclaimed, kissing us on each cheek. Everything about her was captivating: her puppy brown eyes, her wide smile, her attentive, gentle presence. I had to remind myself that she was a journalist. Accompanying her was Claudia, another journalist. She too was friendly, but I felt her penetrating gaze searching, assessing. Instinctively, I put on my marketing face—professional and polite—and we made our way to a nearby café.

The interview began with the usual questions about the physical aspects of our journey, but then their questions turned to our lives before this walk, and what inspired us to do it. This was my first opportunity after our big fight to demonstrate to Alberto that I trusted him, and that he could speak his truth without my trying to manipulate the conversation.

It was difficult at first, hearing him speak so openly, imagining the number of times the word "God" would be mentioned in the article; but then I saw how Anna and Claudia responded. They leaned into him, absorbing his words, their gazes filled with understanding. They put down their pens, and the conversation that we shared that afternoon was one among friends.

Anna revealed that she had miraculously survived a terrible motorcycle accident that had left her driver friend dead. "I believe I am here because my life has a deeper purpose that I am determined to fulfill," she confided. "Guardian angels exist, and it is because of them that I am speaking with you today."

I stood at a crossroads, battling my head's insistence that she was a journalist using kindness to break through to me, and my soul's desire to trust and be authentic. I stepped in gingerly at first, speaking about my divorce and subsequent spiritual awakening. When I began to speak about the miracles and the angels, I knew I had taken a giant leap forward in my inner quest for authenticity and overcoming my debilitating fear of what others thought. Anna's honesty allowed me to be similarly honest, and for that I will be always be thankful.

As it turned out, Anna and Claudia's final articles were full of praise, and my fears were unfounded...again.

* * *

Alberto and I stood at the back of the packed church, watching Father Claudio's passionate sermon. I felt the harmony that pervaded that small church, and the love in every glance and greeting. They were like a big loving family, and we were a welcome part of it.

At that moment, I considered taking communion. We had just symbolically crossed over to this new shore, this land of new possibilities and beginnings, and communion seemed the perfect ritual to complete the crossing. Father Claudio was such a loving priest, and I couldn't think of a better person to do this with. I whispered this desire to Alberto, who agreed to join me. We again left with the parishioners' well wishes and accompanied Father Claudio to his home, where another table overflowing with food and wine greeted us.

"I'm so happy that you stopped here," he effused. "Please stay another day. I would love for you to speak with the people of this community." His offer was tempting, but we couldn't accept. My feet were better and, as pilgrims, we needed to continue on our journey. Father Claudio was disappointed.

"Thank you so much for embracing us so completely," Alberto said. "You have welcomed us into your community, your home. You've treated us like one of your own children and opened your heart to us. We feel very comfortable with you, and wonder if you could give us communion before we leave tomorrow morning."

"It would be my honor," he replied emotionally.

"The only thing is," Alberto continued cautiously, "I haven't confessed or taken communion in years. My ideas and beliefs are also further away from the traditional beliefs of the Church. Still, I feel the desire to go back to this symbolic ritual, something that for me was, in its time, an important and influential part of my life." Father Claudio nodded in agreement and approval, his eyes moist.

"I know I must confess before taking communion," Alberto proclaimed. "Although I have my own views on that, I would still like to confess with you."

"Of course, of course," replied the priest earnestly. "We can go to the church tomorrow, where I can hear both your confessions and then offer communion. I can't think of a more appropriate way to send you off."

When I thought of taking communion, I had not considered having to confess. I had never confessed before and, like Alberto, did not believe in sin. I quietly debated whether I still wanted to take communion.

"I'm not sure if you know, *Don* Claudio," Alberto stated, "but Mony is Greek Orthodox. That's not a problem, is it?" All color dissipated from the priest's face. The ever present smile disappeared, replaced with genuine shock.

"She's not Catholic?" he sputtered incredulously. "She's Orthodox? Well, uh, uh, well…"

"To be honest, *Don* Claudio," I started slowly, delicately, trying to phrase my truth in words that wouldn't hurt or offend. "I am not a practicing Orthodox or Christian. I have not attended church in many years. I respect all religions and believe that they are merely different paths leading to the same God. Like Alberto, I felt the desire to take communion as a symbolic act of acknowledging and accepting God's presence, which to me is love, in my life."

"Yes, yes, of course," he replied. "Don't misunderstand me; I have nothing against the Orthodox. They are our Christian brothers but we do have different sacraments. I don't know if you confess in your church, or if and how you take communion. I really don't know. I don't think it's a good idea."

"But if there is only one God, what does it matter what church I belong to?" I replied, the edge in my voice masking the unexpected hurt that his rejection had caused.

"It's not about God," he replied gently. "It's about rituals. The Catholic Church has certain requirements, as I'm sure your Church does. I'm certain the Bishop would never consent to this."

"These rules should bring people closer to God, not further away from him," I retorted, feeling my face flush with indignation and the one too many glasses of wine that now loosened my tongue. "God places no conditions on his Love, only the Church does. Besides, I don't need to receive something that is already within me and all around me. God is every thing. I am God. You are God. Every thing is God."

Father Claudio looked away, his eyes filled with pain. My words had been overly harsh and had come from a place of hurt, not my heart. I wished I could take them back, but it was too late. I had gone too far.

"I'm truly sorry," he stated sadly but with finality. "I cannot offer you communion." An uncomfortable silence ensued.

"It's not a problem," Alberto finally replied, trying to sound light, but I knew he was disappointed too. "We need to leave early anyways and it would have taken too much time. Don't worry, it's all right."

Our goodnights were melancholy. I couldn't stop my incessant mind replaying the evening's conversation and feeling a deepening regret for not having handled myself with more grace.

"I'm sorry about what happened," Alberto remarked softly later that evening. "Maybe you were a little hard on *Don* Claudio, but you spoke your truth. I'm proud of you."

I didn't feel proud of myself and slept fitfully, waking from dreams I couldn't remember and feeling a terrible knot in my stomach. I heard Alberto moving about, and imagined that he too was struggling with what had just happened. I was happy once morning came.

Our farewell with Father Claudio was filled with sincere well-wishes and blessings, but in his embrace, I felt the sorrow.

"I think I finally understand what that anchor in the church means," Alberto said once when we were alone on a quiet stretch of road. "It represents the things that stop us all from moving forward. For *Don* Claudio, maybe the anchor is the rules by which he lives which cut the wings of his heart. For us, it's the longing to hold on to the love of those we hold dear. I see now that there comes a time when we must allow others to walk their path so that we can also walk ours."

"Even when that path can sometimes feel sad and lonely," I added.

17. The Way of the Wizard

"I don't want to worry you," my father said. I immediately began to worry. "Your mother is in the hospital. She had a mild heart attack a few days ago and now has pneumonia." Alberto and I had arrived in Concordia Sagittaria and were sleeping in a lovely chapel-meeting room. Alberto was buying groceries, and I had decided to call my parents.

In the unspoken words, I heard my father's silent plea for me to come home. The voice of obligation whispered in my ear, accusing me of being a terrible daughter, of abandoning my family when they most needed me. I imagined my father, sisters and brother rallying around my mother for support, while I, the eldest daughter, was thousands of kilometers away on a different continent, living a different existence, completely disconnected from their realities and struggles. My walk for peace never seemed more frivolous.

For as long as I could remember, my mother had struggled with her health due to the various effects of Behçet's Syndrome, the condition that ailed her. It attacked her auto-immune system and made her susceptible to anything. She suffered a heart attack and had double by-pass surgery in the early nineties. She was on blood pressure and heart medication, and had to contend with their side effects which involved various gastro-intestinal problems. More distressing still, she developed uveitis, an inflammation of the fibrous tissue surrounding the eye, which caused her to gradually lose her vision until she became completely blind in 1988.

In her later years, my mother maintained a positive attitude about life which we all believed kept her alive. She came into her own when she joined the Canadian National Institute for the Blind (CNIB). She learned to walk with a walking stick, and began going for walks in the neighborhood and nearby shopping center. She took the bus to get to familiar places, and learned to read and write Braille. She became a spokesperson for a large charitable foundation, and shared her inspirational story with groups and corporations as part of the charity's fund-raising efforts. She even learned to crochet, and surprised us one winter with slippers and coasters.

At around the time that I began to explore my spirituality, she began to explore hers. I shared with her my newfound beliefs, and we spoke at length about the deeper meaning of her life and her illnesses. She read in Braille some of the books that I recommended to her, and began the journey of healing the emotional and spiritual wounds of her life. At times, it was draining for me as I was having a hard enough time dealing with my own issues and felt the added, and guilt-ridden, burden of helping my mother through hers. Over time, however, this experience healed and strengthened our relationship, and I was finally able to see my mother through the eyes of an adult, not through those of a child.

"I'll call Mom right away," I said to my father.

"Oh," my father sighed. I could feel his disappointment from across the ocean. "All right."

I said my goodbyes before my resolve ran out. This path of peace was indeed lonely, and I wondered if those I held dear would ever walk with me again. I dialed the number of my mother's room.

"Hi, honey," she exclaimed happily, even though she sounded weak and congested. "I'm so happy to hear your voice."

"Me too, Mom," I replied softly. "So I see you're putting my tax dollars to good use again." She laughed weakly, interrupted by bouts of coughing that lasted for several seconds.

"Don't worry, Mo. Really, I'm OK," she proclaimed. "The doctors say I'm improving. I'll be out in a few days." In the midst of more coughing fits, my mother recounted the details of her physical condition. I listened quietly, silent tears spilling down my face.

"I want to tell you something," she pronounced seriously. "I have been reading some of the books you've mentioned to me, and I'm beginning to understand why you're walking. You're trying to live what you believe about peace. That doesn't mean I'm less worried about you, but I want you to know that I'm proud of you."

A tremendous love swelled within me. I felt its healing warmth throughout my body, and then sent it to her. I imagined this love enveloping her, entering her very being, and washing away the pain and hurt. In its wake, I saw that love leaving a trail of light and radiant health. I understood profoundly that my presence at my mother's side made no difference because what I was offering her transcended physical boundaries.

I went to sleep that night feeling at peace with my decision to keep walking, and with a strong sense that all would be well. My mother would be released two days later.

* * *

We pressed on past San Michele and San Giorgio, and now headed towards Cervignano. A thick fog rolled in, blanketing us. It had started several days earlier, and was grey and ominous. When it brushed past me, I shivered more from its eerie touch than its dampness. I felt on edge, not only because I feared for our safety on the open road, but because every car or person that passed us seemed to be emerging from another dimension.

At one of our many stops that day to warm up, Alberto started telling me about unusual dreams he was having. In one, he was a student in a School of White Magic in an ancient castle that also served as the student residence. Images of the Harry Potter books immediately came to mind. He described his ageless-looking teacher, who was also the headmaster and most powerful wizard in the land, teaching a class the forgotten importance of magic, imagination and fantasy, explaining that these were all wonderful teachers, and that what people called monsters were merely misunderstood creatures that we must not fear.

"It was amazing and so vivid," Alberto enthused. "I believe this world of magic truly exists, and not just as a fantasy. I want to explore this world, understand it, play with it, master it. It's a path that many before me have walked. It's been called many things, but most commonly, the Way of the Wizard.

"Are you saying you're a wizard now?" I asked.

"We are all wizards, whether we're aware of it or not," Alberto replied. "We are constantly creating our reality with our thoughts and beliefs. You know that. I just happen to call it being a wizard."

I didn't know who or what I was walking with any more, and was afraid to find out. He had gone from telling me he was an instrument of God, to an angel, and now a wizard.

"Are we talking about the world of dungeons and dragons here?" I asked hesitantly, trying to understand his ideas and his metaphors.

"Not in the way you think," Alberto chuckled. "To me, the wizard is God inside. I'm not talking about the mental awareness that God exists within me, but the absolute certainty and knowing that the extraordinary power that created the universe and the stars is the same power that resides within me and every one of us."

"What about dark wizards?" I probed, as if pulled by some magnetic force to know, or perhaps more importantly, to understand my unusual companion.

"They have God within them too," he replied, "but are so far removed from that light and love that they are blindly unaware of its existence. They live in darkness, in ignorance, and misuse that same creative power we all have for selfish gain or to hurt others."

"So you're a kind of Merlin?" I queried, puzzled.

"Not really," he said, "because it's believed such wizards used rituals, spells and potions to achieve their aims; but these are mere objects. They have no power. It is peoples' faith in them that gives them power. Faith, belief, certainty; these are the wizard's tools of creation, not inert objects. All that we need is within. It's getting to that place of absolute certainty that's the challenge."

"I'm trying to follow you," I remarked slowly, "but this is a totally different world for me."

"Magic is the divine power within you, Mony," Alberto assured. "It is God, in action. When you create, you are using that magic. It's a sacred gift to be honored, not something to be feared. Do you know who one of the greatest wizards in the world was?" Obviously I could not think of anyone, and told him so. "Jesus," he answered.

"You mean Jesus Christ?" I gaped.

"Yes," he answered confidently. "He never used potions or spells to heal the sick or create miracles. He had faith in the God within him and around him. From that certainty, he commanded what he desired into being. He taught that the power of faith could move mountains, and promised that we could do the same and more. That's all I'm trying to do; live every moment from the awareness that I am God living a human experience, and consciously create the world I desire from that place of absolute knowing."

"*Now he's telling me that Jesus was a wizard,*" I thought, aghast at the idea. "*So if he wants to be a wizard, does that mean he thinks he can be like Jesus? Who does he think he is?*"

18. Fear

Our walk into Cervignano seemed interminable. Heavy rains pounded us incessantly, almost soaking through our backpacks despite their protective covering. After more than an hour of walking in these conditions, we found a roadside bar, and stopped to dry off.

My phone rang, and I picked it up to find a distraught Hannah on the other line. Unhappy in her work and missing Alberto, she unburdened her loneliness and anguish on me. I consoled her as best as words from a friend could, and then handed the phone to a concerned Alberto whose loving tone eventually turned serious.

"Hannah, I think you should walk with us," he asserted. "I'd like to speak more, but can't right now. Please call me tonight." He handed me the phone, saying, "She's sick and more stressed out than ever. She needs to leave that life and join us. At least here, she would be living her spirituality."

"I don't know if that's the best thing for Hannah," I replied. "She has her own path and that sometimes means having to struggle, even suffer. I suffered for over two years at my job before I finally left. My work was my identity, my security, and I was terrified to step out of that into the unknown. Hannah is going through a process, that's all. I think all we can do is send her the courage and strength to choose what will make her happy."

Alberto's rigid countenance told me he didn't agree, but we were interrupted by a well-wisher. By the time he left, the rain had stopped and the skies were clearing, so we hurriedly left. Our pace was quick and purposeful. I could almost hear the wheels churning in Alberto's mind and dreaded the inevitable argument. We arrived in Cervignano relatively dry and were received at the first church where we stopped. Hannah called again, but this time sounding much happier.

"I was doing a lot of thinking after our talk today," she chirped, "and I've found some new ways to combine my spirituality with my work. You know, Mony, Jerusalem is not for me and…"

"I know, Hannah," I interjected. "You need to do what's right for you."

"Thanks for understanding," she replied warmly. "Can I speak with Alberto?"

Alberto glared at me. I didn't understand why he was so cross. He snatched the phone from my hands and stomped out into the hallway. I ignored him, and searched the bookshelves for anything interesting to read, randomly flipping through the mostly religious, Italian titles. A tense-looking Alberto eventually strode in, and began pacing the room. "How's Hannah?" I asked.

"Fine," he responded tersely, sitting on his mattress and pulling out his diary. I sat in my corner, and began writing in mine.

"Mony, I'd like to speak with you," Alberto stated gently. "I've been hesitating because I don't want to argue or to have you misunderstand me, but we need to talk."

"All right," I responded guardedly.

"I know we've had this discussion before," he said apprehensively, "but I feel that you're still not revealing the entire truth of our experiences. I respect your choice not to speak about it, but in this case, I believe it's affecting Hannah."

"What are you talking about?" I interjected, immediately feeling defensive. "She was happy when I spoke with her."

"She knew I was going to try to convince her to walk with us," he said, "so she invented a story to make us believe she was happy; but I know her. She's not happy. I'm sure she had these ideas before, but she conveniently chose to pull them out today."

"I think you're making a lot of assumptions," I replied.

"Mony, Hannah trusts you," Alberto continued, the edge in his voice marked. "She respects your opinion. Instead of telling her about how we're changing and growing every day, you filled her head with what she wanted to hear. You're encouraging her to stay where she is instead of helping her make a change, now."

"Her idea is good," I shot back in irritation. "It gives her something to work towards. Maybe you can just get up and leave everything behind, but obviously she can't. She needs more time. And you pushing her to quit is not helping her." Alberto stood and paced the room like a caged tiger. I stayed on the floor, watching him.

"At least I'm speaking the truth," he accused. "You only tell her the superficial things like the places we're visiting and the news articles, but not the important things."

"Unlike you, I'm not trying to change her or convince her of anything," I countered hotly. "You think if you keep telling her about all this magic that somehow she will see the light and leave everything behind. Guess what, she won't. Hannah is like me in more ways than you care to see. She does not like anyone telling her what to do or how to live her life, especially her close friends. She's not ready, and all the preaching that you do will not change a thing."

"How do you know if she's ready if you don't speak the truth?" He accused, towering over me. I stood and faced him. Alberto stepped back and took several deep breaths, clearly trying to control his emotions.

"I'm not telling you to tell her what I believe," he said, softening his tone. "I'm asking you to tell her what you believe. Speak honestly. Share with her your revelations. Tell her the things that you and I talk about all the time."

"I am speaking my truth, Alberto," I responded, "whether you believe it or not. I'm Hannah's friend too and I want to see her happy; but I don't know what's best for her. And neither do you."

"*How typically arrogant,*" I silently huffed.

"The real problem here is that you can't accept people for who they are," I said icily, "and have no respect for the path each person chooses to walk. There is no one right way for everyone. Real love is loving and accepting people no matter what they do; especially when they don't do what we want or expect. Maybe quitting is the right choice for Hannah, maybe it's not, I don't know; but I'm not going to be the judge of that. Maybe she needs to experience more pain before she makes the final break. Again, that's up to her; but I will love and support her no matter what she chooses."

"What?!" Alberto exploded. "Do you really believe that's what you're doing, allowing her to be herself? I can't believe it." Alberto shook his head in disgust and again paced the room, muttering to himself in Spanish, before stopping in front of me once again. This time, however, he looked weary.

"Listen to me, Mony," he said. "There are people who need to hear your truth because they are afraid. Hannah is one of those people. When you don't say what you truly think, feel and believe, you are an instrument of fear. Today, I sincerely believe that you did not help Hannah. You helped her fear. Hannah needs to hear the voice of her heart. She needs to hear the voice of your heart. I don't want to pressure her. I only want her to trust. To take a chance. To say *no* to her fear. To say *yes* to her dreams." Alberto looked at me sadly, almost compassionately, and added, "It is the same hope I have for you."

"Don't presume to know me," I fumed. But it was too late... Alberto had already walked out the door.

19. *Ciao, Italia*

The town of Aquilea, sounding like the word *aquila*, Italian for eagle, was our destination the following day. The friendly priest Father Olivo received us warmly, and over coffee, we spent a leisurely afternoon with our astute and well-versed host, speaking at length about many topics, including the conflict in the Middle East.

"The situation is complex, as you know," he stated. "If this conflict is so important to you, surely you must have some ideas about how to resolve it."

My heart beat nervously. I was still refining and testing my ideas of peace, and couldn't believe I was being asked to express them now when, in the lingering aftermath of my argument with Alberto, I was feeling especially uncertain.

"At one point, I thought I knew the answer," I hesitantly responded. "I grew up believing that the only way to peace was through resistance. It was only when I started to go through a profound spiritual change a few years ago that I even questioned those beliefs."

Father Olivo looked at me with interest, as I went on, "Every day, I see the difficulty of being in a state of peace. I still get angry: with Alberto, with myself, with people who judge or reject us. I bristle at injustice. How then must it be for Palestinians, living under occupation? How must it be for Israelis, living in a state of terror? How can they think peaceful thoughts? I can't even imagine their anger, their horror, their hatred."

"Indeed. How can they?" He asked. I paused, waiting for inspiration.

"Perhaps by going through what I'm going through," I mused aloud, "trying to find that peace within their hearts. To forgive. To heal. To see the light in their enemy. I sound naïve and idealistic even to myself, but that's what I feel to be intrinsically true. This walk is my laboratory for figuring peace out, and practicing it. I practice it when I'm rejected or judged. I practice it when I battle my fears and insecurities. I keep thinking to myself: how can I hold on to that light of peace in the midst of all these debilitating feelings? How can I grow from this? Who am I in response to this situation? I'm not always in that state of clarity, and I mess up often, but that's how I'm creating my peace. And since I believe that my peace is our peace, then I must believe that Israelis and

Palestinians are going through the same process; but their laboratory is more amplified and intense. They're experimenting with war and hatred to create peace."

"Do you think peace is possible?" he probed curiously.

"I'm realizing just how difficult the road of peace is to walk," I confessed. "But I'm also seeing that I'm the only master of that road. I control how I react to the difficult situations; no one else controls it for me. It's my choice. I believe these small choices add up, and taken together weave themselves into a collective change. The power to create peace is in my hands, not someone else's. I believe that's true for everyone, Palestinians and Israelis included. So yes, I think peace is possible, but only when individuals become responsible for their thoughts and deeds. I struggle with how to use personal power, how to translate it into effective action to create peace. I don't know when, or if, force is necessary. I still have many questions."

Father Olivo smiled approvingly. "What do you think about all this, Alberto?"

"I completely agree with Mony," Alberto replied, gazing at me with admiration. "For me, the conflict also serves a higher, loving purpose: spiritual growth. How can we know the light, if we don't pass through the dark? How can we value peace, if we don't experience war? I believe this conflict is an opportunity for each of us to reflect on what we believe, and to consciously choose what we want in response to that. That's not to say we just sit there with folded arms waiting for things to happen, but that we act not from fear or hatred, but from love, of wanting to understand."

We spent the afternoon in lively conversation with our host, and when we met him the following day to say our goodbyes, he presented us with a book on the town's famous Basilica that he dedicated and signed as Monsignor Olivo, a rare, honorific title bestowed by the Pope, and usually reserved for Bishops. He also handed me a stamped and self-addressed postcard showing the Hebrew alphabet which he asked us to send to him when we arrived in Jerusalem.

I walked away from Aquilea, my eagle town, trying to assemble these pieces of information into a coherent whole. I met a priest whose name meant olive, the undisputed tree of peace. He had given me a postcard of the Hebrew alphabet, a direct link to Jerusalem. I had spoken about peace in ways that I would have dismissed as rubbish in the not-too-distant past, and espoused, much to my amazement, a spiritual solution to a political problem. A tremendous shift was taking place, of that I was certain.

* * *

We passed Monfalcone and Trieste, and embarked on the final leg of our Italian experience. Yet another dense fog greeted us on a road that was mountainous and treacherous even for motorists; but they could not hold us back. We arrived at the Italian side of the border, breathless from the exertion of the way and our mounting enthusiasm. We joined the line of cars driving up to the incongruous white building, joyfully responding to their waves and honks. The officer at the kiosk examined us, his face expressionless, and demanded our passports.

"Where are you going?" He asked, leafing through the pages of our passports.

"Today to Kozina, Slovenia," I chirped, "but eventually to Jerusalem."

No response. No expression. I wanted to be inside his head at that moment, to know what he was really thinking. Surely he did not see people like us at the border every day. He returned our passports and motioned for us to pass through, wishing us a safe journey. We thanked him and joined the cars that were heading towards Slovenia. I glanced back and tried to contain my laughter. Hanging out the windows and excitedly waving was a group of border patrol officers. Our final Italian wave was for them. Within a few steps we were at another simple building that was the Slovenian border, where we were waved through without question.

I stood for a moment and looked back, hardly believing that we were finally out of Italy. It had taken us nine weeks, and we had walked just over one thousand kilometers. I felt pangs of melancholy, as a child leaving home for the first time, knowing that great adventures awaited us, yet feeling sad to be leaving the comfort of the known.

Italy had offered us many gifts—a language we grew to adore, lasting friendships, hospitality, love—and I knew I would miss her. She wasn't always easy on us. She knocked us down often, and challenged us physically, emotionally and spiritually. From those ruins, however, a stronger foundation was emerging, one more firmly based on trust, confidence, and love. As I looked ahead, those were the qualities I knew I wanted to carry with me. On January 29, 2002, we entered Slovenia.

Ciao Italia e grazie!

20. Invisible Friends

I stared at the billboard by the side of the road, trying to understand these new foreign letters. Uncertainty quickly displaced my previous excitement.

"Do they even speak English or Italian here?" I wondered. *"What currency do they use? Europe just introduced the Euro last month. Do they accept it? Do they have bank machines in small towns? Slovenia was part of Yugoslavia, which was a Communist regime, wasn't it? Are there even churches here?"*

It was difficult to corral the many questions that invaded my mind, but eventually the warm sunshine and pleasant surroundings won over for the short distance to Kozina, a simple village anchored by a gas station, a bar and a grocery store, and adorned with simple unassuming homes. Curious stares followed us.

We stopped at the bar, clear gathering place for the men of the village, and greeted them in Italian. They responded in Slovenian. I had assumed that at least here, so close to the Italian border, they would speak Italian; but they didn't. Alberto crossed himself and I made the sign of the cross with my fingers, trying to indicate that we needed the church. I hoped we weren't offending anyone with our gestures.

A young man approached and held out his cell phone, motioning for me to take it. Speaking in Italian, the man on the line explained that there was no church in town and that the nearest one was at least fifteen kilometers away. He confirmed that Slovenia accepted the Euro but returned the change in the local currency. I thanked this stranger profusely and returned the phone to the clearly pleased young man, thanking him also.

Alberto and I agreed we couldn't go another fifteen kilometers. It was already late afternoon and it had been a grueling day of walking. We strolled about the side streets searching for a sign, heavenly or otherwise, that would lead us to shelter. We finally found a pension, and with the money that Alberto was given that morning from a well-wisher, we split the cost and spent our first night in Slovenia.

We sat in our room the following morning, enjoying a breakfast of cookies and juice. Alberto appeared distracted, so I asked if he slept well. "I did, but had more strange dreams," he replied. I marveled at his ability to recall them so vividly, while I usually recalled snippets. Our last dream talk about wizards had revealed a side of Alberto that I found disconcerting. I wasn't sure why his ideas frightened me so much, only that they pulled me into spiritual territory that I resisted. Despite my reticence, I asked him to tell me his dream.

"I was with a group of about six children, aged between four and ten. I was maybe twelve. You were also there, but younger than me. We were walking to Jerusalem, and were happy and full of life, singing and playing along the way, and wore old, frayed tunics that were our only possessions. Far ahead of us was a giant about three meters tall with long dark hair, dressed in lumberjack clothing and carrying an axe. He walked through towns smashing windows with his axe, and blaming it on us. I felt that he fed from the destruction and fear that he awakened in people. Without even knowing us, people mistrusted us; but when we arrived and spoke the truth, joyfully and undaunted, they understood and welcomed us.

The giant never attacked us directly. I think he was afraid of us because the closer we got to him, the more desperate his actions became. When we finally reached him, we marched towards him and laughingly shooed him away with our hands and sticks, chanting in unison the words *no miedo, no miedo*[5]. The giant shirked away, holding his hands out in defense. With every word we sang, his body became smaller and smaller. He screamed in outrage, but it was too late. His body kept shrinking until it finally disappeared into the grass beneath some nearby bushes."

"It's easy to see that the giant represents fear," I remarked. "We're the children and, with our demeanor, were helping others dissolve their fears."

Alberto agreed, and added, "But it doesn't end there." I asked him to go on.

"From behind those bushes, two figures emerged," he said. "They were short and slim, and wearing what looked to me like terrible disguises—bald heads, fake hair, mismatched street clothes. They came near me, whispering that it was time for me to go. I was excited to join them and knew something wonderful was awaiting me, but felt terribly sad at having to leave everyone. You and the children saw these men,

---

[5] No fear

95

and clung to me, crying, begging me to stay. The two men patiently waited."

I felt the tears welling up in my eyes, as if I were living that moment of anguish. "A carpet appeared beneath your feet," Alberto went on, "and ever so slowly, started to slide, pulling you and the children away from me, leaving a trail of dust in its wake. You were in front of the group, and looked especially dismayed. The last image I have before waking up is of my tear-streaked face watching you disappear in the distance, and feeling such a profound sadness that my heart ached."

"Do you think something is going to separate us?" I asked.

"I'm not sure," Alberto responded.

"Who were the people asking you to go with them?" I asked. Alberto shifted uncomfortably. "Do I want to know this?" I added.

After a lengthy pause, Alberto said, "I believe they were beings from another world or dimension."

"You mean aliens?" I exclaimed.

"*Tranquila*[6], let me explain," Alberto quickly soothed. "These entities are like angels to me, spiritual guides, not something to be afraid of. I see the world as connected, and not just here on the physical plane, so there's no limit as to where love and guidance can come from—the spirit world, other planets, or different dimensions. To me, angels, spirit guides, and masters are all wise evolved beings, loving friends whose mission is to help us in our growth and raise our consciousness. In fact, it was because of them that I made the final decision to walk with you."

"What do you mean?" I asked apprehensively.

"In Germany, I was receiving many clear messages from them to join you on this walk," he answered, "but I was confused and under so much pressure that I started to doubt these messages. I was risking so much and didn't want to make a terrible mistake. Finally, I told them that I needed irrefutable proof that they were speaking with me before I made my final decision. I asked to see them."

I couldn't help gaping, and expectantly awaited his next words. "And I saw them," he concluded.

---

[6] Relax, calm down

"I don't want to know any more," I said firmly, standing to leave. "This is too much. You are scaring me, even if you don't mean to."

Alberto's other-worldly confession left me more spooked than ever, and I vowed to never again ask about his dreams. I knew enough. However, it did make me consider whether his dream was premonitory, somehow foretelling an impending separation. The thought saddened me. I locked away my fears, assuring myself that we were protected on our journey and that my fears would never come to pass.

* * *

Having just arrived from the grandeur of Italy, this part of Slovenia was decidedly uninspiring. Homes were square or rectangular, with no architectural detail. They looked functional and well-maintained, but showed none of the adornments we had become accustomed to seeing in every Italian town and village.

That evening, in Hrusica, we found a church and a most welcoming priest. The next day, we were again mired in mist, and could see nothing until we arrived at the simple shack that made up the Slovenian side of the border. The young officer casually leafed through our passports. "Where are you going?" he asked cheerfully in Italian.

We explained and showed him our signs. He laughed heartily, and excitedly called out to other people. We spent the next twenty minutes surrounded by merriment and camaraderie, speaking with candor to new friends, and receiving their well wishes. Walking away, one of the men ran up and handed us a bottle of wine, putting a cap on our brief, but memorable, experience among the hospitable Slovenian people.

Another white building a few hundred meters later marked the Croatian border. The officer brusquely asked for our passports, his face expressionless as he heard our explanations, then motioned for us to cross. On January 31, 2002, we took our first foggy steps into Croatia.

We walked for half an hour, only able to see the asphalt road, until we came upon a few houses. Looking around for a place to warm up from the damp cold, we glimpsed the words *Bar Mir-Bar Peace*, and could think of no better place to be.

A young man welcomed us in English. An older woman behind the bar nodded at us suspiciously. The bar was cozy and the food fantastic, all home-cooked, warm, and plentiful. At the end of our meal, the young man brought shots of some home-made liquor, telling us they were compliments of his mother at the bar. We thanked him and saluted her. She nodded, but her expression was still serious. We explained our story to the questioning young man, which he translated for his mother. Her expression remained the same. I wondered if something had been lost in the translation.

The village had no church, but thanks to the young man's efforts, a priest in Matulji twenty kilometers away now awaited us with promise of shelter. It was already after two o'clock, so we were certain to arrive at night. The idea of walking in foggy darkness without reflective material in another foreign country scared me, but we at least had a place to sleep.

To our surprise, the mother refused payment for our meal. She never said a word, simply folded her arms across her chest, and gazed at us. She even sent her son after us with a bag full of apples from her orchard. We learned our first Croatian word that day: *huala*, thank you. We would come to appreciate the full depth of these peoples' caring during our unexpectedly long stay in this country.

* * *

The Matulji city lights sparkled like diamonds, a welcome sight for the two weary pilgrims who finally arrived. The priest only spoke German and immediately led us to his car. He drove through the city and then out onto the open highway. We had no idea where we were going or how to even ask; so we sat and waited. He finally stopped in front of a hotel, led us inside, exchanged a few words with the receptionist, wished us a safe journey, and then drove off. The receptionist explained that our room and meal were compliments of the priest.

Over dinner, Alberto and I marveled at how the day had unfolded. We were once again in the unknown, relying on invisible forces to guide us. The Croatian heart had thus far revealed itself to be reserved but grand. I also realized that we were walking in a country that had just survived a bloody civil war, and nervously wondered how the message of peace, along with its messengers, would be received.

With the help of our waiter who spoke English, we translated our signs into Croatian. My sign would now read *Hodajuci prema Jeruzalemu za Mir*, and Alberto's *Hodajuci za Mir*.

We couldn't correctly pronounce the words, but hoped our intentions would be understood.

Our first few days outside the known of Italy were promising, with our concerns, for the moment, unwarranted. The magical seemed to transcend borders, and it was with a renewed enthusiasm that we looked ahead to the adventures that awaited us in Croatia.

21. The Call

We entered Rijeka, an enchanting, cosmopolitan city whose charm begged us to stop and enjoy it; but we couldn't. We were searching for Trsat, a monastery that we were assured would accommodate us. Two hours later, and at the city limits, we arrived at the base of an interminable set of steps where the monastery was supposed to be. A passerby, chuckling, pointed up the stairs, confirming its location. *"Maybe there won't be so many of them,"* I thought hopefully.

Five hundred and sixty one agonizing steps later, followed by a few-hundred meter uphill march, we arrived. My legs trembled. My heart pounded, and my lungs searched desperately for air. A majestic church presided over the city below, its bell tower reaching for the heavens, but I didn't care. My only interest was finding the monastery which, fortunately, was near the church.

The large wooden door creaked open and a young man, looking no older than twenty-five and wearing brown Franciscan robes, peered out. He spoke English, so I presented our needs. "I will have to ask the Superior for permission," he said. "He will return shortly but you are welcome to wait inside."

The young monk led us through an indoor courtyard to a lovely garden whose centerpiece was a cave structure housing a statue of the Virgin Mary of Lourdes. The lights of innumerable candles glowed gently, swaying softly in the breeze, and illuminating the statue. The candles balanced precariously in the wax of countless other candles that had melted long ago, and left their legacy on the stone for others to stand on.

"This chapel is dedicated to Our Lady of Trsat," he explained. "This is a place of pilgrimage. For centuries, pilgrims from all over Europe have come to pay homage here. They climbed the stairs, many on their knees, asking for penance and forgiveness. Even St. Francis of Assisi was here. He was shipwrecked on his way to Jerusalem, and started an Order here with the task of maintaining the chapel. That task continues to this day, here, in this Franciscan monastery."

"What a strange coincidence," I thought, following the monk inside the chapel; *"to be in yet another place of pilgrimage, as if we were following some invisible steps in time."*

The front wall was taken up by a simple statue of Mary. Every other wall was filled with crutches, braces, and walking aids. Hand-written notes, rosaries, and gifts of all types, including replicas of ships and paintings, took up every available space.

"The sick and needy come here, asking to be healed," he said reverently. "These gifts are a testament of their gratitude and devotion to Our Lady. You are welcome to wait here."

I wandered around the chapel, lingering at the hand-written notes, unable to understand the words, but feeling the faith and love of those who wrote them. That feeling emanated from every article, adding to the impact and overwhelming emotion of being in this sacred place.

Another young monk, no more than twenty, excitedly approached. "I am Vlado," he enthused. "When my brother told me about you, I knew I had to meet you. He mentioned you might be stopping in Medugorje."

We had heard about Medugorje, a village in Bosnia and Herzegovina, sporadically throughout our walk. In June of 1984, Mary purportedly appeared to six young children on a nearby hill, and started giving them messages of peace. The Vatican has never sanctioned the authenticity of the apparitions, as in Fatima or Lourdes, but this hasn't stopped people from going. What most attracted us to Medugorje was that she was called the Queen of Peace. "We haven't firmly decided," I responded.

"Oh, you must go," Vlado enthused. "You can feel the presence of the Holy Mother everywhere. I walked there from Zagreb, and felt God's hand guiding my every step. I found my faith and my calling during that pilgrimage, and decided then to dedicate my life to serving others."

We stayed in the garden for over an hour, pilgrims sharing stories and experiences, and remembering difficulties and triumphs. We connected profoundly with this young monk, and in him found a kindred spirit.

"I can speak with you forever," he proclaimed, "but I must leave. I promise to return soon." He was back within a few minutes, excitedly waving a small piece of paper. "Alberto! Mony! Look at this!" he exclaimed. "I found this note on the floor of the Basilica when I went in for prayers. It was the only piece of paper there." It looked like it had been pulled out of a fortune cookie.

"What does it say?" I asked.

"It's a message from Our Lady of Peace in Medugorje," Vlado enthused. "She still communicates with some of the children, or visionaries as they are now called. Her message is published on the twenty-fifth of every month. This message speaks about following your faith."

"This is no coincidence," Alberto said.

"I believe it is intended for you," Vlado affirmed.

Alberto asked me for the map and pulled out a small pocket calendar. With Vlado's help, we mapped out a route to Medugorje. It was near the Croatian border, about six hundred kilometers south of where we were.

"Today is February the first," Alberto said. "If we can average twenty-five kilometers a day without taking rest days, then we can be there for the twenty-fifth."

"I believe Our Holy Mother is calling you," Vlado added reverently. "You must go."

Vlado left us again, and Alberto and I wandered the grounds. I wasn't sure what to make of what had just happened. It seemed like a sign to go, but I needed more proof. Two hours later, Vlado reappeared and hurried us through the halls of the dimly-lit monastery, depositing us into the arms of a motherly nun who led us by the hand to our room, all the while speaking excitedly in Croatian, and then to a dining table filled with hot food.

We sat with Vlado and enjoyed the pasta dish mixed with sour cream, cheese, and onions, along with various local cheeses and fresh bread. Vlado nibbled on some bread, and sipped water. We invited him to join us.

"Our Lady in Medugorje recommends fasting Wednesdays and Fridays," he replied happily. I couldn't enjoy my meal after that.

An older monk joined us. He spoke limited English, and so Vlado was our translator for the evening. Vlado's devotion to Medugorje was evident, but with this other monk, I felt even more deeply the unconditional acceptance of the ways of the Catholic Church. We had stayed in many monasteries in Italy, but I never felt the fervor that I felt here. The Croatians seemed more Catholic than the Italians, so I kept my views to myself and felt I was walking a tight rope all evening. Alberto was similarly reserved, and when he did speak, it was in simple, non-controversial ways. I was relieved to see the evening come to an end.

* * *

Vlado sat with us at breakfast and seemed even more excited than usual. "I had the strangest dream last night," he confessed. "I don't normally remember my dreams, but this one felt very real. A magician came to the monastery."

"Excuse me?" Alberto exclaimed. "Did you say a magician?"

"Yes. You know," Vlado replied, "a wizard."

I glanced at an astonished Alberto. "So what happened?" He asked, trying to sound matter-of-fact.

"I was in a room studying and praying with some of the brothers," Vlado stated, "when someone knocked on the door. I opened it, and invited the wizard inside. He was friendly and open, sharing with us his beliefs about God and Jesus. I felt his words were an attack on our faith, even though I knew that wasn't his intention. The brothers were becoming agitated, but no one challenged him. I was also becoming tense and couldn't listen any longer, so I stood and said, 'Go to Medugorje.' The wizard stopped speaking and looked at me intently. Then I woke up."

"How did you know he was a wizard?" Alberto asked furtively. "Did he perform any magic?"

"No," Vlado replied slowly, his eyes firmly fixed on Alberto. "He spoke more like a philosopher, but I knew he was a wizard."

Vlado announced he had something for us, and pulled out several items from a nearby cabinet, mainly pendants and photos of various Marys and saints. He surprised us with a hand-written list of common Croatian translations to words such as hello, goodbye, my name is, and where is the church. I smiled affectionately when I saw included translations for the full Hail Mary and how to say I'm fasting Wednesday and Friday.

Finally, Vlado handed me a small English bible. I had been receiving continual signs for the name John since Italy; first Giovanni in Italian and now Ivan in Croatian. Since St. John was represented by the eagle, I had wanted to search for a message or sign in this Gospel of the Eagle, but had dismissed the idea of finding an English bible in Croatia.

Now that it was in my hands, however, I was certain that there was something there for me.

"Wasn't that amazing?" Alberto enthused once we were on the road again. "Wow. It's the first time I've ever received a message through someone else's dreams. If this doesn't prove the existence of magic, I don't know what does."

"Do you think Vlado suspects you're the wizard?" I asked.

"Judging by the way he was looking at me, I would say yes," Alberto replied, "but that doesn't matter. His message is what matters. We need to be in Medugorje for the twenty-fifth."

"I don't know, Alberto," I said evasively. "I want to get there but I don't want to push myself."

Alberto didn't seem pleased with my response. Things were changing quickly, in ways I couldn't understand, and they unnerved me. I needed time to reflect. Perhaps Medugorje was calling the wizard, but that didn't mean she was calling me.

22. Guardian Angels

Rocky peaks rose to our left. The Adriatic waters glimmered to our right. The road hugged the mountain, curving gently with it, and making for spectacular views. For the first time in months, I took off my jacket and enjoyed walking in the warm sunshine.

We arrived at our destination late in the day and, practicing our new Croatian words, asked for the church. We walked in the general direction until we arrived at the base of some large, wide steps. I looked up, trying to see where they ended, but the sun temporarily blinded me. In the glare, a small figure appeared high atop the stairs, the light of the sun casting a halo around its body. I blinked several times at what looked like an angel hovering above us, and stepped back. Talk of wizards and aliens was making me edgy.

The figure descended and I could finally see that it was a girl of about ten years. Her chestnut hair fell gently around her shoulders, and framed a lovely face. I greeted her in Croatian. She smiled and returned my greeting, then shyly turned away. Alberto and I started up the thirty-odd steps. Halfway through, I stopped and turned around. To my surprise, the little girl was a few steps behind us, this time with a similarly beautiful girl of the same age. I smiled and waved at them. They raced towards us.

"What is your name?" I asked slowly, in English.

"Anna Maria," answered the first girl we saw.

"You understand me," I exclaimed.

"Yes," she replied happily. "I am learning English in school. This is my friend Tania." Alberto and I introduced ourselves. The girls shook our hands, giggling.

"Can you please take us to the church?" I asked. They nodded excitedly and led the way, all the while whispering to each other. It was dark by the time we arrived. Parishioners milled about the church entrance, and we saw the priest unloading boxes from a car with the help of two young boys. Tania and Anna Maria marched right up to him and began to speak, pointing at us. The priest distractedly glanced our way, so we approached. Ascertaining that he spoke Italian, I began to explain our needs while he continued unloading his car. I wondered if he was even listening.

"Look, I am extremely busy right now," he interjected in irritation. "I cannot help you. Try a hostel."

Discreet whispers of disapproval sounded among the crowd, but the priest took no notice.

"Please, let me explain," I tried again. "We started in Rome two months ago. We have slept in convents, monasteries, at times even the house of the priest..."

"The house of the priest?" He scoffed, cutting me off. "Do you expect me to let you sleep in my home? I don't think so. I don't even know you."

"I'm trying to explain," I continued, flustered.

"Stop," Alberto said with authority. "We're leaving."

For the first time since we had arrived, the priest stopped. He locked eyes with Alberto, clearly surprised; but the moment passed, and he returned to unloading his car. He barked some commands, and then walked into the church. Everyone followed him. Anna Maria and Tania brushed past the crowd towards us, their eyes filled with concern.

"Thank you for everything you have done," I said, kneeling to look at each one in the eye. I hated to see their worry. "You are two special angels. Always remember that you not only helped two strangers in need, but two pilgrims on their way to Jerusalem. We will never forget you."

The girls reached over and embraced me. I held on to both of them tightly, and kissed each on the cheek. Alberto leaned down and did the same. I turned and quickly walked away, weeping. Alberto placed his arm around my shoulders.

"But where will you sleep tonight?" I heard Anna Maria cry out in the darkness.

Her words seared into my heart like a flame. Mustering up the courage to sound light-hearted, I turned and yelled back, "Don't worry. We always find a place to sleep." With one last wave, I hurried away and never looked back. Alberto's lightly caressed my head, trying to console me, but I was inconsolable.

I cried until I was spent, until all the frustration worked its way out of my being. Alberto suggested we try the only hostel in town, but it was sold out for Carnival festivities. We tried several other places that we were directed to, but in the end, had to face the reality that there was no place for us to sleep in town. Looking at our map, we saw that the nearest town was four kilometers away along the coastline. We agreed to continue ahead and search for possible camping spots along the way. At 7:30 PM, in complete darkness, we began our slow march.

I silently begged for help, and recalled the many moments when it miraculously appeared. I saw Alberto wiping away a tear and heard him whisper, "Please help us. If I really am the wizard you keep telling me I am, then why can't I change this situation?" His eyes searched the heavens. "I believe," he said, sounding angry and clenching his fists. Then in a barely audible whisper I heard, "Please. I believe."

A long chain now blocked our advance. Dangling from it was a sign bearing the words PRIVATE. DO NOT PASS. "Where are you going?" A man's voice called out in English, frightening me.

We peered into the darkness. Fishing boats rocked gently in the bay, while others lay discarded along the shore. A wiry, older man, sporting a sailor's hat and cigarette dangling from his lips, stood behind one of the boats on the shore.

"We are looking for a place to sleep," Alberto answered.

"You can sleep in any one of these boats here," he proclaimed, waving his arms about. "That's what I'm doing tonight."

We both shook our heads. "No, thank you," Alberto said, adding that we were trying to get to the next town. The old man took a deep puff of his cigarette, studying us. "Stay on this path along the water and you'll get there," he said, and disappeared into his boat.

We continued ahead, following his directions, ignoring another sign that said PROHIBITED. The street lights ended here. Beyond us was nothing but darkness. We agreed to press ahead, and pulled out our flashlights. The path wound through an increasingly industrialized area. Heavy machinery and cranes towered above us. Large shipping boats stood like impenetrable walls. We realized we were in a port, but the path cut through it. We followed it cautiously, but it ended all too soon at a set of train tracks. The situation seemed to be going from bad to worse. "Do we go back?" I asked.

"There's nothing for us back there," Alberto replied in agitation.

I ignored his tone, and quietly followed him along the train tracks, stepping through a black, muddy gunk that squished under my feet. The smell of oil and solvents filled the air. I walked in Alberto's steps, trying to prevent the gunk from reaching my ankles, and wondering how this night was going to end. A long steel-mesh ramp now appeared. It flattened out into an overpass that floated about ten meters above us, and seemed to stretch out indefinitely. I started up the ramp cautiously, testing my weight on it. It felt solid, so I motioned for Alberto to follow me. The ramp was wide enough for one person, and higher and longer than it looked from below. We walked quickly, bright lights partially illuminating our way.

Several hundred meters later, our detour abruptly ended about six meters above the ground. The only way off was down a narrow steel ladder of about fifteen steps that was encircled by a thick metal spiral. I stared incredulously at this scene, not knowing whether to laugh or cry. Pressing his body against the ladder, Alberto gingerly made his way to the ground. My backpack was wider than his, and I was afraid of getting stuck inside the metal spiral. Alberto climbed halfway up and took my backpack, as I carefully made my way down the slippery steps. Our hands were black. Alberto's jacket was smeared. He angrily cleaned it with a wet towel. I had seen long ago that Alberto was scrupulous about being clean, and I knew this was difficult for him.

The overpass deposited us back beside the railroad track. Beyond it, we could see the waterside path. Blocking our access, however, was a long train that was parked exactly where the ramp ended. We looked for ways under and over the train, but it was hopeless. We began to walk towards the end of the train.

A dog began to bark loudly. I tensed. About fifty meters ahead, a man stood in front of a small building, his flashlight beaming out into the darkness. It was clear that he was the night watchman; and we were trespassing.

"*Mierda[7],*" Alberto exclaimed.

"This is just perfect," I griped. "I hope Croatian jails are warm."

We approached slowly, saying "hello" in every language we knew. The man pointed the light at us, but did not respond. I couldn't make out his features, but he was an older man, possibly in his sixties, dressed in a uniform. Unable to pronounce what we were doing in Croatian, I turned around so he could see the sign on my backpack. The man stared at us quietly, his face expressionless. The dog, a small terrier, ran circles around us, barking incessantly. The man motioned for us to follow him.

---

[7] Shit

We followed him inside the dimly-lit building, and into a small room that had cramped into it antiquated furnishings: corner table, rickety chair, sofa-bed with brown wool blanket, bar fridge. A movie played on the small black and white television. We sat on the bed, he on the chair. I pulled out the list that Vlado had prepared for us, searching desperately for any words or fragments that would explain our situation. The man gently reached for the list, and then silently examined it. Pointing at us and using hand gestures, he asked where we were sleeping. Responding in a mix of sign language, English, Italian, and some words from the list, we attempted to explain what had happened in town, throwing our hands up in a sign of resignation and pointing in the direction of the next town.

The man maintained a calm that was threatening to unnerve me. Finally, he stood and once again motioned for us to follow him. Alberto and I exchanged nervous glances. I didn't know what he was going to do. He could justifiably call the police since we were trespassing, but I was so emotionally exhausted at that point, I didn't care what happened to us. I just wanted to stop moving.

The guard led us out of that building and into one nearby that the darkness had kept hidden. He turned on the lights. The abandoned feeling only accentuated the coldness of the neglected space. He led us down a corridor, and opened a door. The smell of sweat and grime was overwhelming. Empty cans, discarded tissues, and rumpled pieces of paper littered the floor. Oil and dirt mixed to create a filthy layer that coated everything. The windows looked like they hadn't been cleaned in years. Two makeshift beds peeked out from under several dark blankets. The man pointed at the beds, then at us, and made the sign for sleeping.

I stared at him in disbelief, and openly began to sob. Alberto started doing the same. At that moment, the filth disappeared, and all I saw was shelter for two weary souls. Together, Alberto and I reached over and embraced the shocked man. He backed out of the room slowly. I thought he was going to run away, but moments later, he was back with a space heater, which only brought on more tears. The poor man stood there looking distraught, wringing his hands, not knowing how to comfort us.

He led us by the hand back to his room and eagerly motioned for us to sit down. He opened the fridge door and emptied its contents onto the table, gesturing for us to eat; but I was too upset. He cut some bread and cheese, and handed them to me, which only made me cry harder. Singing rang out from the television, and in English the words "sometimes you just need an angel" repeated as part of the chorus. I could barely breathe from the emotion that wracked my body. The distressed man momentarily left the room, and I heard him speaking on the phone. I used that time to stop crying, and when he came back, we finally introduced ourselves. The man pointed to himself and said, "Micho." Michael, like the angel that he was.

I pulled out some of the photos that Vlado had given me and showed them to him in an attempt to communicate. He lingered over the one of Medugorje, so I immediately gave it to him. He smiled happily and lovingly kissed the picture, embracing it close to his heart. I wished I could have given him everything that I owned at that moment for his single act of kindness.

A young man arrived, and in Italian, introduced himself as Donald, a friend of Micho's. Finally able to express ourselves, we explained everything to Donald, who translated it to the increasingly amazed Micho. Shortly after, Donald's girlfriend arrived with her mother. She spoke English, so I was able to communicate even more fully the depth of this incredible gift that had been bestowed upon us.

Donald explained that Micho could neither read our sign nor the note that we had given him because his eyesight was poor and he didn't have his glasses with him. I thought he had helped us because we were pilgrims walking for peace, but the truth that he had helped two strangers in the night was even more incredible.

Joy radiated from Micho. He clapped his hands and spoke enthusiastically, all the while looking at us with the same wonder that we looked at him. Finally, the group stood to leave. We hugged everyone in turn. Donald's girlfriend reached into her pocket and pulled out a small porcelain figure of an angel. I had no idea why she would be carrying an angel with her, but it was the most precious and perfect gift, proof that angels were indeed among us that night.

* * *

We stood in front of the building with Micho. The light of day broke slowly through the grey fog. The path started at his doorstep.

We repeated the word *huala*, not knowing how to say anything else, and wanting to say so much more. The gentle sparkle in Micho's eyes told me that he understood. Micho cupped Alberto's face in his hands and gazed lovingly into his eyes, as a proud father with his son. Alberto's eyes watered, and they embraced. My never-ending tears surfaced again. Micho embraced me, gently stroking my hair. When he released me, he reached into his pocket and pulled out his wallet, but we gently pushed it away. He searched his pockets, and I could tell he wanted to give us something, but the value of what he had given us transcended any physical object. His humanity had restored our faith, and that gift would remain with us forever. We will never forget Micho, our guardian angel.

That incident left me more convinced than ever that angels were walking with us, making things happen. That day, Alberto and I left behind his camping tent as a demonstration of our faith in them.

23. Our Deepest Fear

We continued along the spectacular Croatian coastline, passing Novi Vinodolski and heading towards Senj. Thanks to a roadside interview that we granted a passing journalist, we were greeted in recognition and stopped by many people, all wishing us the now familiar *Sretan Put,* a safe journey. We found our picture on the back cover of the local newspaper, along with a small article, and added this first of many more Croatian articles to our Italian collection.

I was receiving continual signs that day for Ivan, the Croatian name for John. From a car that stopped with an occupant of that name, to a huge wall spray-painted with the word Ivana, to discarded bits of paper at my feet with that word, the Universe was screaming at me. I was attentive. When I stopped at the side of the road to adjust my backpack, Alberto said that he too was receiving signs at that moment. We stood and waited.

Across the road, a young woman stepped out of a restaurant and, in English, asked if she could help us. We answered "yes" in unison and crossed the road, telling her we could use a drink. We chose a table near the entrance of the bright, spacious restaurant. I tried to be patient, but thought I would jump through my skin when I saw a painting of an eagle hanging alongside that of a white dove.

The young woman appeared with our drinks, and asked what we were doing. She looked to be in her twenties, with long, flowing auburn hair and a lovely face. Her green eyes struck me not only for their beauty and kindness, but the sadness they conveyed. She listened politely to our story, but her averted gaze and folded arms told me there was something she didn't agree with. We invited her to join us, and introduced ourselves.

"I am Ivana," she said, sitting down. My heart lurched. Alberto kicked me under the table.

"How is it that you speak English so well?" I asked, trying not to scare her off with my enthusiasm.

"I am studying to be an English teacher," she replied, "and am only home for a few days helping my parents here."

Through our conversation, I learned that her family was Bosnian and that the civil war had forced them into refugee camps for many years. Unable to return to their home, they now lived in a land that did not welcome them and that generally regarded them with disdain and to be of an uneducated, lower social class. After years of hard work building their family restaurant, were they finally being accepted in their new community.

"I think what you're doing is admirable," she said, smiling sadly, "but I don't think it will change anything. One person can't make a difference."

"Gandhi was one man, and he made a difference," I replied. "He said we must each be the change we wish to see in the world. That's all we're trying to do. Every day people stop to speak with us. They honk their horns and wave in support. They invite us into their homes. They offer us food and drink, and often to sleep there. For that brief moment, their attention is on peace. I can't tell you what's changing inside each and every person, but their actions demonstrate that we are influencing them."

"Most people here only think about surviving," Ivana responded. "They don't have the luxury of thinking about creating peace. They've learned that even when they try to speak about peace, they can be arrested."

I could sense that she wanted to believe me, but that she didn't want to have hope, that fragile commodity so easily crushed. "I was in Lebanon for a few months this past year," I reflected. "My father had always described it in such glowing terms, but what I saw were the scarred remnants of twenty-five years of civil war—people living in fear and mistrust, not knowing if or when war will break out again, and taking what they could for themselves, often at the expense of others. Those genuinely interested in rebuilding their country were labeled fools and idealists who didn't understand the complexity of the country's religious and political realities. I've come to understand that they too care deeply for their country, that they want to live in the peace they dream of, but are afraid to hope, to be disappointed yet again. I'm not saying it's easy, but peace remains a choice, even in times of war."

"We've met so many people during this walk who are building peace," Alberto added, "but they think they're alone. They're the ordinary people that Mony mentioned who step out of their daily routines to help us. They're the real heroes of the world. Thanks to them, I believe more than ever in the goodness of people and our power to change the world."

"It's hard to believe that I can make a difference just by being nice to someone," Ivana responded with disbelief.

I asked her for a piece of paper, and while she spoke with Alberto, wrote out words that I had long ago memorized and taken to heart. They were given to me the day I saw my eagle for the first time, and was questioning my audacity to dream of working for peace. They were part of Nelson Mandela's 1994 inauguration speech when he accepted the South African presidency. I asked Ivana to read them.

> *"Our deepest fear is not that we are inadequate.*
> *Our deepest fear is that we are powerful beyond measure.*
> *It is our light, not our darkness, that most frightens us.*
> *We ask ourselves, who am I to be brilliant, gorgeous, talented and fabulous?*
>
> *Actually who are we not to be?*
> *You are a child of God. Your playing small doesn't serve the world.*
> *There is nothing enlightened about shrinking so that other people won't feel insecure around you.*
> *We are all meant to shine as children do.*
>
> *We were born to make manifest the glory of God that is within us.*
> *It's not just in some of us, it's in everyone.*
> *And when we let our own light shine, we unconsciously give other people permission to do the same.*
> *As we are liberated from our own fear, our presence automatically liberates others."*

Ivana's lips curved into a smile. It was a smile of hope, of believing in the impossible, of having the audacity to dream the grandest dream. I felt a tremendous sense of joy and accomplishment, and a deeper appreciation of what this journey was also about. I was giving people back their power. I was giving people back hope. Sitting before Ivana, I couldn't think of a more powerful purpose than to awaken that spark within each person.

* * *

114

We spent the night in Senj and pressed on to the tiny fishing village of Sveti Juraj, grateful to find a priest, and appreciating the storage room that would serve as our shelter for the evening. While Alberto searched for food, I cleared space on the wooden bench that would be my bed that night. Alberto arrived shortly after, smiling proudly. He held out the expected block of cheese and baguette. Next, he pulled out a tube of mustard, then one of mayonnaise, and smiled victoriously.

Perhaps it was the cold night, or the hard day's walk in the mountains, but the sight of yet another block of cheese with bread, garnished as it was, set me off. "That's it," I exploded. "Tomorrow we're eating a proper meal, and I don't want to hear any complaints from you."

"We've had this discussion before," he responded calmly. "You can eat what you like and sleep where you like. Don't blame me if you feel guilty."

"Mustard and mayonnaise are not food," I seethed.

"I appreciate your invitations and have accepted them many times," he answered. "I don't want you paying for everything."

I didn't know what was making me angrier, his words or his attitude. He was calm and confident, while, for some reason, I was spiraling out of control.

"You think you have all the answers," I blurted. "Do you think you are some kind of master? Have you reached some state of illumination that I'm not aware of? What makes you think you're so special?" Alberto quietly stared at me, his arms folded across his chest, as if watching some petulant child having a tantrum.

"Here we go again," he sighed. "I am no more special than you or anyone else. I'm only trying to help others, just as I've been helped. If I wait to be perfectly illuminated to do that, or anything else in my life, then I will be waiting forever. What I know now can serve others, just as what others know can serve me. We are all masters and pupils. We are all teaching and learning at the same time."

"But no one asks for your advice, Alberto," I interjected. "You just offer it."

"It's easy to hide behind the excuse of who am I or what if I make a mistake," he retorted. "People are free to ignore me. I will not hide myself for fear of appearing arrogant. Nor will I be less so that another can feel more at ease. Isn't that what your precious Nelson

Mandela said? Only yesterday were you reciting those words to Ivana. Or have you forgotten?"

Alberto announced that he needed to use the facilities, and headed towards the door. I heard him turn the handle several times, but the door didn't open. "The priest has locked us in," he said incredulously.

The windows were barred, and the priest in another part of the building. I needed to use the washroom too, and didn't know how I would hold it in all night. Alberto scrimmaged through the room and held out an empty Coke bottle. "I can't pee in a bottle," he anguished. "It's just too vulgar."

"I only wish I could," I retorted.

"There are always the flower pots," he chuckled, pointing at one of the larger pots.

I lay in my sleeping bag, pulled my knees to my chest, and shook my feet, trying to think of anything that would distract me from my need to urinate. I heard the trickle of liquid in the bottle, and hated Alberto even more. Alberto switched off the lights and lit a candle. He came towards me and knelt by my side. "I didn't mean to hurt you," he whispered.

I returned his gaze, not knowing what to say and feeling overwhelmingly confused. Alberto reached over and embraced me. Tears hovered in my eyes and I fought the urge to bury my head in his shoulder and weep. I released him and turned away, not wanting him to see my turmoil, but knowing it was evident.

I had nowhere to run, no one to turn to. In my moments of confusion, there was only Alberto, usually the source of that tumult. I needed time away from him, time to gather my thoughts and feelings; but on this journey of peace, it seemed that we were destined to continue together.

24. The End of the Rainbow

Severe rains pounded us the following morning on a road that snaked deep into mountains that seemed to have to end. I screamed at the heavens and pleaded with the rains to stop, but my cries went unheard. With no place to stop along that barren road, all I could do was walk.

I trudged up that mountain, soaked and shivering, questioning the sanity of my decision to ever start walking. Alberto, however, was in an irritatingly good mood, and hummed and sang to himself, which only made me want to scream even louder.

By late afternoon, the sun finally came out. I sat on a large stone at the edge of a cliff, resting. The sun warmed my body and dried my clothes. I watched with amusement the steam rising off my jacket. I wanted to dry my socks, but feared removing my boots. My feet were swollen and blistered, and I didn't know if I would be able to put them back inside the boots. The arch of my left foot also ached, the searing pain shooting up to my knees. My entire body ached and begged me to rest, but I stood, fearing that my muscles would contract and not carry me the rest of the way. Leaning heavily on my stick, I walked the switchback descent in a zigzag fashion, trying to cut the intensity of the incline and take pressure off my screaming shin muscles.

"Where is the rainbow? Where is the rainbow?" Alberto sang out happily.

As we rounded yet another curve, I heard him gasp and turned to see an amazed Alberto gaping at the sky. Above our heads was the largest, most vibrant rainbow I had ever seen. Its colors glowed against the clear blue sky, arching from one mountain peak to another, and completely covering the sky above us.

"I knew it!" Alberto cried out. "I knew we would see a rainbow today. And what a rainbow! It's the biggest one I've ever seen." I walked away, leaving Alberto to sing with his rainbow.

"Look!" I heard him yell. "Now it's a double rainbow! It looks even wider than before! This is so amazing; and all at the end of the day, just as we're arriving! Thank you, Life, thank you for this beautiful gift!"

We would only ever witness such a magnificent double rainbow when arriving in Jerusalem.

With arms outstretched and face gazing adoringly at the heavens, Alberto bounded down the mountain, twirling and leaping. He kept calling for me to stop and enjoy it, but I trudged ahead, feeling increasingly irritated by his joyfulness.

A quaint village sat prettily beside the water, glowing softly in the setting sun. I hurried my steps, ignoring my blisters and body's loud protests. The remaining light guided us to the priest's house. I knocked in anticipation, not even wanting to consider the possibility that we would be refused. No one answered. I knocked louder and stepped back, waiting for the door to open. Still no one came out. I fought the wave of rising desperation. "*Please be home, please be home,*" I pleaded over and again.

We stood at the door for what felt like an hour, knocking, yelling, and waiting. Still, no one answered. The village looked even smaller than Sveti Juraj. The only sign of life was a docked ferry loading passengers and cars. I recalled Micho and the many miracles that had befallen us, and knocked again. This time, the door opened.

A short, older man with balding grey hair looked at us quizzically, while munching on an apple. I presented our needs.

"I hope you haven't been waiting long," he apologized, ushering us inside. "I was upstairs sleeping and did not hear you. I am Father Josip, but you can call me Joso."

I followed Father Joso inside a comfortably appointed home. He led us up some stairs and pointed to one room, indicating it was Alberto's, then down the hall to another room, and opened the door. A clean, ruffled bedspread covered the single bed. An antique lamp sat on a wood night stand. Simple curtains hung in the windows. I turned away, not wanting Father Joso to see my tears. He invited us to freshen up while he prepared dinner.

After the warmest shower, I sat on my bed and examined my swollen feet. Huge water blisters, some on top of each other, bulged around my ankles and between my toes. I couldn't even touch them, let alone put socks on. I forced my bare feet as far as they would go into my slippers, and hobbled down the hall. Together with Alberto, we walked down to the kitchen, where a table full of food awaited us: rice, bread, and a hearty soup that had the leg of some animal floating in it. I inhaled it all, feeling grateful.

Communication was a challenge because Father Joso spoke mainly German and some French and English; but I think we conveyed the essence of our walk. When we mentioned that we wanted to arrive in Medugorje for the twenty-fifth, Father Joso looked away diffidently. "I don't wish to interfere with your plans," he said. "I just don't believe you need to go to any special place to see God. God is everywhere."

I immediately agreed, and waited for Alberto to do the same. He didn't, and the conversation abruptly ended. I shot Alberto an inquisitive glance, but he simply sat with arms folded across his chest, looking at the table.

Noticing the condition of my feet, Father Joso invited us to stay a few days longer. I immediately accepted his offer. Alberto glared at me. Father Joso reached across the table and held out a basket of red apples, indicating for me to take one, and I did. He then offered the basket to Alberto, muttering some words. Alberto's face turned white, and he politely refused. "*What is going on with you?*" I mentally yelled at him.

Our evening finished, I returned to my room and prepared to thread my blisters. It was a technique I had learned on the Camino that involved threading a needle, soaking it in iodine, and then piercing the blister with the needle, leaving the iodine-soaked thread inside. In this way, the liquid drained out and left the blister open to dry, but disinfected.

Alberto peered inside my room, and winced as he watched me care for my blisters. "What do you think about Father Joso?" He asked.

"I think he's an angel," I replied without hesitation.

"Yeah, he seems nice, but I don't know," Alberto said, but he didn't sound convinced. "Still, my intuition says we should continue walking."

"Why do you say that?" I asked, astonished.

"There are some things about him that don't mesh," he replied. "First, he would have to be deaf not to hear us yell at his door for an hour. Don't get me wrong, I like him, but I was already suspicious, and his comments at dinner about Medugorje, as true and well-intentioned as they may be, made me feel as if he was trying to take us off our path. Then he invited us to stay, offering those apples." Alberto's gaze intensified. "He offered the apples to you first, and you accepted. Then he looked at me, and with a twisted smile said, *il frutto proibito*.[8]" Alberto paused, his eyes shining with passion, willing me to understand.

"And?" I asked.

---

[8] The forbidden fruit

"Don't you see?" He exclaimed. "It's as if we were in the Garden of Eden. You, Eve, were already eating the apple of temptation. And now, it seemed as if the devil himself was making me the same offer."

"Father Joso doesn't even speak Italian," I interjected. "I'm sure you misunderstood him."

"All priests know basic Latin, Mony," he replied. "Besides, it's what I heard. I'm not saying he's the devil. You know I don't believe in malign spirits. I think he was just a messenger, and the scene was created for me to get the message. I must go to Medugorje."

"Alberto, there's no way I can walk tomorrow," I pleaded. "Look at my feet. I can't even stand. I need a day's rest."

"If we stay, then we won't arrive on the twenty-fifth," Alberto retorted. An awkward silence ensued. "So are you seriously thinking about staying?" He asked.

"I am staying," I replied firmly, and continued threading my blisters.

"Aside from getting to Medugorje, I've been receiving signs about walking alone," he revealed. I stopped threading.

"I thought we agreed that the way of peace was better served with us together," I said.

"This is different," he replied earnestly. "I feel it's important for me to be in Medugorje for the twenty-fifth. We would only be apart a short while. I would wait for you there."

"Why not wait a day or two until I am well enough to walk?" I replied anxiously. "Father Joso just told us there were no churches or places to stop for at least fifty kilometers. We just left our tent behind, remember?"

"I can't do that if I want to be in Medugorje for the twenty-fifth," Alberto persisted. He stood, and in a firm tone said, "I want to leave tomorrow."

"What kind of signs have you been getting anyways?" I asked, hearing the desperation in my voice. "Maybe you're misinterpreting them."

"I wish I were," Alberto sighed. "I can't explain them to you easily because they only make sense in my head, in the way I see and interpret things…"

"I can't believe this," I murmured.

"This is not easy for me, Mony," Alberto pleaded. "Please try to understand. I'm afraid of making a huge mistake, but I feel this is something we both must do. My signs are clearly telling me to go alone. I also sense that we must prove to ourselves that we can walk alone, and trust that we will be fine even though we are apart."

My mind momentarily went blank, and then started playing out its worst fears. I felt vulnerable and afraid. Father Joso had made me nervous when he said there were few places to stop along the way, and I now cursed the moment we left the tent behind.

"I feel so bad leaving you, especially like this," Alberto agonized, pointing at my feet. "This is not like walking in Italy. At least there, I felt we were still in Europe, but here everything is foreign. The walking is more challenging than in Italy, and there are fewer places to stop. Not to mention that you are a woman walking alone. I don't even have a phone for us to be in contact."

I wanted Alberto by my side, but not from obligation. As my fears ran away with my thoughts, a calming voice resounded within me, reminding me that we were pilgrims, each on their journey of peace; and pilgrims always found their way.

"Blisters, I've had before," I said. "They will heal. I want to go to Medugorje, but it's not important for me to do so by the twenty-fifth. If your signs are telling you to go, then go."

"How do you feel?" He asked anxiously.

"I'd be lying if I said I wasn't nervous," I replied sincerely. "We've been together so long now that I've become accustomed to walking with you, even though I'm ready to strangle you some days." We laughed, releasing some of the tension. I looked at him nostalgically, already feeling the pang of separation. "It's going to feel strange for a while, but I know I'll find my way." Alberto embraced me tightly.

"Thank you," he whispered, then released me saying, "Good night."

How many times had I longed to walk alone, yet now that my wish was granted, the path seemed so uncertain. However, I needed to walk it. I lay in bed, breathing deeply, rhythmically, until I found stillness. There, I felt comforted, accompanied. A profound peace filled me. I was not alone. All was well.

On February 8, 2002, Alberto and I separated.

25. The Master's Invitation

On my first day without Alberto, I rested; but in my thoughts he was ever near. I wondered where he would find shelter, and how he would survive with the little money that he carried. I had given him my eagle pendant to wear, the very pendant he had given me, so that he may carry my energy with him. He left me with one of his favorite keepsakes, a postcard given him by his mother. I held that card, depicting Mary holding a baby Jesus, and asked her to safeguard his passage.

Father Joso had left early and returned late in the day. As I helped him prepare dinner, he said, "I would like you to take communion today."

I had never been offered communion by any priest on this journey, and the one time I had asked for it, was rejected on the grounds of not being Catholic. I didn't want to disappoint Father Joso. "I'm not prepared to take communion," I confessed, building up to telling him that I wasn't Catholic.

"*Mea Culpa, mea culpa*," he responded dismissively. "There, you're ready." I chuckled at his antics. Placing his hands on my shoulders and gazing at me with eyes that were infinitely kind, he said, "You are a pilgrim and an angel, on a journey of peace. What you are doing is very important. You need to receive God, to be one with him."

No priest had ever described us in that way or tried to minister to anything beyond our physical needs. I felt understood, and my spiritual needs genuinely tended to. "I would be honored to receive communion from you," I replied.

"You will be receiving communion from God, not me," he replied matter-of-factly.

My body tingled. His words felt as a foretelling, a promise of something significant about to unfold. Filled with anticipation, I joined Father Joso for the short walk to the church. A light breeze was blowing off the bay, on a night brilliant with stars and whispering of the magical. I followed Father Joso into the dark church and waited for him to turn on the lights. In the soft glow in which I now stood, my breathing momentarily stopped.

High above the altar was a larger-than-life painting of Jesus from the shoulder up, staring at me, holding out a loaf of bread in one hand and a goblet of wine in the other. I trembled from the intensity of that loving gaze, and slid onto the nearest pew. Unable to return that gaze, to receive so much love at one time, I turned away, looking at anything but that painting, those eyes; and fighting the urge to flee and the desire to kneel.

"*You are worthy*," I heard whispered in my ear, and repeated until I felt tears surfacing. The Nelson Mandela words that I so loved were etched in my mind, but evidently not in my soul. Faced with my deepest fear, I whispered,

"I have so many faults, so many fears, so many things I don't know or understand."

The words "you are worthy" sounded insistently, patiently, until they filled my confused heart with a confident calm. I felt I was being invited to understand the life of a great master and the wisdom of his teachings, not to follow blindly or convert to Catholicism. Before me was held the promise of becoming my own master, teacher, and healer.

When I received communion from Father Joso that day, I did so with a heart that forgave its weaknesses and flaws, and that embraced its worth.

"*I accept your invitation*," I silently vowed, returning his gaze.

* * *

The shortcut out of Jablanac that Father Joso promised ended up being a deserted path that wound upwards through olive groves. After the heavy rains, all of nature seemed to glisten in the brilliant sunshine. I strolled happily, basking in the early morning glory, enjoying the melodious orchestra of chirping birds and rustling leaves.

A magazine lay in the middle of the road, its pages flung open and wet from the rains. I stopped, and peered closer. Looking up at me was a picture of Jesus, staff in hand, along a path lined with olive trees, and gazing towards Jerusalem with its distinctive Dome of the Rock. A tide of emotion welled up within me. He was with me and revealing himself in a way I could relate to; as a pilgrim, among olive trees, on his way to Jerusalem. "*I have much to learn, but I cannot have a better teacher.*"

After an hour of climbing, I reached the main road. My legs wobbled. I walked slowly to help them recover from the exertion, but they dragged. The pain in my left foot returned accompanied by new blisters. I stopped at a large clearing, and pulled out my baby powder, one of the many blister remedies I had tried on the Camino and that best kept my feet dry. I stretched my legs and baked my feet in the hot sun before putting my socks and boots back on. The relief was temporary, and I walked with the pain for the rest of the day.

I was unafraid, but felt lonely. Even though Alberto and I hardly spoke on the road, it was still comforting to know that he was there. I glanced back often, so accustomed to seeing him there, and having to remind myself that he no longer was. I missed hearing his Spanish accent, and his repeated admonition that I was not paying attention to the road, to "Mony be careful." I stopped to urinate behind a large stone, and recalled how often he chastised me for not taking enough precautions before choosing my spot. I shook my head at the silly things I was remembering, and missed him even more.

I spent the night in Cesarica in the home of a priest friend of Father Joso, and continued to the Capuchin monastery in Karlobag the next day. I was greeted with recognition, which surprised me, and brought to a room where several men sat, speaking animatedly. One of them, dressed in dark brown robes, immediately stood and came towards me. He looked to be in his early fifties with salt and pepper beard and hair, and a serious, almost stern, demeanor; but when he spoke, I felt nothing but warmth and sincerity.

"Ah, Monica," he jovially said in Italian, shaking my hand. "We have been waiting for you. Alberto was here and told us all about you. Welcome, please, sit. I am *Fra*[9] Ante, the Superior of the monastery." Before I could ask how Alberto was, *Fra* Ante asked, "How are your feet? Alberto told me they were very bad and that you needed to rest. It's good that you did. You will stay here a few days because the road ahead is very difficult."

I managed to squeak out a "thank you" through my stunned surprise. I was introduced to the remaining group and invited to dine with them. Their hospitality and attentiveness reminded me of their Italian neighbors, and from their insistence that I eat, knew I would not go hungry here either.

"Monica," *Fra* Ante said, reaching into his pocket and pulling out a folded piece of white paper. "Alberto left you a note." All conversation

---

[9] Fray or Brother

stopped, and expectant eyes turned towards me. I eagerly took the note, and silently read it.

"*Animo Sarracena*[10]. Yesterday, crows along my way and a large eagle in a special place. Also saw your name written in the sea. All is going well. Your angels walk with me and the mine walk with you. Ultreya[11]! See you in Medugorje!"

I could almost hear Alberto's voice, and felt him very near.

"He should have arrived by now," *Fra* Ante announced, reaching for the phone. "I told him to go to the house of a friend of mine." After a brief conversation, he handed me the receiver.

"*Hola*," Alberto's laughing voice sang through the line.

"I can't believe I'm talking to you," I replied breathlessly. "How are you?"

"Great," he replied happily. "I'm meeting amazing people, like *Fra* Ante, and many more. I have so many things to tell you, so many signs. I'm walking strongly but feel a little lonely. I can't believe how much I miss you."

"Hah!" I cried into the phone. "I miss you too. Can you believe that?" I heard many voices around Alberto.

"I have to go now," he said. "We will see each other soon. Take care and *buen camino*."

"*Buen camino*," I said, longing to speak more. I hung up the phone and turned to face the knowing smiles of all in attendance. "*Prijatelji*, friends," I immediately clarified. They all nodded quickly, smiling, and turned away, but I had the feeling no one believed me.

I was shown to a room with private bathroom. While showering, I lifted my arms to wash my hair and felt a familiar tenderness under my arms. It had started as chafing and then developed into a rash a few weeks earlier. I applied some cortisone cream, believing it to be the result of sweating and the friction of my arms swinging as I walked; but it didn't help. I hoped whatever it was would clear up quickly.

My stop at Karlobag stretched into a three-day mini-vacation. I slept in every day and took afternoon naps. I wrote in my diary. I

---

[10] *Animo* is a term of encouragement. Saracen is an older term used to describe the Arabs who ruled Spain for over five hundred years. *Sarracena* means Arab woman.
[11] Camino greeting meaning "courage".

washed all my clothes in a washing machine for the first time in a month. My offers to help around the monastery were gently refused, and I was reminded more than once that I needed to rest.

I used my ample free time to read the Gospel of St. John, resolving to keep an open mind and an even more open heart. I wanted to feel stirred, to have the words inspire me to new heights of awareness and understanding, but they left me cold and uninspired. I was certain there was a message there for me and was disappointed when I couldn't find it. I put the bible away and never looked at it again.

* * *

It was now February thirteenth, time to start walking again. I sat with *Fra* Ante examining the map of Croatia with him. He advised me to stay close to the coast because it was more populated, and circled the towns where he had friends, assuring me of their help. Satisfied with his work, he refolded the map for me, then reached into his pocket and handed me a piece of paper, saying, "This letter introduces you, and explains that you are a pilgrim on a mission of peace to Jerusalem. Show this to any priest or person, and I promise they will help you."

The note shook in my trembling hands. It was written in Croatian under the monastery's letterhead and address, signed by Fra Ante, and stamped with their official seal. In my hands was a precious gift. From the influence that *Fra* Ante clearly wielded, I knew that anyone refusing me would also be refusing him. "*Huala,*" I whispered sincerely.

Fra Ante's serious face softened, but betrayed no further sentiment. We exchanged phone numbers, and I promised to call if I needed anything. He accompanied me to the front gates, reminding me of the route I must walk. For someone who showed little emotion, I felt all of his concern and caring revealed in those moments. When he placed his hand on my head, I bowed, quietly celebrating the many blessings bestowed upon me. I wanted to embrace him, but there was a line of formality I knew I couldn't cross. Instead, I shook his hand, repeated my thanks, then turned and walked away.

The day's walk was long but uneventful. I rested well that night in Bariç Draga in the home of an acquaintance of *Fra* Ante's, and pressed on towards Starigrad the following morning.

"Monica? Monica?" A man standing at the edge of his driveway called out. To my answering that I was, he began to enthuse in Croatian about something, all the while smiling and shaking my hand. I had no idea what he was saying, but clearly understood the words Alberto and television. I thanked him and continued on my way, only to be stopped a few meters down the road by another man standing at his doorstep.

"Are you Alberto's friend Monica?" he asked in English. When I answered that I was, he went on, "Alberto was on national television this morning. He spoke about your walk, and how you're separating for a while, then meeting in Medugorje. He said it was easy to recognize you because you were carrying a backpack and sign similar to his. I just want to congratulate you. Please, can I offer you something to eat or drink?"

I thanked him for the offer and apologized that I had to continue ahead. I felt like a celebrity that day, waving at drivers who honked or stopping to thank those who greeted me, and feeling more confident than ever that safe passage was being forged for me too.

26. Rescued

I continued southwards from Starigrad on a spectacular coastal road that was mountainous and sinewy, and that passed lovely sea-side villages. The road finally leveled off and I stood facing a long bridge. The Bora wind, a wind that people here claimed could lift a car, blew strongly that day. Feeling as if it could certainly lift me, I hurried across.

Desolate terrain greeted me on the other side. The earth was garishly plowed over and stripped of all vegetation. Chunks of scarred rock littered the ground. I advanced slowly, cautiously, as bunkers on both sides of the road followed my every step. Military barracks, partially blown out and long abandoned, stood a lonely vigil. I felt my blood run cold with fear, and didn't want to think about what may have happened here. I hurried my step. Although I knew that Croatia had just come out of a civil war, I had not seen any evidence of it. This was the first visible scar I had encountered, and I wondered why the Croatians had not healed it.

I was welcomed in Zadar, amazed to hear that Alberto had stayed at the same church as I, and continued towards Biograd the next morning. That day's walk was cut short by torrential rains and heavy winds, but I was glad for it because I was feeling unusually lethargic. My head throbbed and every muscle ached. I had no appetite and wondered if I was catching a cold, but couldn't rest since I was at least four days behind Alberto. I trudged to Biograd the following day, desiring nothing more than sleep, and checked into a hotel, collapsing into bed without even showering.

I woke up in the middle of the night, moaning in pain. I was still in my walking clothes, and could feel the grime on my face and body. As I took off my shirt, a stabbing pain shot out from my underarms and spread towards my breasts. Its intensity took my breath away, and I put my hands down in panic. The pain had never been that intense before. Up until then, my underarms had been sensitive to touch but I could lift my arms without problem. Now, they throbbed as soon as my arms reached waist-level.

I slipped my shirt and bra off with difficulty, and stepped into the shower. I gingerly touched my underarms and felt several large protruding bumps. My head began to spin and my knees to buckle.

Worried that I would pass out, I stepped out without washing and quickly dried myself. The mere touch of the towel against my underarms sent needles of pain shooting down my body, so I left them damp, wrapped myself in the towel and returned to the room. Sitting beside the heater, and through the searing pain, I put on my tights, thick fleece shirt and wool socks. I took two ibuprophen tablets and crawled into bed, but couldn't stop shivering under the blankets.

I woke up later that night, kicking the sheets and blankets off. My body was on fire, and beads of sweat rolled down my face and back. My underarms throbbed. Mustering all the energy I could, I peeled my clothes off, groaning in pain. I lay on one side of the bed, the cool sheets refreshing my burning body. *"Dear God, help me,"* I silently pleaded before falling asleep once again.

* * *

"Your hair follicles are inflamed," the doctor declared, "along with your lymph nodes. Do you wear synthetic clothing?" I explained the sporting clothes I usually wore. "Your skin isn't breathing," she continued. "You probably cut yourself while shaving, and with all the sweat and bacteria that's trapped by the synthetic clothes, developed the infection. Do you feel any unusual lumps in your breasts?"

"What does that have to do with my underarms?" I asked in alarm. As she examined my breasts, she explained that the breasts fed the lymph nodes under my arms, so if the nodes were plugged, then it was possible that the breasts could become infected too.

"You don't have any lumps or unusual swelling," she announced, removing her gloves. "Have you had a fever in the last twenty four hours?" she asked. I nodded, now feeling more nervous. "A fever is usually an indication of an abscess, a serious infection. If the lymph nodes are blocked and fluid builds in your breasts, then the infection may spread to the blood, causing a major complication."

She helped me sit up, adding, "I'm going to prescribe an antibiotic cream for your underarms and antibiotic pills for your infection. The infection is severe. I'm not sure the pills will do anything. I would recommend you rest for the next few days. If you don't feel better by then, then you will need to have surgery to drain the nodes."

With medication in hand, I returned to my hotel and slept, feeling desperately alone and wishing Alberto was with me.

The next thirty-six hours were a blur. I had no concept of day or night, just waking and sleeping, shivering and sweating. I watched endless movies in Croatian, unable to understand anything, but feeling happy for the company. I nibbled on bread and crackers, and sipped some water, hoping that the antibiotics would take effect.

Late the second day, my mobile phone rang. I picked it up expectantly. "Monica, Monica," *Fra* Ante laughed.

I greeted him through tears that couldn't be contained, in a voice that was weary and thirsting for human contact. His laughter turned to concern when I explained about the infection and possible need to operate.

"Do not worry," he assured. "I know several good doctors. I will make some phone calls and let you know." Within the hour, he called again to say, "I have called a friend who lives near your hotel. His name is *Fra* Drago, and he is also a priest. He will come by your hotel at 9:00 AM tomorrow to take you to the hospital. After that, you can stay with him or return to Karlobag to recuperate."

I wept for a long time, my soul unburdening its deepest fears into tears. I would experience many miracles during this walk, but this particular incident holds a special place in my heart for, in my darkest hour, I saw revealed the grace and unconditional love of the powers that accompanied me.

* * *

Fra Drago was picking me up in an hour and I wanted to make a presentable first impression. The face in the mirror that looked back at me hardly seemed my own. My face was ashen, my eyes swollen and underlined with dark circles. My hair was slick with oil and sweat, and stuck out at odd angles. I stank, and so did my clothes. There was nothing to do except sprinkle on some extra baby powder.

I carried my backpack like a suitcase, unable to lift my arms high enough to slip it on. As I finished checking out, a man of shorter build walked in and looked around expectantly. He looked to be in his fifties and wore street clothes, but what most stood out about him was the shock of frizzy grey hair atop his head. Seeing my backpack, he came towards me, his smile wide and welcoming.

"You must be Monica," he said in broken Italian, shaking my hand. "I am *Fra* Drago. I will be taking you to the hospital."

Fra Drago drove quickly and soon we were in the hospital, maneuvering through the gleaming, antiseptic-smelling halls. At one of the doors, he stopped and knocked. The door immediately opened. "Hello Monica," the doctor said in English. "I've been expecting you."

I recounted the details of my infection, as I lay down and slipped my arms out of my sleeves. The doctor lifted one arm above my head and started pushing down on the bumps, pinching them between his thumbs. I stifled a cry and gritted my teeth. He lifted my other arm and continued poking around.

"Some of these nodes are about five centimeters in diameter," he declared, "but I don't want to operate yet. Stay on the same antibiotics a little longer. Ice the infected area. If the swelling has not gone down in three days, or if it gets worse, then we will operate. Today is February the twenty-first. I want you to return in two days prepared for surgery, just in case."

I still hoped I wouldn't need surgery, but knew that if I did, I would do it in Croatia.

I updated *Fra* Ante, who supported my decision to stay with *Fra* Drago in his home near Šibenik, and not return to Karlobag. I needed to feel closer to Medugorje, and to an Alberto who I imagined would soon be there.

I was given a private room and tended to by the two caring nuns. One, named Dolores, only spoke Croatian and especially fussed over me. She taught me some Croatian words, and laughed joyfully every time I used them. The words *moja draga Monica* rolled off her lips constantly, words that I finally understood to mean "my dear Monica". She prepared my meals, washed my clothes, made me cookies and cakes, and reminded me to ice my underarms, and take my medicine. I felt as if I had come home.

During those first two days, my headaches and weakened state persisted. I awoke often at night, alternating between chills and fever. With the antibiotic cream, bits of skin started peeling off. My underarms looked like the stringy insides of a pumpkin. I feared that I would need to operate after all.

I used my time to stretch and practice light yoga postures, but I sensed that my body needed care that went beyond the physical. I sought moments of solitude and sat in stillness, doing nothing more than breathing. Every breath brought a deepening connection to a divine stream of healing that I imagined flowing all around me. Breath became the carrier of that energy, a golden light that I visualized penetrating every cell of my body, regenerating it, restoring it back to its natural state. My body tingled in response, confirming that this beautiful energy was indeed flowing through me.

The evening before my appointment, I was able to touch my underarms without wincing, and lift my arms just slightly above my shoulders. I slept that entire night without fever or chills.

"The swelling has gone down to two centimeters," the doctor confirmed. "Your skin is healing nicely, and the old infected layers are falling away. The fact that you no longer have a fever means that the infection is clearing up. Still, I want you to continue on antibiotics for another ten days, just to be sure." I whooped in delight.

"No more shaving or deodorant," he continued with a smile, "only baby powder on your underarms. Wear only natural fibers. If you continue healing this quickly, you can start walking in two or three days."

The days that followed were a blur of well-wishers and friends of *Fra* Drago, many of whom spoke English, stopping by to say hello. *Fra* Drago also arranged several interviews, including one for the evening news on Croatian national television, all of which fanned the flames of the message of peace I was proclaiming. I delighted in the exchanges and the effort that was being made to make my stay comfortable.

It was finally February twenty-fifth, and Alberto was on my mind all day. We had not spoken since Karlobag more than two weeks earlier.

During dinner, my telephone rang. I picked it up, expecting *Fra* Ante making his daily call. "*Buona Sera,*" I chirped in greeting.

"*Hola, Sarracena,*" was the reply.

"Alberto!" I cried out.

"I can't speak for very long," he said, deep laughter warming his voice. "I just want you to know that I am in Medugorje. I have so many things to tell you. Amazing things. Where are you now?"

"I'm just outside Šibenik," I responded. "I've been here almost a week recovering from a serious infection."

"What?" he interrupted, sounding worried.

"I'm fine now," I replied quickly. "I'm well taken care of. I'll be starting to walk again tomorrow. I have about two hundred and fifty kilometers to go. I don't know how long it will take me to get to you. Will you wait for me?"

"Of course I will," he replied earnestly. "I want you to know that this experience was very important for me. It wasn't always easy, but I know now that I can walk alone. I want to walk with you, though, and arrive in Jerusalem together."

"Me too," I replied warmly. "I have so much to tell you too, but you were right about us separating."

"I have to go," Alberto said reluctantly. "Write down this number, and call it when you get closer to Medugorje. I'll be waiting for you."

Alberto had arrived, and I would be starting towards him the next day.

27. The Lost Sheep

My shins ached. New blisters covered my feet. Only my underarms didn't bother me. Rather than re-energizing my body, the week's rest had depleted it. I had believed I could walk with the same intensity, if not greater, than before, but those first days of walking proved to me just how weakened I had become.

As a result of the newspaper articles and television report, I was stopped by even more well-wishers. Journalists sought me out, and I gave several roadside interviews. One journalist even gave me a candle to light for him in Jerusalem.

The first night found me in Pirovac, and the following one back in the home of *Fra* Drago. My farewells with him and the nuns were emotional, and our tears spilled not merely for our separation, but the promise of our return one day.

I walked past Boraia and Trogir, and pressed onwards towards Solin. A strong sun came out that day, and I soon found myself sweating heavily. Not wanting to hinder my recovery, I decided to cool off under the shade of a grove of olive trees that sat invitingly just off the road.

I chose a tree deep in the grove, away from the busy road, took off my jacket, dropped on the earth, and leaned my head against the gnarled trunk. I closed my eyes, enjoying the feel of the freshly plowed earth under my feet and the smell of spring that seemed to fill the air.

A rustling sound startled me and I turned to see a tall, elderly man walking towards me. He wore overalls that were slightly dirty, and walked with a smile of recognition. I assumed that he knew who I was, and returned his greeting. He knelt beside me and introduced himself in Italian as the owner of the orchard. He looked to be in his sixties with a sturdy muscular build which I imagined came from working the land.

Inviting me to rest for as long as I wished, he took my stick and began to examine it. "It is olive wood," he said approvingly, leaning it once again against the tree. "Light and strong. It's very good for walking."

I joked that it had seen me through many mountains, and watched as he began examining my backpack. For the first time, I noticed that my sign was facing in. The man patted my backpack heartily. From his kneeling position, he lifted it slightly off the ground and put it back down again.

"It must be at least fifteen kilograms," he said with admiration. He curled his arm and pointed to his bicep, saying, "You must be very strong." I laughed. Without warning, he reached under my pant leg and caressed my calf. "This must be very strong too," he said with a smile, giving my calf a squeeze.

I didn't have time to react. He pulled his hand away, then brought it up to my breast and cupped it. "This too," he said, starting to squeeze.

I pushed his arm away and stood in a mix of shock, anger, and fear. I realized in panic just how far back from the road I was, and how secluded I was in this orchard that seemed to go on forever. He was much bigger and stronger than me, so if he were to attack me, I couldn't fight him off. The ground was plowed and muddy, so I couldn't race out to the road either. I took a deep breath and stared hard at him.

"*Hodachastiti*[12], walking to Jerusalem *za mir*," I said, my voice hoarse and cracking.

He stepped back, clearly surprised. Holding his hands up before his face, he apologized and quickly walked away until he disappeared among the trees. I was breathing hard, and didn't trust that he wouldn't return. I grabbed my jacket and backpack, and stomped out of the orchard back to the safety of the busy road.

I continued to Solin, shaken and outraged. I had been met with respect everywhere in Croatia, but that incident made me forget all the good I had encountered and underlined the fact that I was a woman walking alone. I fought hard that day to not allow one ignorant man's actions to influence my faith in the goodness of all people. By the time I arrived in Solin, I was in better spirits but more reserved than usual.

While awaiting the priest's arrival, I decided to call my family in Lebanon to see how a favorite aunt named Yolla was doing. My father had told me a few days earlier that her condition had worsened. I had gotten quite close to her while visiting Lebanon in September of last year, shortly before my walk. During my stay, she suffered a seizure which doctors diagnosed to be the result of a brain tumor. The treatments seemed to be working but, this time, when I spoke with her

---

[12] Pilgrim

family, they told me that all treatments had failed and that the doctors could do no more for her than send her home.

I reeled from the news, and in my despair, began to consider whether I should visit her. I couldn't believe I was even considering it, especially since I was so far behind Alberto. My rational mind could not convince my impetuous heart, one that beat excitedly at the idea of returning.

My distress must have been evident because the following morning, as I was saying my goodbyes to the priest who hosted me, he looked at me with concern and urged me to share whatever was bothering me. I did.

"There is nothing you can do for your aunt now," he said compassionately, making the sign of the cross in the air. "You are on a path of God. Think of all the good that you're doing with this walk. Your aunt is in God's hands now. Walk, and be strong." But my heart was not assuaged.

On that day's walk to Bisko, I pondered a single question: What is more important, the peace that I could bring to one person, or this walk of peace which is benefiting many more?

I had often disagreed with Alberto when he asserted that touching the lives of people who crossed our path was an important element of our walk, a micro approach to peace which I found limited and ineffective when compared to my macro view of carrying a sign and touching the lives of many. On this journey, however, strangers had become my greatest teachers—and pupils. In our often brief time together, we exchanged a precious gift, the gift of expanded vision and deeper understanding. We then shared that expanded part of ourselves with those who later crossed our path, in a chain without end. Although I had uttered the words "peace begins within" infinite times, it was only then that I began to understand them. Yes, I concluded. The peace of one person was as important as the peace of the many.

I stopped to rest on some large stones that lay scattered along the side of the road. The day had turned grey and a light mist now floated past. As if in a dream, a lone sheep emerged from the mist. I looked around for other sheep or a shepherd, but saw neither. The shaggy sheep crept closer, following the bits of greenery that peeked out of the rocky soil, seemingly contemplating me as much as I was contemplating it. Cars and trucks sped past on this busy road, underscoring the contrast. The sheep continued with its grazing. Then, just as strangely as it had appeared, it straggled away and disappeared into the mist.

I recalled Alberto once telling the story of Jesus being asked why he kept company with prostitutes and vagrants. Jesus had replied that if a shepherd lost even one sheep, he would leave the entire flock to find that stray. My heart beat faster. I would leave for Lebanon as soon as possible.

28. Unexpected Detour

Two days later, thanks to the efforts of the amazing family hosting me in Bisko, I was on my way to Lebanon. I arrived on March fourth with a one-way ticket. My godmother and one of my cousins picked me up at the airport, but no one else knew of my arrival. Night was giving way to dawn by the time we arrived at her home and I finally went to sleep.

I joined my godmother and her habitual group of neighbors for their ritual morning coffee, where my presence was both a delight and fodder for the gossip mill. Assuming news of my arrival would make it to Yolla's home before I did, my godmother and I started for the short walk to Yolla's home, cutting through fields as opposed to taking the main road.

My village in northern Lebanon, called Kfarhazir, has about two thousand inhabitants, most of whom work and live in other countries. The village of my childhood was a single country lane flanked by modest homes, each with its roaming chickens, sheep, or cows. Each family had its gardens and olive trees. Most people lived from the land and what their families sent them from working overseas.

The little farming village of my childhood was now larger. Chickens and donkeys were long ago replaced by the luxury cars that everyone seemed to own. Upscale chalets and villas now lined the busy road and surrounding hills. Our family's home, and where Yolla lived, was modest by comparison, with two levels added to accommodate the growing families. Each floor was its own separate apartment. In a mostly modern country, there was still the traditional belief of families living together.

We entered through the kitchen door, and made our way to the adjoining family room. I was struck by the stillness, an experience unusual in a home usually buzzing with neighbors, children, and the boundless energy of its matron, Yolla.

The hospital bed was a new fixture in the family room, replacing one of the sofas and adding to this new, more austere reality. Yolla lay on her side, sleeping. She had lost a tremendous amount of weight, but still carried about eighty kilograms on her large frame. The chemotherapy had left her completely bald, save for a patch of hair just above the neck. I had already prepared myself, so her physical aspect didn't surprise me.

My godmother greeted Yolla cheerfully, announcing that she brought a special visitor. Yolla opened her eyes slowly, the very task seeming a tremendous effort. She blinked several times, as if trying to focus. Her lips parted slowly, and her eyes widened like saucers.

"Mony," she whispered weakly, reaching for my hand. I rushed to her side, astonished that she even recognized me, and embraced her.

"How are you doing?" I whispered.

"Tired," she answered weakly.

Her eyes sparkled with emotion and joy, and she tried to sit up, but groaned in pain and lay down again. My godmother brought me a chair and I sat beside her, still holding her hand. Yolla's eyes slowly began to close. I felt the same weight in my eyes, and so put my head down on the bed and closed them too.

* * *

I spent the first few days integrating myself into the family's daily life. Soon, I was making meals and doing laundry. I was picking up the three children from school and helping them with their homework. I was taking care of the physical aspects of running a household and trying to remain open to signs or anything that would guide my steps here.

In my time alone, I meditated with Yolla, visualizing her body enveloped in a healing white light that penetrated and strengthened every cell. I kept her company when she awakened, telling her about the everyday of her family. A faint smile usually served as acknowledgement that she had heard me, but I didn't always know if she understood me for she often asked where she was and the names of the people closest to her, including mine. I tried not to feel disheartened when I responded, and to hold on to my belief that all was unfolding as it was meant to be.

I cajoled her into drinking or eating anything. She initially refused but one day, took a few sips of pineapple juice, which everyone took as a good sign. I started making fresh juice, first with fruits and then with vegetables, and mixing them into various shakes. I involved the children in the task, and saw how much they enjoyed feeling a valuable part of their mother's lives.

Yolla sipped a little more every day, often from the hands of her insistent children. She was awake more of the time and, although still in pain, trying to sit up. She eventually did, by herself, and it was no longer a surprise to find her sitting alone in bed. She began nibbling on soft foods and purees that we prepared. To everyone's amazement, she asked to be seated on the sofa. With help, not only did she sit on the sofa but even began taking tentative steps. Our jubilation was beyond words as we witnessed the miracle taking place.

My walk, however, was never far from my mind. I wondered if Alberto was still in Medugorje, or if he even knew of my delay. I had called the number he had given me several times, but no one ever answered. I didn't know how much longer I needed to stay, and prayed for a sign to guide my next steps.

It was the tenth day, and I was adjusting Yolla's sheets. A palm-sized wooden book that was normally under the pillow fell to the floor. I picked it up and, for some reason, began to examine it. On one side of the book was a picture of a Lebanese saint and the other, a picture of Mary. I had seen that book many times, but only then did I see the word written under the picture: Medugorje.

"How did she get here?" I thought, trembling. *"Who brought her? My family has never even heard of Medugorje."*

I felt a knowing then, a certainty that my work here was done, and that, whatever the outcome, it was the one that served the highest good of all involved. I booked my flight the following day.

* * *

On March the eighteenth, I was again on Croatian soil and walking. Despite suffering with a terrible flu and laryngitis, my body responded to my urgency and moved rhythmically, swiftly, shortening the distance between Medugorje and I. I was welcomed in every town where I stopped—Blato na Cetini, Lovreć, Imotski—and every priest called the one ahead to alert them of my arrival. I crossed into Bosnia without incident. Had there not been a border, it would have been difficult to say that I was now in a different country since the language sounded the same to me.

Thanks to the priest telephone relay, I was welcomed in Drinovci, and now rushed to Ljubuški, the last town before Medugorje. In the convent that was my home that evening, I frantically called

Alberto, as I had done every night since my return; but the phone rang frustratingly without end. I slept poorly and awakened early to leave. Deciding to try one last time, I dialed Alberto's number.

"*Bog*," a woman's voice replied, using the typical Croatian greeting.

I was expecting to hang up and was momentarily caught without words. She repeated the greeting again. I explained who I was, in Italian.

"Alberto has told me all about you," she said warmly.

"Is he still there?" I asked hopefully.

"Yes he is," she replied.

"Please tell him I will be arriving today," I said through my tears. "I'm leaving now and will meet him in front of the church."

I raced out of town. Miraculously, Alberto had waited for me, and soon we would be reunited.

29. Reunited

I hurried past the souvenir shops lining the main street of Medugorje, and entered the main plaza in front the church, my eyes roaming for Alberto. I finally saw him, standing at the steps, and waved. He waved back, and started slowly towards me. My pace quickened, as did his. I saw his happy smile and the crinkle around his shining eyes. We rushed into each other's arms and locked onto each other like the long lost friends that we were, rocking from side to side, each repeating how glad they were to see the other. After forty-four days apart, I was finally with my friend, and walking partner, again.

I released him and roamed his face, unable to contain my joy. He returned my smile affectionately. His green eyes had the same softness and kindness that I had so missed, but now rimmed with a steely light that was not there before. His hair was longer and curlier. His face looked thinner, but more luminescent.

Our words tumbled out in excitement, tripping into incoherence, and we giggled at our ineptness. I suggested we find a place to sit and speak quietly, so he led me towards an area lined with restaurants. I saw that he moved confidently, but that he had lost weight and that his clothes were hanging off him. I felt a lump in my throat at the thought that he may have suffered hunger and, seeing a pizzeria, suggested we eat there.

"I'm fasting," he said. I stared at him in disbelief.

"What? Why?" I asked.

"This is the last week before Easter Sunday and most people here are fasting," he replied. "I'm not doing it because of that, but for more personal reasons. I've been only having bread and water for the last three days."

"That's why you look so thin," I admonished.

"I actually feel very good," he contested.

"I can't enjoy my pizza while you're watching me, only having bread and water," I retorted.

"You can eat what you like," he said, smiling and shaking his head. "Don't worry about me."

It was as if we had never separated.

We spoke about the routes we had taken, and the people in common we had met. Alberto listened with concern as I told him about my infection, and with wonder at the amazing kindnesses I received during journey alone. He understood my decision to go to Lebanon, and marveled at the amazing coincidence with Medugorje that brought me back. We agreed that magic had indeed lined our path, and that our separation was a tremendous gift.

It was now late afternoon, and I needed to search for a priest named Father Zvetozar who I was told was expecting me. The priest greeted me warmly at the Church office, and immediately inquired after my health. From his hurried movements, I could tell he was a busy man. I would later learn that he was the Superior of the Franciscan order directing the affairs of the Church here.

Father Zvetozar informed me that he had made all the necessary arrangements for my stay, and asked to take some pictures for his parish newsletter. I agreed and motioned for Alberto to join me, explaining to the surprised priest that he was my walking partner and had been waiting here for me for over a month. He shook Alberto's hand and offered for him to stay at my hostel. Alberto politely refused, saying he already had accommodations. Alberto stood beside me, and the priest took the picture.

As a final act, I asked Father Zvetozar to stamp my letter from Fra Ante, explaining that it was a Camino tradition. I had started collecting these stamps in every church and monastery after Brodarica, where I had stayed with Fra Drago. They were my pilgrim credential, a record of where I had stayed. A delighted Father Zvetozar disappeared into his office and returned moments later with my stamp. On March 23, 2002, I officially arrived in Medugorje.

Father Zvetozar held out a small bulky envelope. "This will take care of your expenses while you are here," he said, handing it to me. "You are a guest in our community. Please accept this gift from us."

My insistence that I had enough and that I preferred the funds be used for other activities fell on deaf ears. The laughing priest pressed the envelope into my hands and walked away. Inside was a letter of welcome in Father Zvetozar's personal handwriting, and almost two hundred Euros in cash.

"I would like you to have this," I said to Alberto, offering him the money.

"I don't need it but I know someone who does," Alberto replied, taking it. I wondered why he didn't want the money for himself.

Alberto accompanied me to my hostel. We left the busy center and cut through farm fields on footpaths that we shared with farm animals. We passed humble brick homes and farmers working the land, testament to the town's rural roots. Alberto pointed to one hill, explaining that it was called Podbrdo, site of the apparition. I resolved to visit it the next day.

"Was it very difficult for you being here?" I asked. "I know you didn't have a lot of money when we separated."

"I haven't had a coin in my pocket for a month," Alberto replied casually.

"What?" I gasped.

"During my walk alone, I realized that money was another challenge on my spiritual path that I needed to deal with," Alberto said. "I've told you before, I grew up believing that money and spirituality were incompatible, and that poverty was an honorable path to God. I've done a lot of healing work there, and long ago opened myself to receive abundance. However, walking alone, I realized that to receive that abundance, I needed to release my fears about not having enough money and trust that I would always get what I needed. I couldn't prove that to myself with you by my side, naturally offering me security. So when people occasionally asked me for money, I began to give it to them. I gave away my last ten Euro bill about a month ago, and have been living without money since then."

"How could you give away all your money?" I asked in astonishment.

"Because the following words always came to my mind when people asked for it," he replied, "*I know that the Universe will always give me what I need, but they don't.* It was an important test of my faith because, by giving to them, I was demonstrating to myself that I believe what I say. Now I know that I can walk to Jerusalem without worrying about how much I have in my pocket."

I gazed with wonder at the pilgrim walking beside me. I admired him tremendously, but didn't know if I could ever do what he did.

"So where are you sleeping then, Alberto?" I wondered aloud. "Father Zvetozar didn't seem to know who you were."

"It's one of those magical stories, Mony, that perfectly portrays my experience alone," Alberto replied. "I arrived in Medugorje on February the twenty-fifth feeling strong, full of faith, more confident in myself than ever. I immediately headed to Podbrdo, hill of the apparition. I don't know why, but I noticed planes flying over my head, all going in that direction. They looked like white arrows pointing for me to go there.

When I got to the base of the hill, a building under construction caught my attention. Not only was it physically the closest to the site of the apparitions, but from one of the cement ledges, I saw a small statue of Mary looking down on me. She looked so out of place there that I felt as if she was personally welcoming me. I greeted her and said thank you, then walked up the hill. I won't tell you my impressions until you see it first.

The day passed quickly. I picked up the monthly message that the visionaries had received from Mary, but I found it to be a conservative Catholic perspective and not at all the universal message of peace I had expected. I immediately dismissed it, knowing there was another reason for my being here, and opened myself to exploring what it was.

When night fell, I went to the Church office to ask for help. I began to introduce myself, but the young monk who answered the door cut me off, dismissively asking, 'OK, OK what do you want?' I looked at him firmly and replied, 'I want to speak with someone who is willing to listen.' He looked surprised, and in a more respectful tone asked me to continue. I explained my situation and I saw that he was more open than before. When I finished, he left for a few moments and came back with a large handful of bills saying, 'With this, you have enough to wait for your friend a few days.' I replied, 'I don't need money, only a roof over my head.' He kept insisting I take the money, ever more sincerely. I tried explaining that I was looking for spiritual, not only physical, shelter; but he became increasingly frustrated and abruptly slammed the door in my face."

Alberto paused, and seemed to be reflecting. "I think I made a mistake," he finally said. "In all cases, it paved the way for what happened next.

As you can imagine, I was in shock. I walked away from the Church office, not knowing what to do. I looked around and saw that the square was abandoned. I was completely alone. The night was cold and the wind cut through to my bones. I went to the center of the church square and waited for some miracle to happen. *Here I am, Mother*, I pleaded, looking up at the heavens, *help me*. For the first time, I noticed the full moon. That night, it was radiant and resplendent, shining like a nighttime sun, surrounded by a huge halo of rainbow colors. I had never seen anything like it before. I felt a tremendous love, knowing that she, my Divine Mother, was shining down on me, watching over me.

With my feet beginning to freeze and my body to shiver in the bitter night's cold, I decided to walk around the church to warm up. I was waiting for something to happen, and repeating over and again, *I trust in You, Mother*.

I was thinking about looking for an abandoned house when I heard a noise overhead. It was a plane, one of many that I had seen earlier, flying in the direction of Podbrdo. I took it as a sign and decided to follow it. My head was arguing that the hill was rocky and there was nowhere to sleep, but I shut it down. *If you hold to the known, you can never discover the unknown*, I thought, remembering one of my favorite quotes.

I had only walked to Podbrdo during the day, and now in the total darkness of the night, on a country road surrounded by open fields, I didn't know how to get there. I heard dogs barking behind me, and hurried my step.

Suddenly, a small dog passed me, its nails clicking distinctly against the pavement. *Guide me to the hill*, I whispered. The dog stopped and looked at me, as if it had heard me. We gazed at each other for a few moments, then it turned and continued ahead. I had no idea where it was going, but at that moment, that dog was my angel and I was following it. It led me down one road after another. Whenever it got too far ahead or arrived at an intersection, it would stop and look back, then wait for me to catch up. Every hair on my body was standing on end.

A van passed me on this road, surprising me. Its driver stuck his head out the window and stared at me, but drove onwards. The dog continued ahead, and soon we arrived to what I recognized to be the small village at the base of Podbrdo. The dog stopped at the final intersection, and waited for me to arrive. To my left was the hill of the apparitions, to my right was the village, and ahead the road continued. The dog went to the right, and again turned its head and looked at me, its eyes gently asked me to follow. I hesitated, my heart pulling me towards the hill, but decided to continue with my angel instead. I took my first step towards the dog.

Hello, a voice called out in English. I turned to see the driver of the van getting out at that moment. I returned his greeting and told him I was Spanish. He answered '*que necesitas?*'[13] He spoke Spanish, can you believe that? I replied, '*solo un techo*,' only a roof over my head, and briefly explained what I was doing. The man was amazed by my story and asked me to follow him. He started towards the hill, in the opposite direction of the dog. I turned to say goodbye to my little canine angel, but he was already gone.

I walked in a daze, feeling as if I was in a surreal movie. 'Only a roof?' The man asked again. 'Yes, nothing more,' I said. He stopped in front of a building under construction. I stared at it in bewildered amazement. It was the last building on the hill, the very same one I had seen that morning. And there she was again, on the ledge, the statue of Maria, lovingly staring down at me in the night, welcoming me back. I trembled with emotion.

The three-story, brick-and-cement building was bare. The wind howled through the cavities that would one day become doors and windows. The man was its night watchman, and led me up the stairs to a room with fully-constructed walls. He cleaned out some of the materials, assuring me that I would be warm here. He covered the open window with a wooden plank, and unfolded a discarded bamboo curtain as a mat. I felt as if I was in a dream, watching him moving about the room, preparing it as if he were readying it for an honored guest. I repeated the word *gracias* over and again, not knowing what else to say. The kind man just kept saying it was nothing, and when he finished, shook my hand, promising to return the following morning with hot coffee.

I lay in my sleeping bag that night, warm and comfortable, grateful beyond words, emotions pouring out of me that I can't properly articulate. After a seventeen-day initiatic journey of magical experiences and revelations, I was in Medugorje on the night of the twenty-fifth, as I had intended. I was sleeping at the base of Apparition Hill, symbolically the closest that I could be to my beloved Holy Mother. I was miraculously guided here and helped under the most amazing full moon that I can ever remember. I could see Her there, radiant in the dark sky, crowned by that mysterious night rainbow and draped by innumerable

---

[13] What do you need?

stars. I felt totally submerged in Her presence. I felt at peace. I felt in love. It was the grandest day of my life."

Alberto's face glowed softly in the setting sun, and radiated some of the emotion that I was sure he felt that miraculous night. We had arrived at my hostel and so said our goodnights, agreeing to meet the following morning. There was so much more to say, but for now, it was enough that we were together again.

30. Medugorje

"There's a surprise waiting for you at the top," Alberto declared, stopping at the base of the steep hill that was Podbrdo, Apparition Hill.

He pointed out the building where he slept his first nights in Medugorje, and the small porcelain figure of Mary perched on the second floor. "Sentry," he smiled, before adding, "This is an experience you need to have alone. I'll wait for you here."

The stones were large and uneven, almost discouraging attempts to climb them, but their shine stood testament to the many pilgrims who had indeed taken those steps. I added my steps, climbing slowly, meditatively up the hill. A few pilgrims passed me, some barefoot. Others climbed on their knees, passionately mouthing prayers or clasping a rosary. Not even at the Vatican did I witness such fervor and devotion.

The higher I climbed, the more that my vision turned inwards. I saw only my path, the steps I needed to take. Everyone else receded into the background, and I arrived at a large clearing, aware only of my feelings of anticipation. A large white statue of a robed woman stood in the distance, its back to me, looking out over the valley below. I knew it was Mary, standing on the site where she appeared. Shivering from the cold, or perhaps the unknown, I moved closer and finally faced her.

She gazed upon me, her smile serene and loving. One hand was poised over her heart, the other extended to the world in offering. To my astonishment, I saw that she stood inside a white marble, six-sided star—my star, the star that was guiding me to Jerusalem. *"This must be the surprise that Alberto promised,"* I thought, smiling at this message from the heavens that I was indeed on the path of peace, well-accompanied, and that love, with all that Mary represents, was at its heart.

I lingered in that feeling of certainty, filling myself with it, and knowing that I would need it in my moments of doubt and weakness. I eventually made my way to the edge of the clearing where, among some trees, I found a stone and sat down.

I reached for my diary, and opened to the list of people who had asked me to pray for them. I had started this list in Rome when a nun asked me to pray for her. *"Dear God, I'm not sure what they're asking of* you, but please hear their prayers. Bless them and protect them on their life journey."

I spoke the name of each aloud, with each name closing an invisible circle of trust. I went to the start of my diary and day by day, added a prayer for those who had helped us on our way. Certain people, such as *Fras* Ante and Drago, Micho and many more, stood out; for them, my gratitude and love overflowed.

"*Thank you for bringing these angels into my life, and for showing me the face of goodness. I am forever enriched for having met them. They are your instruments of peace on this earth, the creators of the world we wish to see. Bless them and guide them always on their journey of peace and love.*"

At the names of those who rejected us, I paused. I wanted to pass them by, to not dwell on the hurt they had caused; but the more that I reflected, the more that I realized that they too were angels along my path and no less a gift than those who had embraced us. Their hard attitudes and inflexibilities showed me mine, as did their fears and judgments. I wanted to believe that I would act differently if our roles were reversed, but now I wasn't so certain. I saw my frailties, and in consequence, saw theirs.

For the first time, I felt stirrings of compassion towards them. Inexplicably, memories of those who had hurt or betrayed me in the past emerged, their cruelties playing out in my mind, taunting me back to judgment and rigid condemnation. I wanted to remain the victim, to hold on to the feeling of injustice and righteousness, but in that holy moment, something inside of me lifted and I felt a gratifying peace that had long eluded me.

"*Thank you for coming into my life,*" I silently said. "*I have learned much from you about myself. You have no power over me. I now release you from my heart.*"

I closed my diary and, with it, an important part of my pilgrimage.

* * *

Aside from going to church, there was frustratingly little else to do in Medugorje. I began to appreciate how bored Alberto must have been, and the enormous sacrifice he had made waiting for me. Peoples' lives revolved around prayer and the messages from Mary. I was invited to attend mass and pray the rosary at least twice a day. I accepted in the beginning, wanting to respect their beliefs, but stopped when I felt it become an expectation, not an invitation. I felt a continuous pressure to conform to their beliefs and rituals, and was suffocating under the constant barrage.

"This is the most conservative place I've ever seen," I erupted in frustration at Alberto one day. "How did you survive?"

"It was not easy," Alberto confessed seriously. "I can tell you that I almost lost myself here."

"I can see how it can happen," I replied. "It's insidious."

"I didn't really see it happening until it was almost too late," Alberto continued, then stopped. I sensed something important had happened, and so waited for him to reveal whatever was in his heart. "I was waiting for you in my abandoned building near Podbrdo," he eventually said, "but providentially met another Spanish-speaking man named Gerardo who invited me to his home. We became instant friends, but I quickly realized that he, like everyone in this impoverished area, had little money and I had none to offer him.

Walking around one day, I started receiving signs which led me to a Catholic community. I introduced myself and our walk, not knowing what to expect from this encounter. They received me kindly, and asked about my spiritual beliefs. I expressed them briefly but sincerely. They listened respectfully and with interest, but I saw that it was difficult for them to understand some of my open views, especially my belief that Jesus was not the only son of God. Yet despite our differences, they invited me to have lunch with them daily and to spend as much time as I wanted with the community. I thought it an ideal way to be less of a burden to my friend Gerardo. The gardens were also beautiful, and the setting peaceful and idyllic for meditation and reflection, so I accepted their invitation, feeling happy to be part of their small paradise.

The kind members invited me to join in their songs, rituals and prayers of the rosary. I did, but quickly realized that many of the ideas they expressed differed greatly from my view of God Love. Their prayers were filled with devotion and kindness, but also with self-humiliation, sin, fear of the devil, even fear of God. However, I continued participating, believing I was strong enough emotionally and spiritually to perform their rituals without them affecting me.

The days passed. We spoke no more of my spiritual beliefs or even my pilgrimage. Coincidentally staying at the community was a group of young men contemplating becoming members. I thought that perhaps the community was trying to protect them from my ideas, so I kept my views to myself, especially the conflictive ones.

Ever so subtly, I found myself trying to please them. I prayed and sang with them whenever they asked, even when I didn't feel like it. I bent my knee every time I walked in and out of their chapel, trying to respect their beliefs. I felt the need to somehow repay what they were giving me, so I tended the garden and did various handyman tasks. I did the same with other people in the village who, in one way or another, were helping me. My daily existence became a payback to others. I was feeling miserably unhappy and wanted to leave, but I didn't know where you were or when you would arrive. *Your will be done*, I repeated over and again. *I can endure this. I know you have brought me here for a reason.*

I tried to focus on the community's positive aspects such as their loving devotion to God, their faith in providence, their camaraderie, their sweetness, their simplicity of life. I fought to ignore their prostrations before God, their constant self-blame and self-proclamations as sinners unworthy of God, their asking for protection from the temptations of the devil. I missed my authenticity, but wanted them to feel that they could trust me, and so continued the lie.

My confidence and courage began to waver. I felt weak and emotionally sensitive, and worried about what people thought of me not only in the community, but in general. I felt lost, unsure of what I believed, and no longer recognized the confident pilgrim who had arrived in Medugorje. I blamed myself for feeling weak and fought to change, but the harder I fought, the weaker I felt. I begged the Universe to end this pretext, always ending with my new mantra, *Your will be done.*

One day, while fervently praying for a sign, I saw some horses roaming free, but then noticed a lone horse grazing quietly by itself, a short rope secured around its neck so it wouldn't stray too far. I immediately understood the message. I was chaining myself to this community for security, for a measly plate of food. I wanted to leave right away, but still hadn't heard from you.

That afternoon I lamented my case to Gerardo, who firmly reproached me, saying, 'You have forgotten why you are here. You have forgotten your purpose, your mission. What you are doing is very important. Stop feeling obligated. Stop feeling unworthy of asking for help. Do what you came here to do.'

The following morning, instead of going to the community, I headed to Cross Mountain, another pilgrimage hill here, alone. I stood at the first Station of the Cross, where a large plaque showed Jesus in the Garden of Gethsemane with a quote saying, Your Will be Done. It had always inspired me, but that morning I felt something stir within me, a certainty that I hadn't felt in a long time.

No, I declared. *No longer will I delegate everything to you. Never again will I say your will be done because I now know that your will is precisely that my will be done. I will no longer use those words for fear of making a mistake. You and I are one. You support any choice I make. The only way to know if my will benefits me or others is through experience. That's the only way I can grow. That's your highest will for me: that my will be done."*

I wasn't sure that I agreed with Alberto, but didn't interrupt him. I knew I was the creator of my reality, but also believed that there was a loving wisdom guiding me, and that listening to it benefited my soul's growth. I now wondered where the balance lay. Does my life's purpose lie in surrendering it to a higher will, or taking full charge of it and creating the life I want?

"That same day, I decided to fast until you arrived," Alberto continued, "only eating bread and drinking water to discipline myself and release my dependency on others. I immediately felt free. I resolved to wait one more week for you, or to receive a clear sign, before continuing alone. I also recommitted to speaking my truth under all conditions. I continued participating in the community's rituals, but stopped praying their words. I stopped kneeling and prostrating myself. More and more, I refused to go to church, citing other commitments or my need to pray alone. Nobody asked, and I offered no explanations, but I saw them becoming more and more uncomfortable.

One night, the acting Superior asked to speak with me. I knew what was coming, but felt sad nonetheless. Her reasons for asking me to leave were feeble and I could see that she was nervous. I told her I wished we would have had the opportunity to really know each other, and then walked away, feeling melancholy but grateful for my experiences there. *You and I, together once again,* I whispered affectionately. The following morning, Gerardo burst into the house announcing that you were arriving at noon."

"That is amazing," I exclaimed.

"You know, I came to Medugorje expecting to have an intimate encounter with God," Alberto contemplated. "I did, but not in the way I expected. God was, and always will be, in me. Medugorje forced me to look at myself, to trust in my path and my choices, and to take the reins of my destiny. That is Medugorje's greatest gift to me, one that I will forever be grateful for."

31. What Love would Do

In my hostel, I struggled with an awkward situation. Its owner, an Italian woman named Isabella, had received me politely but formally, and despite my best efforts, had staunchly maintained an air of formality and distance between us. I was at her large hostel with only two other guests. From the outset, I sensed their tension around Isabella, their desire to please her, or perhaps not raise her ire by infringing on the many rules she had imposed. Every item had its designated place. Dishes were to be washed in a certain order, at a certain time, and stacked in a certain way. Silence was to be observed at mealtimes. She pointedly asked me not to speak about my travels or share my experiences, even though the others wanted to hear about them, believing such stories to be boastful. She chastised me more than once for being too happy, reminding me that the week leading up to Easter was a serious time of year, a time of contrition and suffering, and that my joy was the height of disrespect.

Her harshness had at times reduced me to tears. I didn't leave because I felt there was a purpose for my being there, something that was important for my spiritual journey. I wanted to understand why she was bringing out such powerful emotions in me, but in my weakened physical state, fighting with an unrelenting cold and feeling bottled up in this restrictive environment, I didn't always have the energy to handle her criticism with grace.

"You're not doing this right," Isabella rebuked one night, yanking the plate from my hand and rearranging the food. Guests were arriving at the hostel, and she wanted everything to be perfect.

I walked away, weary of her attacks and angry at myself for allowing her comments to hurt me. I was about to enter my room when a sliver of golden light at the end of the corridor called my attention. It seemed to be beckoning me in the darkness, its slim finger held out in invitation. I followed it to its source, an intimate chapel whose walls glowed in the candlelight that filled the room. I sat down and began to cry.

"Why is she being so hard on me? Nothing I do is good enough. Nothing I do makes her happy. She only seems happy when I obey her commands, like a good little girl. I want to leave but instinct tells me to stay, that this is an important part of this way of peace. But what is it?"

As my emotions calmed, images began to flash in my mind's eye: the little girl trying to get the best grades, only to be told there weren't the highest; the young woman disappointing her family by choosing the business world and not becoming the doctor they all desired; the over-achieving adult seeking success as a measure of her worth.

I saw so clearly then that Isabella was my mother, my father, my ex-husband, and every other person whose approval I had so desperately sought. She was the rebellion against authority, and the anger that seethed at injustice. She was the pain of rejection and inadequacy that hadn't yet healed.

I tried to look past her harsh mannerisms, to see the human being well-hidden behind the mask of authority and confidence. I began to wonder about her story, and what would make her so controlling. The most controlling people I ever knew harbored fear and insecurity so deep that the only way they knew how to deal with it was to control their world, to protect their vulnerability with the appearance of invulnerability. I understood Isabella perfectly because I too was like her, a control addict... but a recovering one.

As my heart grasped this truth, that she and I were one, my image of her began to soften. Behind the hard task-master, I glimpsed a child, frightened and desperate for love, longing for approval. I wanted to reach out to that child, to comfort her.

"*What would love do?*" I heard whispered in my ear.

"*Love is a beautiful ideal,*" my mind contested, "*but it doesn't always work. I have a right to feel angry.*"

"*Love would see the light in the other,*" my heart insisted. "*Maybe she is as much a child as I am. Maybe she is hurting as much as I am. When a child is hurt and afraid, you hug them and tell them that you love them. You tell them that all will be well. That's what love would do.*"

"*There's no way I'm hugging her,*" my entire being retorted. "*It may be what love would do, but not me. What if she laughs at me? Or worse, pushes me away? I couldn't handle that rejection.*"

I stood and left the chapel, happy with my latest revelation even though I wasn't prepared to act on it. I stopped in the washroom to splash some cold water on my face, and glanced in the mirror. The image that stared back at me was the one of the little girl I had glimpsed in my mind only moments earlier.

"This isn't about her, it's about me. I need to let go of my pride. I must take this step forward or be forever stuck in the past."

I rushed to the kitchen, before my mind could contradict my heart. Isabella was still moving about quickly, and glanced at me distractedly. I waited for a pause in her movements, then walked up to her and awkwardly hugged her. Her body tensed. I held my breath. Slowly, she wrapped her arms around my back in a strong embrace. We held on for a long time, neither letting go.

"I think you're doing a great job here," I whispered, finally releasing her. Isabella's face was alight, her eyes shining with tears.

"I'm sorry I'm so hard on you," she said, still holding my hands, "but I think you're just too full of yourself."

"Really?" I answered mischievously. "I was thinking exactly the same thing about you." To her hearty laugh, I added, "Perhaps we're more alike than we care to admit."

She gave my hand a squeeze before finally releasing it and returning to her work; but her movements seemed to me more relaxed and the smile never left her face. I floated out of the kitchen, feeling higher and lighter than I can ever remember. On Podbrdo, Apparition Hill, I had released my fears; with Isabella, I finally embraced them.

* * *

On our last evening in Medugorje, Alberto and I climbed Podbrdo. We watched the sun set, and the lights of the town come on. I recalled the village of Villafranca del Bierzo along the Camino, and its famous *Puerta del Perdón*, the Door of Forgiveness, and main entrance to the Church of Santiago there. For those pilgrims who couldn't continue to Santiago de Compostela because of sickness or injury, it marked a point of completion. By arriving at this door, pilgrims received the same blessings they would have, had they made it to Santiago. I knew I would make it to Jerusalem, but Medugorje felt like my Door of Forgiveness. I had carried the hopes and prayers of those who couldn't be here and delivered them intact. I had carried a message of peace, and appreciated the weight of that choice. And most miraculously, I had discovered that what I most disliked in another was also within me, and that love was the surest way to heal it.

Standing on that hill that evening, with the canvas of lights at my feet and the gaze of Mary at my back, it was easy to believe that the children did see something here, something beautiful and radiant that filled them with hope and love. It was certainly what I felt; but to me, that energy was beyond form or religion. It was what Mary represented: the divine feminine energy, unconditional love, infinite peace and compassion, and unwavering grace. That energy was timeless and eternal, and was what I wished to carry with me to Jerusalem.

On April 1, 2002, Alberto and I took our first steps together again.

32. Heavenly Gifts

Alberto and I fell into an immediate rhythm, and walked with renewed purpose and vigor. We crossed back into Croatia and continued along its winding coastline towards Serbia and Montenegro. We were greeted with recognition wherever we went and usually welcomed without reservation.

"Can I borrow some money from you?" Alberto asked one morning during one of our breaks.

"Of course," I answered immediately. He had never asked for money before.

"I just smoked my last cigarette and I don't have enough for a new pack," he added casually.

Alberto had started smoking while in Medugorje. Although I didn't agree with his choice, I tried to respect it but often failed, slipping into lectures about the dangers of smoking. He would listen patiently while lighting up another cigarette, arguing that cigarettes could only harm him if he believed they could.

"There's no way I'm giving you money for cigarettes," I huffed indignantly, walking away. "For food, clothes, or anything else, fine; but I'm not contributing to your habit."

Alberto eventually caught up to me, grinning like a Cheshire cat, proclaiming, "I told you I always get what I need."

"Congratulations," I retorted sarcastically.

"After you left," he went on, "I began speaking with Life, asking for cigarettes and trusting that if it wasn't hurting me or anyone else, I would receive them. I let go of my doubts and expectations, and walked. A short while later, something off the side of the road caught my attention."

He reached into his pocket and pulled out a packet of cigarettes still in its original wrapping, unblemished and undamaged. They were the full-strength Marlboros, not the lighter brands he usually smoked.

"It was just lying there," he beamed, excitedly motioning with his arms. "There were no cars or other people around, so I have no idea how they got there. They're even full strength. Ironic, don't you think?"

I stared at him, incredulous. Not only did he always get what he needed like food, shelter and money, but now he was getting cigarettes.

It seemed such a frivolous request when he could be asking for more important things; yet there he was with his cigarettes in hand.

"Don't you see, Mony?" he continued. "This is ultimate proof that magic exists, and that to receive, all you have to do is believe."

I didn't know what was making me angrier, the fact that he got the cigarettes or the possibility that he was right, that what he called magic worked, and that we could receive any thing that we asked for, no matter how trivial or inappropriate it may appear. I stormed ahead.

"I can't believe you're angry," he protested. "You're missing the whole point. Mony? Mony!" He called out after me.

I gave up on the whole cigarette issue that day and left him alone whenever he lit up. This simple but remarkable incident would stand out for Alberto as a highlight of his journey.

* * *

April 5, 2002. It was Alberto's birthday, and we were staying in the lovely monastery of Slano. Its kind priest had tended to all our needs, even machine-washing our clothes, and now we sat with our host sharing stories of our walk.

I had hoped to slip out for a while to find a small cake to make Alberto's day complete, but had not yet found the opportunity. A knock on the door interrupted our conversation, and the priest went to answer it. When he returned, he held a white rectangular cardboard box.

"Would you like some cake?" he offered, opening the box. "I'm performing a wedding this weekend, and the couple just dropped off this cake as a thank you."

Between cigarettes and birthday cake, I didn't know if I was starting to lose my grip on reality or if Alberto was indeed a wizard.

The round, chocolate cake was beautifully decorated with flowers and garnish, its center emblazoned with two interlacing hearts made of tiny silver pearls. We were speechless but shameless as we dug in and helped ourselves to two large servings, all to the priest's amused glance.

"I'm now working on more money," Alberto winked between mouthfuls.

We continued southwards along the Croatian coastline and arrived in spectacular Dubrovnik. We were now less than forty kilometers to the Serbian border. We stayed in a convent that Fra Drago had directed us to and where, much to Alberto's delight, learned that one of the nuns spoke Spanish. I followed most of their conversation, which naturally focused on our beliefs. As Alberto attempted to explain to this elderly nun our faith in the essential goodness of people, she interjected bitterly,

"Not in all people, there isn't," she pronounced. "Not in the Serbians. There is no goodness in them. They are a race of barbarians. You can't trust them. They massacred people in a village not far from here, including the women and children. They decapitated the children and hung their heads on poles in the middle of the square. Children," she reiterated, her voice cracking.

My blood froze as terror ran through my veins. She relayed even more horrors, explicitly underlining the brutality of her Serbian neighbors. By the time we bid our goodnights, I was feeling less than enthusiastic about leaving Croatia. Croatia, like Italy, had become comfortable. I had become accustomed to the people and the land. They had embraced us and our message, and thus woven a web of protection that accompanied us wherever we went. I was now reluctant to leave that security, and once again walk in the unknown. Despite my intention not to be influenced by the judgments of others, I found myself doing exactly that. The nun's vivid and grotesque descriptions mingled with continued warnings from our friends and family about the deteriorating situation in Jerusalem haunted me that night.

Our hosts invited us to spend an extra day in Dubrovnik, which we used to tour this historic city. In the evening, we met Neda, an energetic woman who headed the local Franciscan women's order. In a voice cracking with emotion, she explained that our story had resonated deeply within her, and that she felt the desire to help us. We spoke for a long time with this engaging woman, feeling in her a kindred soul. She excitedly informed us that a small group wanted to show their support by accompanying us on our walk out of the city the following morning. I was thrilled at the idea, of witnessing my grand dream of a peace march in Jerusalem becoming real in this small way.

Neda reached into her purse and pulled out a stuffed envelope, sliding it across the table. "We took up a collection in our parish. Please accept this on behalf of our community," she said. I slid the envelope towards Alberto, unable to hide my amazement.

"Thank you," Alberto said sincerely.

* * *

A decapitated statue of Jesus hung over the display case. A similar one of Joseph stood nearby. To one side was a statue of Mary with her eyes poked out. All their bodies were chipped and nicked. Scarred remnants of various relics sat in the display case, all testimony to clear atrocities. A small plaque explained that this was the work of Serbians. Their presence inside a village church along our way made this scene all the more disturbing.

We finally arrived in Gruda, on the doorsteps of the Serbian border, and where we would spend our last night in Croatia. We were guests in the home of a spry, witty woman named Pavica who looked much younger than her seventy one years, and who was a friend of Neda's in Dubrovnik. Her home was comfortable but scarred. Parts of the cement façade were missing or marked with bullet holes. The edges of the windows were roughed out, and the windows didn't fit properly. The furniture looked badly worn and torn. Pavica explained that Serbian troops had occupied her home during the civil war, and that she had returned a short while ago to start reparations.

Perhaps sensing my tension, Pavica fussed over every detail of our stay—what we would eat, where we would sleep, provisions for the next day. She entertained us by playing the piano and singing traditional Croatian songs, all of which endeared her even more to us. I admired the courage of the woman who would return to rebuild when she could have easily stayed away, and the effort she was making to assuage my fears when I should have been doing that for her.

Her son Miro, a fortyish man with a quiet disposition, joined us. Through his obviously-proud mother, we learned that he was a sought-after artist who specialized in restoring works of art. After much gentle prodding, the shy artist finally acquiesced to us seeing his works.

In his small studio were broken and decapitated statues of various religious figures. On the floor were partially destroyed or faded paintings. Their sight still disturbed me, and I turned away. Miro removed a sheet from a figure on the table, revealing a statue of Mary with lovely, vibrant colors.

"I restore religious artifacts that have been damaged during the war," Miro said quietly.

We spent the following hours going through photos that showed in great detail the painstaking process that each object underwent to be restored to its original glory, its beauty a permanent witness to the great love that Miro poured into that effort. With every statue repainted or painting retouched, I saw him restoring something infinitely more beautiful and rare—hope.

Being with Miro, I was reminded that the work of peace required patience, dedication, and infinite love, a task very few are willing to take on, but one that I felt privileged to know in the figure of a humble artist named Miro, a man whose name means peace.

33. The Serbians

Congratulations and well-wishes followed us through the Croatian side of the border, but could not quell my trepidation in entering Serbian territory.

The first thing I noticed about the Serbian guard was just how physically large he was. His body, head, face and hands all seemed gigantic to me. He peered down at us, his face expressionless. We handed him our passports.

"What are you doing here?" he asked politely in English, leafing through my passport.

I turned to show him the sign on my backpack, knowing that the Serbo-Croatian languages were almost identical. The guard asked many questions about where specifically we had walked, and listened intently to our responses. He was courteous in his treatment, and although showed no emotion, I did not feel threatened or unwelcome. With a stamp dated April 11, 2002, we entered the country of Serbia and Montenegro, about to experience for ourselves whether all we had heard was indeed true.

Our destination was Herceg-Novi, a short fifteen kilometer walk from the border. We didn't know where we would be sleeping, but were assured that a large Croatian community lived there. Fra Ante called that day, as he regularly did, to check in on us. When he learned of our destination, he told us that he had a priest friend there and would call to notify him of our imminent arrival. I wondered if his influence extended all the way to Jerusalem. I was now certain that if I told him I was walking to China, he would tell me about a friend he had there as well.

As we settled in for the evening, my phone rang. I answered, expecting Fra Ante, and was surprised to hear Hannah's voice. We had not spoken in over a month, nor had she called Alberto. After we caught up on our lives, it was only natural that we speak about him.

"He sent me an email from Dubrovnik," she said, "saying he was worried about me and wanting to know if I wanted to end our relationship. There's still a lot of caring between us, but I don't feel the same love and passion that I did when we were together. I don't know if I can ever feel them again, but even if I could, could never live with the risk of him leaving again."

Alberto had been out of the room and when he returned, I mouthed that it was Hannah. He asked if she wanted to speak with him, to which she replied a sad, "Yes." We said our goodbyes and I handed Alberto the phone. Alone, I busied myself with washing and hanging clothes. I also checked my underarms for the first time in a long while, and was pleased to see there was no swelling or tenderness anywhere. As I prepared for bed, Alberto returned.

"Things are not well between us," he said, handing me the phone. "They haven't been for a long time, since before Valentine's Day. We're talking more seriously about separating, but neither wants to take the first step. I care for her deeply, but my feelings have changed, and so have hers. It's not just about me going back to her. It's her expectations of me and the guarantee she demands that I will never leave her to do something like this again. I can't promise her that. I need to feel free to continue my spiritual journey inside the relationship. I need to keep growing."

"I never really understood that before," I replied. "I thought freedom meant giving the other person time to pursue their interests, but I see now that it includes supporting them in their personal quest, even when it sometimes means having to separate. Now that I have my freedom and am pursuing that path, I can't imagine giving it up just to be in a relationship."

"Exactly," Alberto responded, distractedly arranging his clothes on the heater, before lying down on his bed and turning off the lights. "It's over," he whispered.

* * *

The Serbian coastline was just as magnificent, and mountainous, as the Croatian. In the towns of Risan and Kotor, we were guests of the Croatian communities living there. Our contact with the Serbian population was thus far confined to the road. The occasional car honked and some people waved in support but, in general, we were left alone.

We now moved towards Budva, along a road that was fast and dangerous. Our map indicated a path parallel to the highway but it snaked off in unusual ways. Soon, we lost the main road and found ourselves wandering along a deserted path that continued forking in various directions.

As we re-examined our map, a car drove past and stopped ahead. The driver, a middle-aged man with graying hair, approached and speaking in English, introduced himself as Zelko. He said he recognized us from the Croatian television programs and had driven the main road several times these last few days, hoping to find us. "What's strange," he added, "is that I never take this road, but for some reason today I did."

Quiet strength emanated from him, and I sensed a man of deep integrity and conviction. We agreed that our meeting was no coincidence, and accepted his invitation to meet his family. He assured us that his home was easy to find and showed it to us on the map, assuring us that the quiet country road was ideal for walking.

The route he indicated was indeed scenic, but he failed to mention the steep mountains. The path snaked through lovely villages that peeked out from the surrounding lush forest. Shepherds greeted us, their curiosity leading them to attempt communication. We simply said "Zelko," and they nodded in recognition before shepherding us like their sheep in his general direction. The forest canopies were a welcome haven from the blistering sun, but our legs were shaking by the time we arrived.

Zelko's family had gathered in the dining room and affectionately welcomed us. He proudly introduced us to his wife and young daughters, and then to his parents and other relatives. Home-made cakes and cookies were brought out and served with ice-cold drinks and water. The girls, who looked to be around eight and twelve, sat on their father's lap and occasionally cast a shy glance in our direction. He spoke softly with them, obviously referring to us because their eyes kept darting over. We waved, but they quickly buried their heads in their smiling father's neck. It was easy to see how much they loved him, and just how much he adored them. I felt genuinely welcomed by this close-knit and gracious family.

"I am Serbian," Zelko declared. "I am proud of my country and its people. I know what the media says about us and the atrocities that have been committed in Croatia. Croatians have also committed their share here, but that is not why I wish to speak with you. I want you to know that those barbarians don't represent the heart of the Serbian people. We are not the cold-blooded monsters that we are portrayed to be."

"Many years ago," he continued. "I was a sailor. I've been all over the world, including Jerusalem. One time, we were docked at a port in the southern United States and I had the chance to meet some American sailors. When I told them I was Serbian, one of the men told me that he had heard we were savages, and that we massacred and ate children. I thought he was joking, and was horrified to see that he was not. I can't tell you how outraged and impotent I felt. His comments have haunted me to this day. I still cannot understand how he could think such things about us."

This dignified man paused and looked at us earnestly, "I am now a father, and I don't want my daughters growing up in a world that believes these terrible untruths. I want you to know that we are a peaceful people. We have the same dreams and aspirations for ourselves and our children as everyone else. We want to live in peace."

My lasting image of this unforgettable encounter was of Zelko standing on the terrace, a smile of contentment on his face, balancing a girl in each arm, and the girls waving at us.

I renewed my promise to myself that day to never again be drawn into the fears and opinions of those I meet, and above all else, to trust in the human heart, for its hopes and dreams transcend borders and nationalities.

I couldn't imagine how quickly I would forget that promise.

34. Dreaded Albania

We walked up the wide steps and entered the simple white building that made up the Albanian border. A rotund patrol guard sat behind a long, marble counter. A few old chairs were against one wall, a table with miscellaneous forms against the other. A feeling of chaos reigned here as people rushed in and out, many impatiently demanding things from the unperturbed guard behind the counter.

He peered at us with suspicion and barked some words in Albanian. I asked if he spoke any other language, and he answered a firm "no." I held out my hand, palm up, and with the index and middle fingers of my other hand, ran them across my palm. The guard just responded with more Albanian words.

"What he's saying is that you need to fill out the visa forms on the desk over there," I heard a man's voice say in a clear Australian accent. I turned to see a slight man in his forties wearing khaki clothes and a safari hat. "*I'm talking to Crocodile Dundee*," I chuckled to myself.

"The cost is really only twelve Euros," he went on, "but he's asking you to pay twenty. These people are very poor and in desperate need of money. This guy probably hasn't been paid in a while. If you want to enter the country, that's the price you've got to pay."

I didn't know if he was talking about the monetary price or the emotional price of walking through my fears. From the earliest days of our pilgrimage, we had been warned about the dangers of walking in Albania—from ruthless violence to corruption on all levels—and were encouraged to avoid it altogether. But there was no way to get to Macedonia and Greece without passing through Albania. After all that I had gone through, and especially after Zelko, I should have known to trust my personal experiences and leave the rest behind… but somehow I couldn't.

The Australian exchanged a few words in Albanian with the guard. I didn't have the impression that they were friends or friendly, only that this man knew the rules of the game. He handed us the papers and hurriedly explained how to fill them out before rushing out the door.

The guard took our passports, and after an hour of waiting, finally called us over and handed us each a small piece of paper.

"Very important," he said earnestly, waving the paper and slipping it into the passport. "Never lose. Always keep in passport. Twenty Euros please."

"So you do speak English," I said encouragingly.

"No," was his smiling reply.

We paid the fee, and he stamped our passports. On April 19, 2002, we entered Albania.

We started towards Bajza, a town where the ever-resourceful Fra Ante had friends waiting for us. The road, narrow and uneven, was marked with huge potholes and looked like it hadn't been paved in years. There was not even a hint of a sidewalk, only a ditch separating the road from the scorched fields. Garbage littered the landscape, and was pushed into piles every few hundred meters. The few buildings that we passed were bombed out or in desperate need of repair. It was a shock to see all this, and harder still to believe that we were still in Europe.

The people drove aggressively, honking and gesturing at us to get off the road. One driver slowed down and hung his head out the window, stared at my breasts, nodded in appreciation, and then drove away. I didn't know whether to laugh or scream. My nerves were frayed by time we arrived at the church, a newly built structure that stood in stark contrast to the general poverty around it.

The attending priest welcomed us, and offered to escort Alberto to get groceries, telling us that Alberto would be taken advantage of as a tourist if he went alone. They returned quickly, laden with local bread, cheese, olives and tomatoes, and the priest bitterly complaining that, despite his presence and complaints in Albanian, Alberto was still charged double the normal price.

"I would never attempt what you are doing here," he proclaimed. "This country is coming out of an oppressive dictatorship, and the people are desperate. They have no regard for the law or for human life. You can't trust any of them. Thieves stop cars in broad daylight, then rob and kill the occupants. Even I've been robbed, and I'm a priest. The police don't care. They're useless, and you have to bribe them to get anything done. If I were you, I would take a bus out of here."

I tried to ignore his comments when I meditated that night. I replaced his vision of this country with that of peace and harmony, and nothing but goodness in every person we met. Alberto cut out the words for our new Albanian signs, written for us by the priest: *Ecim për në Jeruzalem për Paqe* for me, and *Paqe* for Alberto.

A glorious morning greeted our thirty-kilometer walk to Skadar, the next town where Fra Ante had friends. The road took us through mainly tiny villages that I imagined sustained themselves by farming the land and tending to livestock. Garbage continued to dominate the landscape and the stench, which was often mixed with that of human waste, was intolerable. Barefoot children in ragged clothes played in the streets and chased after us when we passed by. Men of all ages sat at tables in front of bars that measured no more than a large closet. Most called out for us to sit and talk, which we did the first few times, until it became apparent that these men had nothing else to do in this impoverished part of the country. They were friendly and respectful, speaking to us in Italian, a language they acquired from watching Italian television programs.

From them, we learned more about the history of this country, and their shared dream of leaving it to find better work opportunities elsewhere. They were awed by our ability to leave our countries at will, a luxury most here will never experience. Without exception, they all warned us against trusting any Albanians, especially the police.

So, of course, when a police car stopped ahead of us later that day, I was terrified. The young police officer asked for our passports and flipped through the pages slowly, examining the entry visa in great detail. When he asked our destination, I turned to show him my sign and briefly explained our walk.

"I stopped you for your own safety," he said, returning our passports. "You must be careful on these roads. Never walk at night. This is still an unstable part of the country and anything can happen to you. Don't trust the people. I will call in your details so that the police on this road will not bother you. Have a safe journey."

"This is too funny," Alberto chuckled. "We only find good people who are afraid of each other." But that still didn't allay my fears.

We continued along what was supposedly the main road to Skadar, sharing it as equally with horses, donkeys, and mules as we did with cars and buses. Most people stopped to offer us a ride, and appeared confused when we refused. We would later learn that for people here, only the poorest of the poor walked. Even riding a donkey was a step up from walking.

We finally arrived in Skadar, where the crowds, filth, and stench mixed with the late afternoon heat, exhaust fumes, and dust, suffocating me. People bumped me as I walked past, or brushed up against me. I felt invaded, as if I had no personal space around me, no space where I ended and they began. Some people followed us, asking for money in English. One young man pointed to my ring. An old woman pointed to my Tau necklace, then at Alberto's watch. In comparison to their meager existence, we must have appeared the wealthy tourists. It was all too overwhelming.

I began to withdraw then, to put up a barrier of self-preservation. I stopped greeting people and avoided all eye contact. I charged ahead, pushing my way through the crowds, trying to create a safe space around me. Some people pointed at our signs and laughed. Others stared angrily at us. For the first time since entering Albania, I felt physically unsafe. My fear mounted, and I found myself responding in agitation to some people, curtly telling them in English to get out of my way.

"Hey, relax," Alberto said at one point, grabbing my arm. "What you're doing is not helping the situation. Either change your attitude or take off the sign."

"Leave me alone," I yelled, yanking my arm away.

Alberto grabbed my arm again, this time a little more forcefully. He had a look of anger that I rarely saw. "I know you're tired and upset, but you must control yourself. You're not carrying a product ad on your back. Remember what you're doing."

I jerked my arm away and charged ahead blindly. Anger, fear, and exhaustion all played themselves out in my body, and I felt their effects in every one of my muscles. Alberto caught up with me and walked ahead, leaving me to follow him and to trust that he would find the Franciscan monastery where we were expected.

Atop a small hill, we found it. With its lush trees and manicured gardens, it appeared as an oasis in that desert of a city. We were shown to a clean room with several beds, where I dropped my backpack on the floor, yanked out my change of clothes, and headed to the showers.

I stripped off my clothes and soaked them in the sink, watching with disgust the water turn black. I stepped into the shower, eager to wash away all the unwanted, physical and non-physical, which had accumulated that day. The warm water cascaded over my head and shoulders, and then down my weary body. Its caress was warm and soothing, its whispers gentle and reassuring. My tears, too long held in, flowed freely. I leaned my head against the porcelain wall and began to weep.

"I don't know if I can do this. I don't know if I'm strong enough. It's only my second day here and I'm already biting peoples' heads off. Alberto is right. I need to get a grip. This is not my way, and definitely not the way of peace."

I sat in the shower, drained on all levels. The gentle whispers and soothing caresses continued falling, more tender and real in that moment than the kindest mother. The waters washed away my failings that day, and by the time I came out, I was ready to try again.

Leaves rustled gently in the refreshing breeze, while birds chirped happily, welcoming me in my renewal. Alberto showered, and then we went to join the monks who were expecting us for dinner. There, we met a Croatian priest named Marcello, a short burly man who reminded me of a pit bull. He listened with interest to our stories, and seemed especially interested in Alberto's views of God and his experiences in Medugorje. I still felt emotionally fragile, and so was happy to have Alberto lead the conversation. When I mentioned my fears about walking in Albania, Father Marcello said,

"What you heard was true five years ago, but not today. I've been here nine years now and lived through the worst of it. You can trust the people here. Albanians are some of the most generous and hospitable people in the world. Most have nothing, but will give you what little they have from the heart. I'm telling you not be afraid. You're safe here. If you need help, ask for it. They love to help."

Father Marcello spoke with a directness and authority that I trusted, and I promised to heed his advice. With maps difficult to find, he sketched out a route that would get us into Tirana, the capital city, and pointed out the places where he had friends who would receive us. I went to sleep that night holding on to Father Marcello's vision of Albania and trying to forget the trials of that day.

* * *

Father Marcello's map led us to friends in Bushat, Lezhe, and Laç where we were readily welcomed. We met missionaries from around the world—Filipino nurses with their mobile hospital, and Indian monks representing Mother Teresa's work among the poorest of the poor— who were all working to rebuild Albania. Their humility and love for the people truly touched us. We saw their spirituality, one that went beyond religious dogma, in action.

I envied their passion and commitment, and hoped that being with them would rekindle that spark within me. But it didn't. With each passing day, I felt myself growing weaker.

At one of our stays, we met a retired English gentleman named John who coordinated humanitarian aid from the U.K. to Albania. John spoke at length about his many accomplishments and accolades, but never once asked about our journey. The few occasions that we did try to speak, his eyes wandered and he seemed uninterested in what we had to say, until he brought the conversation back to himself.

As I contemplated our meeting, I couldn't help but feel that he was sent as a warning that I was in danger of becoming someone superficial who told amusing stories and anecdotes, but who lacked sincerity. I could imagine peoples' reactions to his stories: wow, what you're doing is great; wow, the BBC interviewed you about your work; wow, they've made you an honorary citizen of a small town in Albania. Wow.

He was a well-intentioned man who was doing important things, but what I really saw was myself. I was tired of speaking about our walk, of repeating the same stories over and again. My words were becoming rote, well-rehearsed, and I spoke them with little passion or authenticity. My mind at times wandered in the middle of conversations. People reacted to me in the same way that I was sure they reacted to John, but I was feeling increasingly empty and a fraud.

I wanted to stop walking, to take a break, but would not allow myself to do so. To me, that would mean failure, and I knew that would haunt me much worse than any emotional fatigue I was feeling at the moment. I was touting a message of inner peace that I felt so very far away from, and feeling ever more fearful that people could see through me; especially Alberto, who appeared more confident than ever. Although he tried to comfort me, in his eyes I saw his looks of disapproval and disappointment in me, and so withdrew deeper, praying that Albania would not destroy me.

* * *

If it was possible, walking into Tirana was even more horrendous than walking into Skadar. Despite my best efforts, I found myself slipping into despair and angrily pushing my way through this interminable hell.

As we got closer to the city center, the path became a freshly paved road with lines that traffic actually obeyed. The shacks and corrugated metal roofs were transformed into real brick buildings, some with Spanish tiles. The conditions continued improving and eventually, we found ourselves along a main avenue where freshly painted and colorful buildings, rivaling any in historic Europe, lined the street. A divide of trees and flowers added a splash of color and elegance to the wide lanes. Upscale shops displayed the latest fashions.

"Where did Albania go?" I asked Alberto incredulously.

He shook his head, his eyes as wide as mine, taking in the stunning view and trying to adjust to this new reality. A few blocks in any direction, chaos and squalor were the norm, but this area in the center was pristine. I could not believe the contrast, and wondered why the government would leave the outskirts in such a disastrous state.

Father Richard, the priest who was hosting us that evening, was most accommodating, inviting us to spend an extra night. We used our time to rest and to send home some of our heavier winter items; but keeping our sleeping bags. My daily uniform would now consist of my usual pants, a t-shirt, a lightweight long-sleeve shirt, and a summer hat. Alberto did a similar cleansing of his backpack. We shipped over four kilograms that day, a difference I knew we would feel when we walked. And in the country where I least expected it, my bank debit card worked, and I was able to withdraw Euros from an ATM.

Father Richard appeared later that evening to take us to dinner. It shocked me to be riding in the new Land Rover which he proudly explained was the Church's property; but I couldn't find words to say. We drove in silence along tranquil, winding roads, finally stopping at what appeared to be a private gated estate. It was a restaurant. Small tables filled the intimate space, each adorned with embroidered white table clothes, gleaming china, and sparkling crystal and silverware. The soft lighting and flickering candlelight added to the cozy feeling. Patrons were dressed elegantly, some of the men in jacket and tie. I looked at my dusty well-worn boots and clean, but always-slightly-soiled, pilgrim clothes, and felt completely out of place.

The seating host greeted Father Richard by name and led us to a table by the window. The cuisine was Italian and the dishes easily recognizable. Father Richard ordered a bottle of red wine, and we ordered our food. The waiter brought us a lovely assortment of breads, and then placed the napkin on my lap, and then on those of the men. I was accustomed to this level of service and attention, but I couldn't help but feel that we were doing something wrong.

I desperately wanted to ask about the atrocious conditions in this country but didn't dare, fearing that I would too easily reveal my true feelings at that moment, and I didn't want to hurt our host. I knew that he wanted to treat us well, and that his intentions were honorable. The battle of inadequacy was my own.

Time passed quickly, and we spoke a great deal about our spiritual beliefs, which Father Richard seemed to agree with.

"You're a man of deep conviction," he said to Alberto at one point. "Perhaps you too will become a priest at the end of your pilgrimage."

"I only have one small problem with obedience," Alberto laughed. "I could never go against my conscience, no matter what any person or authority figure tells me to do."

"But...then that makes you a Protestant," Father Richard exclaimed in disbelief. "They don't believe in the hierarchy of the Church either."

Alberto appeared taken aback by the response, but calmly replied, "I don't like labels. I will listen to the advice of others, and am even open to follow a teacher or master, but will ultimately listen to my heart because that's where God is. If that's what a Protestant is, then maybe I was always one and never knew it."

The rest of the evening was subdued.

On the morning of our departure, we searched out Father Richard to say our goodbyes, and found him in the Church's administrative offices. The marble floors and gleaming crystal left me astonished. In light of all the poverty we had seen, this extravagance, combined with our dinner experience the night before, to me seemed insulting to the people of this country. In that moment, I forgot all the kindness and assistance we had received from the Church. I forgot about *Fras* Ante and Drago, and the long chain of priests who had helped us. I forgot about the good they were doing, and only saw the failures. I shared my frustrations with Alberto.

"I'm the first to agree that you don't have to be poor to help the poor," he said. "I believe in helping others awaken their unlimited power to create abundance in their lives, and to change their consciousness from poverty to wealth. The Church speaks of helping the needy and sharing everything with the poor; but how can they live in such luxury when they're surrounded by so much misery, and then preach that message?"

The contradictions that we were seeing, and worse, participating in, were causing us tremendous angst. We spoke more seriously about staying in hostels when we could find them, and exploring other options for shelter. Alberto agreed. With that simple pronouncement, I felt a freedom that I had not felt in a long time.

* * *

We continued eastwards, passing Eba, Elbasan, Librazhd, and Prrenjas, the conditions improving the further east we traveled.

One evening during those days found us in the company of three young Evangelist missionaries. They had seen us on the road, and invited us to have dinner with them.

My patience with all things religious was already thin, so I left it to Alberto to carry on the theological discussion they were eager to have. I did find it interesting to learn that Evangelists didn't venerate Mary as did the Catholics, and didn't believe she was a virgin. They also didn't believe in the hierarchy of the Church and allowed their priests to marry. What they fervently believed, however, was that Jesus was the only way to salvation—and they spent the better part of the evening trying to convince of us of that.

The one named Edona, the youngest and most passionate of the group, asked me directly why I believed peace was a choice when peace only came from God. I looked at Alberto with desperation. "Of course peace comes from God," he said, coming to my aid. "Everything comes from God, but he also gave us the free will to choose any path we wish to follow. So even if we walk paths where we are oblivious to God's existence, we can still find peace. Peace doesn't come from believing in God, but from loving ourselves and the world in the same unconditional way that he loves us."

Alberto continued patiently with them as I slunk further away into the corner. I watched with envy the couples in the restaurant, eating quietly, some laughing, others speaking intimately. I was certain they weren't speaking about Jesus and salvation, and longed for that kind of carefree evening.

"I'd like to say a prayer for you," Edona declared over dessert. We held hands as requested. She closed her eyes and began speaking fervently in Albanian. The words Jesus, Alberto, and Monica were frequent.

I felt spiritually violated, my beliefs disrespected, and hers foisted upon me. I glared at her, and saw her face turn red. The others exchanged nervous glances. Alberto quickly read my reaction and the general shift in the mood.

"Thank you, Edona," he said kindly. "Even though we don't completely agree with your beliefs, I still appreciate your prayer."

Dinner finished quickly after that, and we stood to say our goodbyes. I hugged each person in turn, trying to be sincere in my well-wishes, but knowing that I wasn't. Alberto did the same, with sincerity, and stopped with Edona, his hands resting on her shoulders, and gazing compassionately into her eyes.

"I don't want you to feel bad about your prayer this evening," he said. "What you did was good because, above all else, I know that it came from love."

Edona's eyes brimmed with tears, and I wondered if Alberto's last words had finally reached her. Alberto was a spiritual gentleman that night, and had treated them with a kindness and caring that went beyond anything that I could have mustered. I admired him for being able to maintain his composure, and at the same time, never felt further away from him.

* * *

Our last day in Albania was magnificent, with spectacular views of lush valleys and a crisp air that invigorated all my senses. I heard birds chirping and streams gurgling, all offering their farewell song.

My excitement at leaving was tinged with the sense that I was somehow running away from the battle. Albania had pushed and tested me in ways I had never expected, and I was sad to admit that I had failed many tests miserably. I had left Croatia a celebrity, confident in myself, my walk, my purpose. Now, I questioned everything, and hoped that a new country with its different culture and ideas would inspire me with the love I once felt for this walk. It was the only way I knew of handling what I saw as a defeat.

I was so emotionally despondent then that I didn't even stop to appreciate that none of the warnings about Albania ever materialized.

The border patrol guard took our visa without comment, and stamped our passports. We walked into the neutral zone. I did not look back. I never wanted to look back.

However, the further I got from the border, the greater the nagging feeling that I had neglected to do something important, something that I had done consistently at the border of every country. I stopped and turned around. The border crossing was barely visible. "Thank you, Albania, *faleminderit*," I whispered.

The breeze that blew that day carried no response, but I knew one day it would. I turned and faced forwards once again. Together with Alberto, we walked towards the Macedonian border. It was May 1, 2002, a new month, a new country, and what I hoped would be a new beginning.

35. The Explosion

We crossed the Macedonian border without incident and walked towards Struga, the nearest border town thirteen kilometers away. The mountains descended into lush farmland that stretched towards our destination. We had learned that a sizeable Albanian population lived in Macedonia, especially near the border, so we decided to keep our Albanian signs. Our trajectory through Macedonia into Greece was a short one hundred kilometers, and we agreed it wasn't worth the effort translating the signs.

As we neared the city, Alberto and I started receiving signs in rapid succession to stop. Moments later, a taxi pulled up beside us and a man stepped out.

"Hey, do you guys speak English?" He asked. He was attractive, and looked to be in his forties with short, dark, combed-back hair, a goatee, and a clear American accent.

"Yeah," I answered in surprise.

"That's great," he replied. "Let me buy you guys a drink. Come on. I'm Robert."

We followed Robert to an outdoor patio, where we ordered our drinks. We learned that he was an Albanian-born American who was in town for the summer with his wife visiting friends and family. He was an outgoing, gregarious man who everyone seemed to know. It was a light, superficial chat, one that made the hot, lazy afternoon pass easily into evening. Robert invited us to stay at his home, where we met his wife Denise, an American-born Albanian, and several family members.

We joined our engaging hosts for a stroll through the quaint downtown area, slowly making our way to the restaurant, where even more family members awaited us. Dinner was a raucous affair, with people talking over each other and laughing. Food and wine flowed freely. Most of the conversation was in Albanian, but I sat beside Denise and spoke in English. Alberto ended up in one corner of the long table, while Robert sat at its head.

In the beginning, I translated some of what was happening to Alberto; but as the evening wore on, I tired of it and spoke with Denise and Robert directly. Alberto sat quietly in the corner the whole evening, trying to follow the rapid-fire conversation. They asked about our walk and I answered the questions lightly, superficially, avoiding any deep discussions. Whenever Alberto tried to interject or offer an opinion, I downplayed his response or rephrased it into something superfluous. His gaze became increasingly harder, warning me to stop; but I didn't. I was having a good time, speaking in my own language about trivial things for a change, the things ordinary people speak about such as their lives, their families, and their work. I wanted to be in that world, and for one night, far away from the world I was living.

"With all of your stories, you could probably write a book at the end of all this," Denise enthused at one point.

"I wouldn't have much to write about really," I replied casually, "just meeting different people with different ideas."

"No, that's not true," interjected Alberto softly, ice dripping from his every word. "Although Mony doesn't want to admit it, our walk is also a spiritual journey. She's not talking about what we're really living, the miracles that we experience every day. Those are the realities of our walk because without them, we wouldn't be walking."

I glared at Alberto, who glared right back. Denise cleared her throat and quickly changed the subject. Few words were spoken on the long walk back to the house. Alberto and I didn't even look at each other. When we arrived, I said my goodnights to everyone and hurried to my room, where I collapsed into bed, drunk and dreading the argument I knew was coming the next morning.

* * *

We said our goodbyes to our hosts, and began the hot day's walk to Ohrid. A surprising peace reigned between Alberto and I which I hoped eliminated the need for an argument. Entering the city, we were delighted to find a campsite on a large lake, and that rented trailer homes. The trailer was cramped but clean, with two rooms separated by a sliding door. The grounds had common shower facilities with hot water and a shared kitchen. For six Euros, it was a great deal.

We sat at one of the park benches overlooking the lake, enjoying the scenery. Alberto pointed to a cloud formation over the lake and, with his finger, traced out a mushroom cloud, the kind that appears after a nuclear explosion. Then, he traced out a dragon that was laughing and pointing at the explosion, and finally two large eyes that seemed to be observing the whole scene. It was easy to see once he pointed it all out.

"Something big is going to happen," he said. "Something important, something that will empower the dragon of fear; but behind it is the hand of God. He's watching what's happening. It's all in his plans."

Alberto went for a stroll while I stayed behind enjoying the serenity of our setting. The prophetic clouds dissipated with the sunset, and the stars came out to share their splendor. By the time I returned to the trailer, I was feeling relaxed. The night was warm, so I opened the small window, turned off the lights, took off my clothes, and slipped in under the sheets.

I heard Alberto come in, go into his room, and close his door. I was drifting off to sleep when I heard our separating door slide open.

"I want to talk to you," he announced in the darkness.

"Tomorrow," I responded.

"No," he said firmly, turning on the light. "Now."

I was acutely aware of the fact that I was naked under the sheets. I pulled them up over my breasts and sat up in bed, hugging my knees. Alberto stood in the doorway, his face angry.

"I can't take this anymore," he exploded. "Last night was the final straw. How can you possibly look at Denise and tell her you have nothing important to write about? How can you lie like that? I'm tired of all your lies and half-truths. Now I understand many things, like why you wanted to start alone in Rome. You wanted to be able to brag that this was your walk, and that you, and you alone, started it. You wanted to show them how brave and fearless you are. But you don't fool me. You are nothing but a weak and insecure woman, desperate for approval and recognition. If you want to do this alone, fine. I will not be playing along any longer."

His words felt like daggers, but I was not about to let him see that.

"Even after all this time, you still know nothing about me," I said, my voice frustratingly cracking despite my attempts to appear strong. "If it's so difficult walking with me, then go. I don't need you."

I wanted to have this argument once and for all, and be done with it. I didn't care if he left that instant.

"Do you have any idea what the past weeks have been like for me?" I blurted, my words rushing out before I could censor them, my tears rolling down my cheeks. "Do you think I would have suffered what I did for publicity, especially in Albania? Do you think I enjoy not showering for days, eating the same foods every day, and sleeping on cold floors? Do you think I enjoy having pain in every part of my body?" Alberto looked at me doubtfully, his face still hard.

"Maybe," he responded. "It just makes you more appealing to the media. It makes for a better story."

"I would be terrified if any of them contacted me right now," I retorted. "I wouldn't know what to say for fear they would think we were freaks. If I had wanted the spotlight, I would have allowed a friend of mine to do press releases and invite the media to start with me in Rome, like he wanted to do. I obviously didn't because the walk was never about that for me." I suddenly felt overwhelmingly tired. I covered my face with my hands and began to weep, rocking my body back and forth.

"I'm tired of being stared at," I spat out. "I'm tired of carrying this sign. I can't do it anymore. It's too much. I had a normal life. I had friends. I gave all that up to do this. I feel stuck. I don't know if I can go forwards, and I don't know if I can go back. Last night was a chance for me to have some fun, to talk about silly things that have nothing to do with God, spirituality, and world peace. I just wanted to be my old self for a change."

My head dropped between my knees and I wept for a long time, feeling a tremendous aching in my heart that no amount of tears seemed able to lift. My crying finally stopped, and silence once again filled our trailer. All I could hear was the sound of the waves crashing against the shore.

"I'm so sorry," Alberto finally said quietly. "I think I've been too hard on you, and unfair in many things." He sat on the edge of the bed. I lifted my head to look at him. His face was weary, his eyes soft. With his finger, he gently wiped away my tears. "Can I hug you?" He asked.

"Uh," I replied, smiling nervously, "I'm naked under these sheets."

"Please," he said, reaching over and tightly embracing me. His hands were warm on my bare back. It felt good to be held, to be comforted. I buried my head in his shoulder and continued sobbing. He held me even tighter. Our masks were finally off, and the people that held each other that night were nothing more than two frightened and lonely human beings. I took a final quivering breath and released him. He smiled faintly, then finally released me and stood.

"I need to go for a walk," he said. "Good night."

I heard his feet crunch on the sand until they faded. I dropped back into my bed and closed my eyes, exhaustion mercifully overtaking me before I could think about the impact of what had just happened.

36. Resistance

The events of the previous night had left us emotionally weary, so it took little convincing for us to spend an extra day in Ohrid. We explored this lovely town, our steps carefree, matching our mood. Our newfound ease saw us leaning into each other, the protective barriers that recently guarded our deepest sentiments now abandoned. I didn't mind the intrusion into my space, and accompanied Alberto in laughter and merriment. That day, the companions finally became close friends.

From the local post office, we sent home our winter sleeping bags. It was a difficult decision to make, but they were simply too hot in the increasingly warmer nights. We reasoned that we would find summer sleeping bags in touristy Greece. Weighing about twelve kilograms each, our backpacks now felt as light as a feather when we began to walk again.

We also made another important decision—not to carry our signs. Although I would not allow myself to stop walking, I felt it necessary to put away the message of peace until I was strong enough to carry it again. That simple act liberated me, and I walked to Zavoj that day feeling emotionally lighter as well.

The evening found us as guests in the home of a close-knit family and community. When they showed us to our room for the night, I paused. Aside from a chair and end table, the only other furnishing in the room was a double bed. Alberto and I did not speak or look at each other. I took off my fleece jacket and socks, but left my tights and t-shirt on. Alberto did the same. I got into the bed first and slid towards the wall, but realized with horror that the bed sunk in the middle. Alberto got in, and we said awkward goodnights. I clung to the edge of the bed, and hoped we wouldn't meet in the center.

I opened my eyes. My body was pressed against Alberto's, my face buried in his chest. His one arm extended over my head, and the other rested against my hip. I heard his heartbeat, and felt his soft breath on my hair. I pulled away with effort, the dip in the bed pushing me back towards him, and hurriedly slid off the bottom edge, announcing to a groggy Alberto that it was time to start the day.

We spent that night in Resen in separate beds, and the following one in Bitola, near the Greek border. On May 7, 2002, we crossed that border, and officially began what would become an unforgettable Greek experience.

We had just turned out the lights of our hotel room in Florina when Alberto said, "Can I tell you something?"

"Sure," I answered.

"Ever since our talk in Ohrid," he started slowly, "I feel that I know you better. I see now that I had so many prejudices about you, and misjudged you. As I told you before, I'm sorry. You really are a good person. You're funny and open. I really like that side of you. It's very attractive."

"Thanks, I feel the same way about you," I replied casually.

"That's not what I mean," he responded. "That night, I feel as if I saw your light, your soul, the real you; and I loved it immediately. I think I have feelings for you."

"*This cannot be happening*," I thought, feeling my heart in my throat. "*I must be misunderstanding him.*"

"What exactly are you saying?" I asked.

"I'm not sure," he said. I waited for what felt like hours for Alberto to elaborate. "Well, I feel better for having said the words," he declared. "Good night."

I stared at the ceiling, trying to absorb this new bombshell. From his breathing, I knew Alberto wasn't asleep either, but I certainly wasn't about to continue this discussion. It was the one complication I did not want or need, especially with Alberto.

* * *

We sat at breakfast the following morning, having exchanged no more than awkward "good mornings." Each went to the buffet several times, briefly commenting on how good the food was, only to return to silence.

"So did you think about what I said last night?" Alberto asked with trepidation.

"I think maybe your feelings for me are a little confused," I answered sincerely. "We had a very powerful experience in Ohrid, and a lot of emotions came out. It was all good and it brought us closer. Maybe you're responding to this new openness between us."

"No," he contested, shaking his head. "I don't think that's what it is. I think I'm attracted to you."

"Who wouldn't be?" I joked. He laughed and continued gazing at me softly, tenderly and which could only be described as love-struck. I looked at him determinedly.

"Look, I don't think you're really attracted to me," I asserted. "I think you're lonely and maybe miss Hannah. We're together twenty-four hours a day and there's no one else to share all this with, so it's natural that you would reach out to me. I feel lonely sometimes too, and it would be easy for me to go to you too because you're here. You're convenient and available, but I know I wouldn't feel good about it. I wouldn't be doing it for the right reasons and would be jeopardizing not only my friendship with you but with Hannah as well."

"You know things are finished between us," he interjected.

"She's still my friend," I replied. "I think she would be terribly hurt." Silence, long and awkward, filled the space between us. I didn't want to hurt Alberto's feelings but I needed to be absolutely clear. "I'm sorry, Alberto," I said gently, "but I just don't see you in that way. You're like a brother to me. I'm attracted to you as a friend and companion, but not in any other way, do you understand?"

Alberto gazed at his plate and picked at his food. "Look," I continued. "I think this is just a terrible case of hormones. It's spring, and love is in the air. What we both need is to go find somebody and just get that energy out of our systems." He cracked a slight smile, but his gaze was still sad.

"Maybe you're right," he finally said. "It's probably just hormones."

With storm clouds hovering in the sky, we agreed to spend the day in town. We bought a map of Greece and some groceries. We searched for lightweight sleeping bags, but without success. I had every intention to walk the following morning, but my period started, and I felt tired. Alberto left me to rest, and came back at dinnertime. Our earlier awkwardness seemed to have eased, and we returned to our natural easy flow.

I sat on my bed, watching Alberto on his bed bounce a small plastic cup in his hands to see how long he could keep it in the air; pilgrim entertainment. I occasionally picked the cup off the floor when it got close to my side, and tossed it to him. Soon, I was kneeling on my bed, he on his, and swatting the helpless cup between us in a make-shift game of volleyball. Our laughter, and the competitive nature of each trying to win the point, filled the room. Alberto's playful gaze softened once again, and I felt uncomfortable. I stopped the game, and lied that I was feeling tired. His disappointment was clear.

I turned on the television and absently flipped channels, trying to occupy the time. The movie *Magnolia* was starting in English, so I began to watch it.

"Can I sit beside you?" Alberto asked.

"I don't think that's a good idea," I replied seriously.

"We're just two friends, sitting together, watching a movie, that's all. I promise," he grinned, crossing his heart. I stared at the screen.

"What is going on here? Where is the line between us? We have to keep a line; otherwise things can get out of hand. I may not be attracted to him, but I'm not made of stone."

"I just want to sit beside you, nothing more," Alberto reiterated.

I shifted over on my bed, my gaze still fixed on the television, my legs stretched out straight in front of me, my arms folded across my chest. Alberto sat beside me and similarly stretched his legs and crossed his hands on his lap. Our arms touched. I could feel the warmth of his body and smell the freshness of his soap.

Without warning, the television and all the lights in the room went out. We tried the switches, but nothing happened. I searched for my flashlight in the darkness. Alberto lit his candle and placed it on the nightstand. A warm glow filled the room. My awkwardness returned. I slipped under the sheets, and with my back turned to him, whispered, "Good night." He wished me the same.

I tossed and turned, not knowing what he was thinking or feeling; worse yet, not knowing what I was thinking or feeling.

"It felt good having him close."

37. Nice to Finally Meet You

"Let me carry some of your things," Alberto offered.

"Not to worry, I'm fine," I replied.

"Really, I'd like to," he insisted. "I'm not carrying a lot of weight now. Besides, I see that you're limping a bit."

We were on our way to Vevi along a quiet road that undulated gently. I had somehow overstretched my left calf during one of our many climbs, and despite my best efforts to keep my weight off it, it still hurt terribly. Alberto persisted in his pleas until I finally gave him my water bottle, camera, phone, and small bag of toiletries. They weighed no more than one kilogram, but I felt the difference immediately and walked more comfortably.

Alberto walked beside me most of the day, pacing me, keeping my attention on our rhythm, distracting me from my pain. Occasionally, I would glance over and notice him looking at me with soft intensity. I felt myself weakening in his presence, and felt stirrings of desire that confused me.

"What is happening to me," I scolded myself. *"I can't believe I'm even considering the possibility of being with him. I'm not even attracted to him, or am I? How can I even be thinking it?"*

We arrived in Vevi having walked a solid twenty four kilometers, but my left calf now burned with pain. I was happy to find an open hostel, where I immediately showered, then sat on my bed to massage my calf. It was too sensitive to touch, so I stretched it as gingerly as I could and reached for an ibuprophen tablet. Alberto came out of the shower and sat on his bed, watching me in silence.

"Would you like me to massage your calf?" he asked. I gave him a suspicious look.

"I've told you that I know massage," he continued earnestly. "I offered it once before, and you almost bit my head off because you were so angry at me. That day, I swore never to offer it again."

I hesitated, trying to weigh the hidden motives behind his tempting offer. I finally reasoned that anything that could heal my calf would help me walk better the next day; and so, choosing to trust his purest intentions, I accepted his offer. I rolled my pant legs to my knees, lay down on my stomach, turned my head to one side, and closed my eyes.

I heard him rub his hands rapidly together, and felt their warmth on my calf. He gently caressed the area, spreading the olive oil. His thumbs pressed gently into the base of my calf muscle, then traveled up almost to my knee. I winced in a mixture of pain and pleasure, trying to contain my groans, but finally releasing them into the pillow. Over and again he repeated the motion, each time more deeply, until my calf melted under his touch. When he rested his open hands on my calf, I felt a penetrating heat that radiated all the way up my leg.

It got cold when he pulled his hands away, and I wished that he would put them back. I stayed with my eyes closed, bathing in the sensations. When I opened my eyes, Alberto was lying on his bed, gazing at me wistfully.

"Can I please hold your hand?" he asked softly. He looked so sad that, without thinking, I responded, "yes."

I rolled over onto my back and slid to the edge of my bed. I reached my hand into the divide that separated our beds, and placed it in his waiting hand. I wanted to hug him, but feared the consequences of such a simple act. In the confused state he was in, and increasingly unstable state I was in, I thought it better to simply hold his hand.

"What are you thinking?" he whispered.

"I was thinking you could use a hug," I whispered, mentally kicking myself

"I would very much like that," he said, his voice filled with emotion.

I stared at the ceiling for a long while, and then said, "OK."

Alberto joined me on my bed, and we sat facing each other. My heart beat wildly. I was no longer worried about how Alberto would feel when we embraced, but rather, how I would feel. His gaze filled mine, the light in his green eyes shimmering. I awkwardly placed my hands around his neck. He wrapped his arms around my waist, and pulled me closer. Our heads rested on each other's shoulders. His heart raced as furiously as mine, but we did not move, and I wasn't sure if we were breathing.

I waited for sparks to fly, for passion to take over; but the longer I held him, the quieter my heart became, the more tranquil I felt.

"This feels very odd to say," I said softly, pulling away, "but I feel strangely calm with you. I don't understand why. I'm sorry." Alberto lowered his gaze, and then slowly released me to lie back on his bed.

"Thank you for being honest," he said.

I had tried to touch the fire, only to discover there was no fire there in the first place. I was contented at the success of our little experiment, and confident in the knowledge that I can now concentrate on my walk without distraction.

* * *

The twenty-eight kilometer walk into Arnissa the following day was long, made longer by the distance between Alberto and I. We hardly spoke, and when we did, it was strained. The previous evening's experience had clarified my feelings, but I wasn't sure it had done the same for him.

The cold freeze continued into Edessa the following day. The road was narrow with no shoulder, and we were sharing it with cars and trucks that drove way too quickly. The heat was stifling and, mixed with exhaust fumes, made breathing difficult. Our only reprieve was the fruit vendors that now dotted our path, selling the various fruits of the season. We stopped at one, and enjoyed a large bag of strawberries and cherries under the shade of a heavenly fig tree.

We easily found a hostel in this large town, and treated ourselves to pizza for dinner. Our camaraderie had returned, making for an enjoyable evening. Back in our room, I could feel that my stomach was queasy. I tried to ignore it, but gradually felt the need to vomit. I rushed to the bathroom and dropped on the cold tile floors, my head poised over the toilet. Alberto hurried behind me. I heaved and heaved, but nothing came out. I felt the cold sweat on my forehead and began to shake. Alberto held on to me and helped me lie down on the floor. I curled up into a ball and hugged myself, the tiles refreshing my clammy skin. I heaved over and again, and sat up each time, but couldn't vomit.

Alberto spoke soothingly, reassuringly, and tried to convince me to stick my fingers down my throat. I shook my head vigorously. I hated vomiting. It was always a tremendous effort. I breathed deeply, trying to keep it down, but couldn't. I finally felt it rising up into my throat, but I only had enough energy to crawl to the stand-up shower. Alberto was on his knees with me, holding my hair out of my face and rubbing my back. The smell of it was overpowering, and only made me vomit some more. Alberto held on to me with one hand and with the other, turned on the shower tap and washed my face, my neck, my mouth.

"I'm so sorry," I kept repeating between my tears.

"Don't worry," he soothed. "I'm here. You'll feel better soon."

I vomited once more. Alberto held me tightly and again washed me. I watched in growing embarrassment as he cleared the drain with his fingers from all that had already accumulated. Suddenly, I felt a gurgling in my stomach, and ordered Alberto to leave, as he helped me onto the toilet. I groaned in agony as cramps swept through me. What came out was liquid. My teeth chattered, and I could not stop trembling.

At the sound of the toilet flushing, Alberto knocked on the door, and came in. He helped me to the sink, and washed my hands and face as I leaned against the sink for support. He brought me my toothbrush, forcing me to brush to get the taste out of my mouth. I followed his instructions without thinking or questioning, happy to have him with me at that moment. With my body still trembling, Alberto led me to my bed, helped me under the sheets and covered me with several blankets. I closed my eyes, and heard Alberto cleaning up the mess in the bathroom.

"Alberto, don't," I called out weakly. "I'll clean it up later."

"Just rest. I'm almost finished," he called back.

I fell into an exhausted sleep. When I awakened, it was dark. I had no concept of time, only that I had slept for a long while. The pressure in my stomach had eased, and I felt much better. I glimpsed Alberto on the balcony, gazing out onto the street, and felt even more embarrassed, knowing that he had cleaned my vomit. It was a wretched task at the best of times, and barely tolerable when it was my own. I had only ever done it with people I loved. As I watched him on the balcony, I realized that only love would do what he did. Warm tears slid down my face, melting my previous resolve.

Seeing that I was stirring, Alberto came into the room and sat beside me on the bed.

"Thank you," I said.

"It's nothing," he replied, his eyes filled with caring, and what I had refused to see before: love. His hand caressed my hair and smoothed some strands off my face. He gently wiped away my tears and caressed my face, his hand warm and his touch as soft as a feather. It all felt so good.

I held out my hand and whispered, "Please stay with me".

He kissed my hand, slipped in beside me and lay on his side, facing me. He gently kissed my forehead, his lips barely touching my skin. He kissed one eye, then the other. He kissed my nose. He kissed one cheek, and then another. I wanted to weep for the love and tenderness with which he was treating me. I reached up and gently kissed his lips.

Time seemed to stop. I closed my eyes and again kissed him. Something felt familiar. I gazed into his eyes, trying to see behind them, to glimpse a timeless moment of recognition. Alberto's face momentarily changed and I had a fleeting image of someone I knew, someone close and beloved, but the image disappeared. Bursting with emotion, I pulled him to me and hugged him tightly.

"I know you," I whispered in confusion and joy.

We spent the rest of the evening in bed, touching, exploring, feeling. There was a magic and chemistry between us that took my breath away. Electricity shot out from every part of my body. I had never experienced anything like it before, and Alberto was certainly the last man I would have expected to feel it with.

We did not have sex that night. We didn't need to. The love that we made was infinitely more powerful than anything physical could have ever offered. As he wrapped his body around mine for the night, he whispered into my ear, "It's nice to finally meet you."

38. Lovers

I awakened the following morning in the same position as I had fallen asleep. Alberto's breath was warm against my neck, and his body pressed tightly against mine. In the light of day, the events of the previous evening didn't seem quite as magical. My fears immediately took hold and made what happened feel like one big mistake.

I turned around to face him. He looked like an angel sleeping beside me. I brushed the curls off his face and saw him smile. He slowly opened his eyes and grinned at me.

"*Buenos días,*" he said in a throaty voice, pulling me closer in his embrace. I lay on top of him for a while, listening to his heart beat and feeling the warmth of his body. His hand lazily stroked my hair.

"You know we have to talk about this," I said.

"Hmm, hmmm," I heard him murmur, feeling the vibration in his heart. I reluctantly pulled myself away and looked into his smiling eyes.

"*That's not going to help me focus,*" I thought. I sat up, crossed my legs, and then looked at him, trying to be resolute. I pulled my hair behind my ears and put my best business face on.

"I'm not sure what just happened is good for me, for you, and especially for the way," I declared.

"Anything that comes from love is good for the way," he purred, stretching out on the bed.

"I'm serious," I responded. "You know how important this walk is for me. I don't want anything or anyone taking me away from it. Do you understand?"

"Of course," he said, sitting up and leaning against the headboard. "This walk is important for me too. I have no intention of losing my way either."

"Good, so we're in agreement then," I replied. "*Check one,*" I listed mentally.

He didn't seem to be taking our conversation nearly as seriously as I was, and was gazing at me with the same eyes that had caused us to have this discussion now.

"I also want to make it clear that I'm not sure how I feel about you," I said slowly. "Last night was incredible but I'm not sure if I love you. My biggest fear is that you're going to fall in love with me. I can't give you any commitments or guarantees. I don't know what the future will bring. All I can offer you is this moment."

"That's fine," he replied casually, shrugging his shoulders. "I don't need any more than that. I was more afraid that you would fall in love with me and try to hold on to me."

"That will never happen," I said confidently.

"And I'm sure it won't happen with me," he said cheerfully, placing his hands behind his neck and gazing at me again. "So where's the problem?" I couldn't immediately think of one. "*Check two.*"

"And what if someone else comes along that is better for me?" I asked. "Someone who I feel is better suited for my life work?"

"Then I will willingly and lovingly let you go, knowing that you are happy and living the life you want," he responded confidently. "*Check three.*" I couldn't think of any more arguments at that point and snuggled into his open arms.

"And if I feel at any point that this pulling me away from the walk, will you let me go?" I said, remembering this last question.

"Shut up," was his only response before bringing me closer.

* * *

Our excuse for not walking that day was that it was raining and that I wasn't yet strong enough to walk. I slept alone most of the morning, but accompanied the rest of the afternoon. We were like children, joyfully playing and exploring. It was as if neither of us had ever been in a relationship before, and we were discovering these intoxicating feelings for the first time. It went beyond sex. That would have been easy to understand and handle. This was much more intimate, more intense, and more loving.

The following morning found us walking towards Giannitsa, forty kilometers away from Edessa. I felt strong for the first hour, but quickly began to lose energy. The diarrhea returned, repeatedly forcing me to stop. I took some anti-diarrhea pills, but with hardly any food in my stomach and the crushing heat, I felt drugged up and walked even more slowly than usual.

The nearest town was Skidra, so we decided to stop there. Our route was lovely. We passed orchards bursting with cherries, plums, apricots and apples. The trees were in bloom with every colored flower imaginable. Wildflowers painted the landscape, their vivid expressions perfectly complementing the many hues of green around us. Every house that we passed seemed adorned with roses of all shapes, sizes and colors. They were too beautiful not to stop and appreciate. I did so often, luxuriating in this simple pleasure and gift.

I slept that entire day again, and awakened when it was dark. Alberto was sitting beside me, writing in his diary. I was hungry and chanced some bread. I saw that Alberto had already washed our clothes and hung them around the room to dry.

"I don't understand why this is happening to me," I said, sipping some water. Alberto gazed at me, as if weighing his next words.

"Is it possible you're manifesting it?" He finally asked cautiously.

"What do you mean?" I replied, trying not to get defensive.

"I know you believe that physical ailments are a manifestation of emotional conflicts," he said gently. "Maybe your diarrhea is trying to tell you something."

"Like?" I asked impatiently.

"Is there something you can't digest?" He continued in the same gentle voice. "Like our relationship, for example. Maybe you're tired of walking, but don't want to admit it to yourself. Maybe you'd like to stop and rest for a while. An illness is the perfect excuse to do so without feeling guilty."

I wanted to contradict him, but couldn't. He held me in his arms for a long time. I didn't need to say the words. Alberto was right.

"Let's see what the Universe says," Alberto suggested, reaching for a coin. "Heads, we stay for a few days and enjoy our time here without thinking about the walk or feeling guilty about stopping. Tails, we leave tomorrow and walk with the same joy and passion that we had when we started."

The coin came up heads. Elated, I reached for Alberto in a tight embrace. I needed to rest, but more importantly, to explore more fully this blossoming relationship.

39. Turbulence

The days and nights passed quickly in Skidra. Our feelings intensified, and I found myself abandoning my reservations. I had hoped to wade into this relationship and navigate slowly, but I was swept away in a tidal wave of emotions that with each passing day seemed more permanent. I felt my heart and soul opening in ways I never could have imagined with him, or with any man. There were times when I felt we were one on all levels, no place where I ended and he began, and that our bodies were the vehicle for our souls to make love.

I didn't want to leave the intimacy of our small haven, but by the sixth day, feelings of guilt started to creep in. I was feeling much better, and walked strongly to Giannitsa...until the last ten kilometers. My backpack felt as if it loaded with stones and my legs as if they were trudging through mud. Alberto started complaining of pain behind his knee, and worried that it was tendonitis. We straggled into town like defeated warriors. We didn't even discuss if we created that situation.

The peace pilgrims once again disappeared. I left my guilt with them. We became a couple, crazy in love, strolling hand in hand, sharing ice cream, watching the world go by over coffee at outdoor cafés, going out to movies and to dance. Without agenda or places to be, we now obeyed an invisible rhythm that guided us to eat, sleep, and move. We were giddy with love, and many people asked if we were on our honeymoon. Strangers smiled and greeted us. A bakery owner gave us an extra cheese pie for no reason. A shop owner gave us incense as a gift. A bartender invited us for drinks. It was as if we radiated love, a powerful energy that appeared to touch people; and they responded, returning this blessing in myriad forms. Overwhelmed by this unexpected love, I would often weep at the fortune that had befallen me, and felt a calm and peace that I never imagined possible in a relationship.

Alberto's knee continued improving, but slowly. He encouraged me to try a healing, to send him the loving energy we were feeling through my hands. I focused on that feeling, and felt a tremendous energy coursing through my body. I felt charged, and my hands were hot when I placed them on Alberto's knee. I had done healings on myself, but never as powerfully as this. It was as if love was opening up dormant channels in my body so that I could transmit this energy without barriers. I marveled at this new discovery, and started directing it to people who I felt could use it, such as my mother and Yolla, and then spread it outwards until it covered the entire earth and suspended it in a ball of radiant loving energy that permeated the earth and every one of its inhabitants. I felt magnificent, connected to every living creature on this earth, and now desired to explore this form of healing even further.

* * *

After another six-day rest, Alberto's knee was strong enough to attempt walking again. Upon learning that most Greeks understood English, we felt inspired to carry a new sign that read: "Jerusalem in Peace". With that novel message, we were once again on the road.

In the days that followed, we passed Gefyra, Thessalonica, Langadikia, and were on our way to Loutra Volvis. On this spectacular day, we found ourselves stopping more than once to bask in the sunshine and breathe in the sweet perfumes that the spring air carried.

"Look at this," Alberto enthused at one of our stops, pointing at the grinds in my coffee cup. "It's you, holding a baby in your arms." Even I saw it clearly.

We had spoken about building a future together, even having children, and in the throes of passion, it seemed a beautiful idea. Seeing that image, however, made it seem too real. We had gone from friendship to babies in less than two weeks. I panicked. I was evasive with my response then, as I was that entire day, and withdrew into myself. Alberto kept asking what was wrong, and I kept lying that it was nothing. The more he insisted the more trapped I felt, and the further I withdrew. By the time we arrived in town, there was a clear distance between us. When I suggested we get separate rooms, he exploded, "What is going on with you?"

"Maybe I just don't want to get too attached to you," I blurted. "Maybe I'm afraid that one day you'll leave me too." Alberto stared at me with disbelief. Not even I believed my own words.

"I think you're looking for any excuse to push me away," he replied angrily. "Are you saying you don't believe we have a future together?"

"I don't know what I want," I retorted, "but all this talk about our future scares me. I need you to back off a bit."

"Fine, I'm going for a walk," he said and stormed out of the room. For a change, I decided to go for a walk too.

I knew that I was afraid of commitment, but what I feared more deeply was the other side of that some coin—losing my freedom. I wanted to finish my walk first, to get clarity on my life, and then share whatever that looked like with Alberto. I didn't want him influencing me or taking me off my path. I refused to allow him, or our relationship, to define me. Only I would do that.

By the time I returned to the room, I felt more centered and ready to speak honestly. Alberto was waiting for me. "I can sleep in another room if you'd like," he said dejectedly.

"It's not necessary, but we need to talk," I answered. We spoke well into the night, and although it was at times difficult, I revealed to him my deepest fears. Alberto listened, and understood, asking only one thing of me; to include him in my journey.

All I could do was promise to try.

40. Family Matters

"I'm going in for surgery next week," my mother said. "The doctors found a fifteen-centimeter-long cyst on my ovary, and another smaller one on my kidney."

I listened in stunned silence. We were in Alexandroupoli, a stone's throw to the Turkish border, having traversed the towns of Paralia, Kariani, Kavala, Xanthi, and Komitini.

"The doctors think there's a less than ten percent chance it's cancer," she continued. "They are doing tests to see if my heart can survive the operation."

My mother rarely asked me to come home, but there were occasions when I sensed her fear, and did so anyways. I never felt my presence was needed, or that it added anything, since it was my younger sister Sue, by default the doctor in the family, who facilitated all medical necessities. This time, however, I heard my mother's silent plea for me to return. I explained the situation to a sympathetic Alberto, who urged me to go.

My parents were thrilled with the news, but I couldn't help but feel that I had made this decision primarily to please them. After all, I had gone to Lebanon to see my aunt; how could I do any less with my mother? I wanted to tell her that I would be meditating for her, as I had done on other occasions, but would not physically be there. I also wanted Alberto to join me, but knew that my still-traditional father would never accept into our home a man who was not my husband. I felt like a coward, driven by guilt and obligation, the flight tickets in my hand confirmation of that cowardice.

For the second time during my pilgrimage, I boarded a plane that separated me from Alberto and my walk for peace to be with my family. As I boarded that plane on June 16, 2002, I hoped that all that I was leaving behind would still be waiting for me.

Four connections later, I arrived in Ottawa, Canada, overwhelmed with exhaustion. My father greeted me at the airport, looking older and more haggard, but clearly pleased to see me. Beyond the basic details of my flight, my health, and my mother's condition, we drove in silence, and I was grateful for that. It was my first time home in over eighteen months, and I needed time to adjust to this reality.

Everything was clean and orderly. Cars drove in their designated lanes and obeyed traffic laws. Pedestrians crossed at green traffic lights or crosswalks. I understood every road sign I saw and conversation I heard. I had spent six months trying to communicate in languages I had never heard before, and now felt overwhelmed at being able to understand everything.

The bombardment of my senses continued the following day. The road, the houses, the neighborhoods, all looked familiar, but at the same time, foreign. I felt nauseous and disoriented, and stopped several times to heave, hoping that whatever was happening would pass quickly.

My mother sat in her hospital bed, her eyes closed, her lips curved in a slight smile. Despite her ill-health, my mother's face looked young and belied her sixty years. I was relieved to see that she had no tubes or devices strapped to her. At the sound of my cheery, "Good morning," she turned towards my voice and reached her arms out to me. I hugged her tightly.

"So tell me about Alberto," were the first words that came out of her mouth.

Chuckling, I sat on the edge of her bed and recounted how we had met, and how our relationship had recently evolved and was still developing. Her questions were direct but sincere, as were my answers, and she only stopped when she was satisfied she had the entire story.

We spent that day, and the days that followed, speaking about my pilgrimage and the people and experiences that had forever changed my way of thinking. The hospital room became the meeting place for people I hadn't seen in years. Cousins, aunts, relatives and friends all stopped in to wish my mother well. Many knew I was walking and wanted to know the countries I had visited, but rarely seemed interested in knowing my real intentions for peace. Even when I tried to explain, I still had the impression they thought I was on a grand adventure. I also perceived the hidden judgments in some comments, and how these individuals believed themselves to be the responsible ones, while I was running away from responsibility. Perhaps, more truthfully, they were only reflecting my deepest concerns, but it only served to isolate me even further from them.

My mother's surgery went well, and the doctors removed the cysts without any complications to her heart. I meditated that entire time. She was out of intensive care almost immediately and back in her hospital room. I asked if she would like me to do some healing on her. I didn't know how she would respond, and feared she would think it too far-removed from the practical medical surroundings she was in; but to my great surprise, she said, "What do I have to do?"

"Just relax and be open to receiving it, that's all." I responded, delighted by her desire to actively participate. I explained that I would be envisioning her body enveloped in a light that was so loving and caring that it healed and strengthened everything in its way. "Imagine that light yourself, and feel it moving within your body. If you want, you can direct it to any part that you feel needs it. I'll just focus it with you."

After a few deep breaths, I began to feel the familiar warmth flowing through me. I moved my tingling hands over her body, hovering them over her heart. My hands pulsated with energy, as if keeping rhythm with her heartbeat. My mother placed her hands first over her stomach area and then over her eyes, before resting them on my hands above her heart. I felt tremendously happy. I had helped my mother in her healing journey, but more importantly, shared with her an emerging part of myself, a part that longed to express itself beyond the protective boundaries of my relationship with Alberto, and declare its presence to the world. It took its first step that day.

Alberto was never far from my mind, but in the hustle of all that was happening, and the time difference, I couldn't call him. We e-mailed, but I felt the edge in his words and the indirect accusations. I didn't know what would be waiting for me when I got back.

My mother continued to recover quickly, amazing her doctors. However, two days before my scheduled departure, she began complaining of chest pains and difficulty breathing. She was re-admitted into intensive care, where doctors discovered that her heart was not pumping efficiently and filling her lungs with liquid. I did more healings with her, which she told me made her feel better, but her condition remained unchanged.

My last day approached. I stood by her bed-side, looking at her frail body. An oxygen mask covered her nose and mouth, while countless tubes stuck out of her arms. I centered myself as best as I could and did one last healing, holding her hands in mine.

"Mom, I have to go," I whispered in her ear. She nodded weakly.

"Be safe," she murmured.

I hugged her, my tears mingling with hers, and rushed out of the room to my waiting family. My composure failing me, I hugged and kissed each in turn, and saw their eyes as watery as mine. My father held on to me the longest, and told me to be safe. I ran out of the hospital, blinded by my tears, and stepped outside into a fierce thunderstorm. The wind lashed the rains against my face and the thunder rumbled threateningly, the heavens themselves reflecting my inner turbulence and despair.

My youngest sister Laurie expertly negotiated the storm to the airport. We cried in the car, and then hugged and cried some more when she dropped me off. I boarded my flight more drained than ever, images of my mother burned into my memory, augmenting feelings of guilt that no amount of reasoning could assuage.

Twenty-four hours later, I was back to my other reality, and to Alberto. They had both waited for me. I rushed into his waiting arms and stayed there, craving safe haven from the raging storm I had just left behind, and relieved to receive such a loving welcome.

After a seventeen-day hiatus from our walk for peace, Alberto and I took our first steps out of Alexandroupoli for the remaining forty kilometers to the Turkish border. Another month had ended, but what a month! The gifts that Greece offered were many, but she had surprised me with the most unexpected: one that had been walking alongside me the whole time. I will forever associate Greece with this new love that I found. Thank you, Greece. *Efharisto.*

41. The Turkish World

People rushed and spoke loudly, gesturing at each other. Chickens and other farm animals sat with their humans on the dirt ground. A haze lingered over the area from the dust that people and animals alike kicked up. This was the Turkish border—chaotic, disorderly, and loud— and I loved it. It vibrated with an energy that reminded me of the Arab world. On July 1, 2002, we entered the Republic of Turkey.

I was in high spirits and filled with a sense of adventure, imagining Turkey to be a mix of the Arab and European worlds into which I could fit easily. A slim minaret in the distance directed us into Ipsala, our destination. Riding donkeys and tractors, villagers of all ages passed us on their way to and from the surrounding fields, their curious gazes direct and unwavering, unlike the Europeans who were more discreet. Most of the women and young girls wore the *hijab*, the typical Muslim dress covering the entire body and head. Some only showed their eyes.

In town, the men gathered in coffee houses, drinking tea from miniature glass flasks and playing *tavla*, or backgammon, the favored board game among Arabs. I recalled the many days of my childhood when my father would sit with his friends, banging the chips on the board in the heat of a close game, and throwing his arms up in the air in disgust or triumph depending on which way the game ended. I saw those memories reflected in the faces of the men that we passed that day, and felt even more at home.

To me, this was all familiar territory but I could see that Alberto was overwhelmed. With my dark coloring, I could pass for a Turkish woman, but my clothing gave that away. Alberto, however, with his long hair in a ponytail and fairer features, stood out and was an even greater magnet for curious stares. He had said he was excited to be in this new world, but I felt his discomfort at being the object of so much attention.

From a bank machine along the main street, I readily pulled out Turkish Lira, the local currency. I found the Lira confusing, with one U.S. dollar worth about one million six hundred thousand liras, and had to think quickly to do the conversion. At the pharmacy, we bought mosquito repellant and a plug-in diffuser with disposable repellant tablets, now indispensable items. With the stifling heat, it was impossible to sleep with the windows closed, and with most homes lacking screens on their windows, we were being bitten alive by mosquitoes.

Our first night found us at a hostel advertising itself as a three-star, but which European standards would consider a one-star. It didn't matter though. We were in Turkey, a land straddling modern Europe and ancient Arabia, a land whose contrasts and contradictions would play themselves out in our myriad experiences here and forever leave their mark.

* * *

We now started walking at 5:00 AM to avoid a heat which by 10:00 AM was insufferable. Our map indicated long distances between towns and we now wondered where we would sleep. Although we had chosen to stay in hostels in Greece to have intimacy, we always knew we could turn to the Greek Orthodox Church if we needed to. Now, we were in a predominantly Muslim country and unsure of how accepting they would be of an unmarried couple asking for accommodations. Without even attempting to ask at any mosque, we concluded that they would not accept us, and decided not to approach them for help.

We passed Keşan, following endless sunflower fields and orchards of every color, and headed south towards Bahçeköy, which we were disappointed to find was nothing more than a smattering of houses. It was already noon and too hot to walk the twenty kilometers to the next town, so we stopped at a road-side restaurant to eat, and then rested under the shade of a large tent on the grounds. The *raki*, Turkish firewater, was working its magic. We had tasted the firewater of every country we had walked in, and were even advised to drink it throughout the day as a remedy for the heat. I wasn't convinced we would still be able to walk after drinking it, and so never put that theory to the test.

I awakened to the sound of footsteps near us. I sat up quickly, and nudged Alberto. A slight, fifty-something man with dark hair and mustache peered at us curiously, saying words in Turkish, pointing to a nearby house. I had earlier noticed the three-story house as a sleeping possibility because two of the stories were still under construction, and two eagles presided over the entrance.

The man was Huseign, the owner. Unhurriedly, he led us into the gazebo on his property, indicating for us to sit while he brought a water hose and turned it on for us to wash our faces. He brought us fresh water and cucumbers from his garden to munch on, delighted by our gestures of appreciation. In a mix of basic German, English, Arabic, and plenty of sign language, we managed to make him understand that we were walking to Jerusalem and needed a place to sleep for the night. He simply pointed to his home and led us inside, up the stairs to a spacious, fully-furnished bedroom.

Huseign invited us to visit the main town, a few kilometers away. I donned the floor-length beach wrap I had bought in Greece and matched it with a sleeveless button-down shirt, my new summer change of clothing. The weather had cooled considerably, but the sun was still brilliant even though it was after 7:00 PM. After a half-hour walk through mainly open fields, we arrived at a small village of simple, white stone homes.

Everyone greeted Huseign, but their eyes were fixed on us. I heard him use the word *haci* several times which sounded similar to *hajji*, the Arabic word for pilgrims. We bought some cookies and almonds at a small market, but I felt awkward and self-conscious as people stopped all activity to look at us. I realized that I was wearing a sleeveless shirt when the few women who happened to be in the street showed absolutely no skin. I mentally kicked myself for not thinking of this small detail, especially in the villages where I knew norms were usually more conservative, and resolved to find a long-sleeved shirt as soon as possible.

We entered a small bar and sat at a table near the door, once again under observation. I was the only woman there. Huseign ordered us a *pide*, a piece of flat bread with cheese or meat baked on it. We tried to calmly enjoy our food, but it was difficult under the persistent stares.

A tall man entered the bar, holding a drink in his hand and laughing loudly with his two companions. Seeing us, he brought a chair to our table and sat among us. I was surprised at this intrusion into my space, and didn't know how to react. Alberto's entire presence emanated rigidity.

"Beers, yes?" he asked, turning to order them from the bar.

"No, thank you," Alberto and I replied in unison.

"*Raki*, yes?" the man continued. We again politely refused. I sensed his irritation, but he persisted and leaned in even closer. I could smell the liquor on his breath and wanted to leave, but didn't dare to stand first for fear of aggravating the situation. After yet another offer to drink, Alberto stood up and in a loud, firm voice said, "No."

All conversation stopped at the force with which Alberto spoke. He stared down at the man, his normally relaxed face hard, and his soft eyes blazing with anger. I had never seen that side of Alberto. The man stared at him in confusion, and then laughingly said some words in Turkish before walking away. I gulped down my remaining food. Alberto ate agonizingly slowly, and we eventually stood to leave.

Alberto marched ahead. I trotted alongside. Huseign struggled behind. No words were spoken until we arrived at Huseign's home. We said our goodnights and retreated to our room. Alberto lay down on the bed, staring up at the ceiling.

"Are you all right?" I finally ventured.

"I don't like how I reacted tonight," he replied. "I was actually furious, can you believe it? I don't know what's happening to me. I had so much patience before, and if I saw a guy like that, would laugh it off. Tonight I was ready to fight him. Where did my patience go?"

"He was probably harmless," I reflected, "but I'm glad you stood up to him."

"Yeah, but is that the way of peace?" he answered. "This is not the peace I'm walking for. I left that world of the warrior behind a long time ago; but the warrior's fire is still inside of me, and in situations like this, just wants to explode. It scares me that it's still so strong. This is not the man I want to be, or the behavior I want to demonstrate to the world."

"*Does a person of peace never fight under any circumstances?*" I silently pondered.

42. Old Married Couple

My body was swollen and my fingers looked like sausages. My feet were blistered and chafed, and my underarms red and irritated; all the after-effects of walking in the midday sun. We had arrived in Çanakkale, an arduous forty kilometers from Lâpseki, and were in a hotel with air conditioning, a feature that was now becoming a necessity. Even with my feet up, I needed almost an hour to deflate.

We only ventured out in the early evening, joining the multitudes in their strolls along the water-side promenade. Our steps led us to a small restaurant with a view of the impending sunset. I sensed that the worst of our initial insecurities were behind us, and looked forward to a peaceful, although hot, summer.

"I want to tell you about something that happened while you were in Canada," Alberto said after we had ordered our drinks. I looked at him expectantly. "I was about to leave you," he said. I couldn't contain my surprise. "I waited for your call every day after you left," he continued, "but you never called."

"I told you before," I interjected defensively. "I was very busy and couldn't use my credit card when I did try to call."

"It doesn't matter," he replied softly, but clearly it did. "The hotel owner saw me there every day, and sat with me while I waited." My stomach lurched. She was an attractive woman, not much older than me, and I had not paid her the slightest attention…until this moment.

"We talked about many things," Alberto went on, "including relationships. I confided to her that I was so in love with an old girlfriend that I forgot myself, and that I vowed never to repeat that mistake again. She asked why you hadn't called, and I made excuses for you day after day, all of which sounded shallow even to me. That was when she said that when a story repeats itself it's because we still haven't learned the lesson. I defended you, but the seed of doubt was planted. When you didn't call, I began to wonder if her words were true."

I wasn't sure if I was breathing. I waited, bracing myself for the worst.

"I received a strong sign to go without you," he said. "The idea of walking alone in a mainly Muslim country where I didn't speak the language and had no money scared me; but then I remembered walking alone to Medugorje and knew I could do it. Despite all that, I still worried about leaving you alone, and fought with God and the angels, tormented by what I should do. I told them I refused to go without at least speaking with you."

I was relieved that nothing had happened with this woman, and now wondered if I could have tried harder to reach him. My excuses were true, but in my heart I knew I was testing him, looking for ammunition to hold back from giving myself completely. My mind had given him all the logical arguments before, but now my heart needed to speak.

"I'm sorry," I said sincerely.

"I considered never telling you," he responded, "but it was too heavy a secret to keep. I'm happy I waited." Now it was my time to be honest.

"Before I started this walk," I revealed, "one of my girlfriends had a vivid dream with me. She saw me in a white tunic, leading thousands of people in a peace march to Jerusalem. I was in the Arab world with an Arab man who had tattooed on his arm a sword with two eagle wings. My friend knew nothing about how important the eagle is for me. This man had power and money, and was passionate about peace. In this dream, we traveled throughout the region, working together for what we both believed in."

I had been excited by the dream, taking it as a sign for me to walk; but now, sitting before Alberto, I felt embarrassed, a woman naively following a friend's dream.

"I'm nothing like the man your friend described," Alberto responded softly. "So is that your fear? That I am taking you away from your destiny? That I'm not the man of your dreams?" I nodded.

"It was only a dream," I said.

"What if you get clear signs in the future about following your path to Jerusalem without me?" Alberto asked.

"I don't know," I replied honestly.

"It's funny," Alberto replied with a sad chuckle, "that's the same fear that Hannah had with me. It's so much easier to understand her now. I guess you and I are more alike than we think."

"I believe that a future together with each following their dreams is possible," Alberto said, "but we must feel free to do it, and to know that the other person supports us in our choice."

"I promise you that my greatest desire in this relationship is that you feel free to follow your own path," I said.

"That is my greatest desire for you too," he replied, kissing my hand. "But you must bet for this relationship too, or it will not survive."

We lingered over coffee, and then meandered back to our hotel, hand in hand. Street vendors now lined the promenade, enticing passersby with their glittery and colorful wares. Alberto disappeared among them, and then emerged, grinning. He asked me to close my eyes, and when I did, felt him slip a necklace around my neck. I opened my eyes and held the small pendant in my hand: the peace symbol inside a heart. He also wore one.

I kissed him and contentedly slid under his arm. That evening, I bet for a relationship with Alberto alongside my walk for peace.

* * *

The days started to look the same: waking up at 4:00 AM, walking in the dark, and rushing to arrive before 10:00 AM. It made the long days of summer feel even longer. We stayed close to the coastline, seeing that it catered to tourists, which made it easier to find mid-range hostels with air-conditioning. Aside from an impromptu interview with a journalist at a campsite where we were staying, our interactions with people were limited to negotiating the price of our hostel room and ordering food.

We now also battled regular bouts of diarrhea, the consequence of questionable water quality and the battering heat. More than once, too weak to walk, we took a bus to the nearest city. I didn't know how I felt about my walk any more, and only cared about arriving quickly so that I could rest.

I was also convinced that our physical recovery was being hampered by persistent arguments between Alberto and I, which took their toll on me emotionally. The comments had started innocently enough, and I even thought them endearing, but they quickly became annoying. They were typically variations of the following themes:

"Mony, make sure the curtains are tightly closed," Alberto would say. "Someone might see us."

"I think you're over-reacting and trying to control everything," I would reply.

"Mony, you can't go out without a bra," he would say. "Have you forgotten where we are?"

"Oh, so now you're trying to tell me what to wear," I would retort.

"Mony, we can't go into that bar. It's full of men and they're not used to seeing women there."

"We've always walked into bars without ever checking to see who was there," I would counter.

In barely two months, we had become an old married couple. Worse yet, all the arguments that couples would typically have over the course of their relationship were now compressed into the pressure cooker that was already Turkey. Alberto admitted that these feelings of insecurity and jealousy had taken him by surprise, and that he was fighting a hateful image of himself, one that he likened to a terrible wolf that he didn't know how to control and that he thought he had long ago healed. He asked me to be patient. Watching my once-confident companion—my all-powerful wizard—suffer stirred deep feelings of compassion for him, but I didn't always succeed in controlling my anger, frustration, and above all, hurt. We rode an emotional rollercoaster that seemed to have no end.

When we arrived in Izmir, we decided to rest for a few days to allow our bodies to fully recuperate. We slept a great deal. We moved slowly, without destination or hurry. We lost ourselves one afternoon in the immense open bazaar in what seemed like a stroll back in time. Perhaps it was the exotic smells and dazzling colors that assaulted our senses; or the artisans in their frocks and robes working their trade; or the little boys that flitted past us balancing tea trays; or the Arab music that filled every space. Whatever it was, it was cathartic, and we allowed ourselves to be swept away by it.

A silversmith working in a small tent motioned for us to stop, eagerly displaying his jewelry. His designs were interesting, and we were drawn to a silver ring with rounded edges and an inlaid criss-cross pattern. He had a matching set and when we tried them on, they fit perfectly. We engraved them with our spiritual names, names that we had chosen which we felt represented the best within us and which gave expression to our spirit. Alberto's ring carried my name, while mine carried his.

We returned to our room, and lit the many candles that we had purchased in the bazaar. In the soft glow of our simple room, we sat cross-legged on our bed, facing each other. Alberto reached for the rings in his pocket, and placed them side by side on the bed between us. He picked up mine and reached for my left hand.

"This is a symbol of my infinite love for you," he whispered. "It has no beginning and no end." He slipped it onto my finger and kissed it. I reached for his ring and held it over the finger of his left hand.

"This is a symbol of my infinitive love for you," I whispered. "It has no beginning and no end." I similarly slipped it onto his finger and kissed it.

"Will you marry me?" He asked softly in Spanish, his beautiful eyes sparkling.

"*Si*," I replied lovingly, throwing my arms around him.

We lay together for a long while, admiring our rings. They shone in the candlelight and seemed even more brilliant against our tanned skins. Alberto stroked my hand, tracing the silver edges with his finger.

"One day, I'd like to buy you a better ring," he promised.

"I love our rings," I answered. "They're more precious to me than gold or any other metal."

To this day, they remain our wedding bands.

43. Children on the Path of Peace

The Roman ruins of Ephesus now beckoned, a mere two kilometers from our lodging in nearby Selcuk. We agreed that we couldn't leave such a culturally rich area without seeing all the sights, and so joined tourists from around the world exploring these magnificent ruins, snapping photos, and eavesdropping on guides explaining to their tour groups the history of this area.

From them, we learned of an important pilgrimage site nearby called Meryemana, believed to be location of the house of Mary, who was brought here by St. John the Evangelist after the death of Jesus. During my travels in Egypt, I had learned that Mary was one of the most highly regarded women in Islam, and seen as a symbol of virtue, piety, and submission to God's will. No other woman is given more attention in the Koran. Jesus is similarly respected as one of the great prophets. I knew of no other site besides Jerusalem that was venerated by both religions, and wanted to see it.

The site, a simple brick home deep in the woods atop a nearby mountain, was moving in its simplicity, and infused me with serenity. There, we learned that the tomb of St. John, considered one of the most sacred pilgrimage destinations of the Middle Ages, was also nearby. My signs with John, symbolized by the eagle, had faded over time, but whenever they appeared, I paid attention.

On a lonely hill near Selcuk, among forgotten and discarded bits of stone, I found the tomb, a marble slab measuring no more than fifty square meters, and adorned by a small identifying plaque. I knelt and caressed it, feeling inexplicably sad. Monuments as grand as the ones we had seen weren't necessary, but somehow this didn't seem fitting either.

"Thank you for sharing your energy with me. I see that you too were trying to teach the way of love and brotherhood, the way that Jesus taught. My eyes are straining to see the essence of those teachings, my heart to understand them. May eagle wings one day deliver me to that place of higher vision."

When a breeze kicked up in that blistering mid-day sun, I couldn't help but feel that my plea had been heard.

I would learn that St. Paul of Tarsus had also preached in this area, and that Tarsus lay on our route. I reflected that, from the beginning of our journey, without knowing it or planning it, we were walking in the footsteps of the great saints and apostles. It struck me that they had left Jerusalem to spread a message of peace and love, and that we were now returning to Jerusalem with that same message. The message had not changed in all these years, only the messengers. I didn't know what had led us to these sites, or what we had received being there, but I had a distinct feeling that these great spirits had called us there, wanting to whisper their secrets and inculcate us with their unique wisdom and energy for the way. It would leave me with a powerful sensation of knowing that they were indeed with us, and guiding us.

* * *

"There is something hiding within you, something that you loathe," Alberto said, concentrating on the image in the coffee cup and twirling it in his hands.

We were having dinner in a quiet restaurant in Söke, about forty kilometers south of Ephesus, and Alberto was reading the waiter's coffee cup. He had seen Alberto reading my cup, and insisted that he read his as well.

"It looks like a terrible wolf that you want to escape from," Alberto continued. "It's inside of you. You trapped it there for no one to see. You feel ashamed of it, and have judged and condemned it. It's the part of you that you don't like, that you wish didn't exist. You are afraid that people will discover it, and refuse to allow them to know this side of you." The mesmerized waiter leaned in.

"However, it is only an illusion," Alberto asserted. "It is an image that you have created in your mind. Don't hate this monster. Look at it closely, directly in the eyes, and you will see that what you thought was a monster is really a neglected creature that desperately needs your love and acceptance. It is like a frustrated and angry child who doesn't understand why you have jailed it, why you don't love it. If you have the courage to open the gate of its jail and embrace it, you will see that it is an angel, there to help you grow."

I wondered if the words Alberto spoke were for that waiter, or for him; if he was receiving a vision, or a reminder. Our arguments had persisted, and I thought more than once of leaving him, of abandoning this way of peace; but I didn't. I wanted to see where I and this relationship were going to end. So, I walked.

Our bodies continued to deteriorate. Even though I was wearing pants, the area between my thighs was badly chafed and raw, as was the area on my buttocks where the elastic of my underwear rubbed my skin. I had similar chafing and a rash under my breasts and underarms where my bra was rubbing. Whiteheads, pimples, and all kinds of skin eruptions littered my backside from the salt of my sweat. Alberto suffered similar chafing and irritation between his legs and down his back. We were physically stronger than ever, capable of walking at least thirty kilometers a day effortlessly, but I felt the heat conspiring against us and prolonging our stay.

As a consequence, our rest days became longer in areas that were increasingly touristic. We heard English, German, and Dutch spoken frequently. Bars only closed when the last patron left, and the music could be heard well into the early morning hours. In several beach-side restaurants, the male waiters went topless and served our food dangerously close to their hairy chests. Many even joined us at our table, uninvited, trying to make conversation. It was an intrusion into our space that I didn't like. I was already convinced that they only cared about our dollar value, and these blatant actions only reinforced my beliefs. The outer message of peace, along with its messengers, receded, leaving in its wake two people struggling to hold on to their emotional integrity.

August was passing quickly in an interminable routine of waking, walking, and sleeping. We passed towns such as Didim, Milas, Bodrum, Marmaris, Dalyan, and Fethiye. We heard of floods and heavy rains pounding most of Europe and parts of Turkey, and I found myself longing for the days of walking in the pouring rain. We noticed the sun rising later, giving us longer periods of freshness. I actually shivered some mornings and relished the thought of cooler weather ahead.

With September dawning, it seemed that the worst of our arguments had run their course, and that our relationship had weathered the storm. I radiated a more positive energy, one that attracted people of like heart and mind. Thanks to a bleaching accident during that time, we walked the roads dressed completely in white, drawing renewed attention and accentuating the image of the peace pilgrims. The sign that we now carried simply proclaimed *Barış*, the Turkish word for peace. We were stopped more often, and offered not only meals and drinks, but the more precious gift of understanding and support.

Our walk wasn't always easy, but our renewed sense of purpose and peace made the kilometers disappear quickly beneath our feet. We were reaching the first southerly peak of Turkey and eagerly looking northwards to Antalya. To me, it marked the end of the first half of Turkey, and meant only a tantalizing one thousand kilometers to Jerusalem. The number looked large, but we had already walked almost four thousand kilometers, so in my eyes, we were in the home stretch.

We moved towards Kale, which we learned was the burial site of another important saint, St. Nicholas, upon whom the legend of Santa Claus was based. We were assured that a well-marked trail existed that saved many kilometers off the highway, so we took it. The unmarked rocky path was grueling, but filled with the type of magical moments that were reminiscent of our early days of walking. From a friendly dog appearing to show us the way when we were lost, to a woman in an abandoned village offering us food and drink when none could be found, to a secluded cove where we bathed for hours...we were in a flow that we hadn't felt in a long time, and couldn't remember when we had had so much fun.

Finally in Kale, we decided to end that memorable day with a visit to the tomb of St. Nicholas. His remains were purportedly stolen by Italian sailors during the tenth century, and were now housed in the Basilica of Bari, Italy. The ruins were well-maintained, but only parts of the tomb remained, along with fragments of a sculpted figure believed to be that of the saint.

In the courtyard, we were drawn to a large bronze statue of Santa Claus with a sac of toys over his shoulders. He stood on a round pedestal base that was covered with flags from various parts of the world. Searching for the Canadian and Spanish flags, we hit upon an engraved inscription that read:

"16th International Santa Claus Activities and the Call for World Peace. Children on the path of peace".

I smiled at the message. Santa Claus, the bearer of gifts, was delivering a precious reminder; that we were still on the path, children discovering the way of peace. I couldn't help but feel that our difficulties were part of that path, and that our task was to remain on it despite them; but as children, joyful, adventurous, filled with curiosity, always in the moment, and trusting that all worries are taken care of. Ho ho ho!

44. End of a Dream

We celebrated our arrival in Antalya, the midpoint of Turkey, by resting a few days before continuing towards Alanya. Our three-month visitor visas were expiring, and the fastest way to renew them was to take a ferry from Alanya to Girne, Cyprus, and to buy new visas upon our return.

It was during this time that Alberto and I decided to re-enter Turkey not in Alanya but in Tasucu, a coastal town two hundred and fifty kilometers ahead. The decision was mine, and it was agonizing to make. Our map indicated not only a mountainous route between Alanya and Tasucu, but long distances and few places to stop. My battle, however, was not with the kilometers. The perfectionist side of me demanded that we walk, and looked at other options as cheating. When we took a bus, it was because we were sick. When we accepted a ride, it was for a purpose that served the way of peace. No such purpose existed now. I finally accepted the fact that there was no right way to walk, and there was no such thing as a perfect pilgrim. I made peace with my inner tyrant, and felt liberated.

The rough waters tossed our small ferry mercilessly in its crossing to Cyprus. I felt nauseous despite the anti-nausea medication, and endured the retching and vomiting of passengers for the entire five hour trip. The crew passed out the vomit bags and sprayed cologne to kill the smell, but with little success. Alberto seemed strangely unaffected by it all. I was happy to see dry land.

At our hostel that evening, Alberto confided that he was beginning to understand why he had been struggling so much.

"From the time I was a child, I was taught to place God above all else," he explained. "Any time that I did anything for simple pleasure, and that did not include a higher purpose, I began to feel guilty and subconsciously sabotage myself, fearing that I was moving away from the right path. I thought I had overcome all these feelings after my spiritual awakening, but I see now that I have slipped back into that pernicious habit of feeling guilty and judging myself. I think it started with our relationship, and the natural desire to focus on us. We began sleeping in hostels, eating out in restaurants more often, and rarely calling on the churches. We were also walking at an hour when most people are still asleep, so we had even less outside contact. Even when I refused to admit it, I felt I was turning my back on God."

"I don't believe we need to suffer just because we're pilgrims," I said. "Wealth and comfort are not incompatible with a spiritually-fulfilling life."

"I know you're right," Alberto reflected. "I see now how much my Catholic upbringing has influenced my beliefs. I can almost hear their voices saying: *how can you spend so much money on hotels and food when so many people are homeless and dying from hunger? How can you be happy when so many are suffering?* The better I was living, the guiltier I was feeling, forgetting all that I had learned. Today, I know that the best help I can offer the poor is to show them that scarcity only exists in our minds, in our vision of things. An old proverb says give a man fish and feed him for a day; teach him to fish and feed him for a lifetime. God denies us nothing; we alone do that. True abundance, just like love and peace, is inside of us."

"I'm not sure the world is ready for this message," I answered. "We can't tell those who are suffering that the real problem is in their minds."

"Probably not," Alberto agreed, "but true help cannot be material only. Even as we nourish the hungry, physically or emotionally, we must pass along our intention that they learn to feed themselves, and that they awaken to the abundance within them. If we help them from the same vision that they have of themselves, we only reinforce the mistaken belief that they are powerless victims who need to be saved. Feeling guilty for their circumstances is a warning bell that we are falling into their same perspective. I see that so clearly now. That's why tonight, I broke that oppressive pact, and renewed my true pact with God. From now on, I welcome all abundance that comes into my life, and will enjoy it."

It felt good to hear him speak with such conviction, like the Alberto of old, and hoped this episode marked the return of the man I had fallen in love with.

On October 2, 2002, we re-entered Turkey with another three-month visa that I hoped we wouldn't need to complete our Turkish experiment.

* * *

Alberto's restored confidence seemed to impel him to pursue with even greater intensity his interest in the Way of the Wizard, the world of magic. He had been practicing throughout our time in Turkey, but now pursued it with vigor. Despite his assurances that he was simply developing his mind potential, to me it was still a world that I associated with darkness and sorcery. Able to easily see symbols and interpret them, Alberto read the coffee grinds and tea leaves of anyone who asked. He read the clouds, and received with greater frequency messages from all that surrounded him. He practiced with regularity guessing the suit of playing cards, accurately guessing more than half the cards correctly. He focused on picking a specific card from the deck, and did so with increasing precision. He even affirmed that he moved a pencil with his mind once.

I wanted to share his enthusiasm, but resisted, fearing delving into an unknown that could slip beyond my control. I also found no practical purpose in pursuing this. Alberto, however, was as a child with a new toy, pestering me to play along; and so I did, trying to guess the suit of a card he held in his hands or to pull out a specific card from the deck. I wasn't taking it seriously, and looked at my ability to guess correctly as owing to chance. When we finished each other's sentences or guessed what the other was thinking, I took it as nothing more than the result of two people spending too much time together.

More disconcerting to me, however, was that I was receiving signs suggesting that I follow this path. Billboards I would pass, or pieces of paper at my feet, would speak in English of psychic powers and changing realities. The most impacting, however, was a dream that I had where a man's voice, someone who I was convinced was an angel, was telling me to support Alberto in this important work because he needed my help. It had felt so real that I woke up trembling.

One afternoon in our room, I absently turned on the television and saw the word Alberto in large rainbow letters appear on the screen. Surprised, I called out for Alberto to watch with me. The program, called *Alev Alev Alberto*, was a live call-in show to a psychic named Alberto who read the caller's tarot cards. Beyond my initial shock was the outlandish manner in which this psychic was dressed: large wig, garish makeup, and colorful clothing. I was prepared to live with a man who read tarot cards, but not one who looked like Dame Edna. My Alberto's hearty laughter and assurances that he owned no wigs or dresses was little comfort to the clear and humorous message I was receiving.

As if to underline the point, as soon as that program ended, the movie *Matrix*, a favorite of Alberto's, began.

I had yet to see it, mainly because I dislike violent movies, but Alberto coaxed me into watching, explaining that, beyond the conspiracy plot and fight scenes, it spoke beautifully to the illusory nature of reality and the infinite potential we all possess.

"Now imagine," he enthused, holding out his hand for me to sit beside him, "that behind this Matrix or illusion in which we live, are hidden not the dark world of machines shown in the film, but rather the wise and divine love that you and I already know."

I did watch it to the end, and found that it helped me better understand the inner world of Alberto, a world I still didn't fully comprehend and which left me with many concerns.

We walked, Alberto ever more confident in his abilities, and now trying to manipulate clouds and create refreshing breezes, while I grew more silent and begged for clarity. "*Surely you're not asking me to follow Alberto's way. What happens to my way? What happens to my Jerusalem? That was the dream that launched me on this walk. Am I to give it up now to pursue something I don't understand and see no use for?*"

My battle with the Universe raged into Mersin, with no clear answers. A long shower soothed me, and when I came out to our room, it was with a renewed calm...until I saw a man on the television screen using his mental powers to make his pipe float in the air.

"I was trying to move a coin with my mind, and saw this when I turned on the television," Alberto said cautiously, yet unable to hide the sparkle in his eyes.

I never felt as trapped as I did in that moment. There was nowhere to hide or flee, for the Universe would find me and haunt me with its signs. So, I sat beside Alberto and watched the movie.

The scene continued with this grandfatherly-looking man explaining that he moved the pipe by concentrating his mind on it; that it was something anyone could do if they focused their attention and understood that they and the pipe were one; that no separation existed between them, just as no separation exists among human beings and the Universe. He was able to guess cards accurately, bend spoons, and move objects with his mind. His parting advice was that there comes a time when one must be willing to risk everything without fearing what anyone else thinks.

I couldn't speak. The movie credits rolled past, and soon another movie started. Its title was *Turn of Faith*. "Enough!" I yelled, turning off the television and rushing out of the room, Alberto close to my heels, and into the waiting elevator. The lone advertising was of two angels, each blowing a trumpet, the word "believe" between them in bold, colorful letters.

"Stop it!" I yelled.

I wandered the busy streets of Mersin. Alberto occasionally reached for my hand, but I pulled it away. We entered bookstores and browsed their selection of English books, but I wasn't paying attention. We stopped at an Internet Café and checked email.

"Look at this," Alberto exclaimed, motioning for me to look at his screen. In bold, capital letters was an email from a charitable organization with my name in large, bold letters stating: *Monica still needs your help*. I stood and walked away. I wanted to keep going, to disappear among the crowds; and I did, for a long time. I eventually stopped at a small café. The anguish had dissipated, and I now felt weak and exposed.

"I don't know my purpose or mission any more, Alberto," I whispered. "I see the signs, but I don't know what the Universe wants me to do. I feel as if it's asking me to support something that I don't understand, and that scares me. Magic has a dark side too, and I don't know if you're wise enough to handle something so powerful. I don't know if I am either."

"I think you're being invited to be a more conscious creator of your life, nothing more," Alberto assured. "You started walking by following signs and believing in what you were doing; and that's great. But I think there comes a time when you have to take control of the tremendous gift that we have all been given, and to exercise the power of God that is within us. "

"What about my dreams, Alberto?" I pleaded. "What happens to them? Do I abandon them and follow you in your quest? I don't know if I can, or want to, do that. I don't even know if our missions are still compatible."

"I don't think you have to give up your dreams of working for peace in Jerusalem," Alberto reassured. "Maybe the signs are just asking you to be open to other possibilities beyond just physically being there. Working for peace can take many forms that you can't even imagine right now." I shook my head sadly.

"I feel as if my dream is dead, and all I have is your dream to follow," I wept. "I feel unimportant, and all that I wanted to do cast away." Alberto held my hand and let me cry. All I could hear was the pounding of my head. All I could feel was a terrible ache and emptiness in my heart. "Maybe I don't want to admit it," I sniffed, "but I guess I'm afraid of what people will think when I tell them you're a wizard, a psychic, or whatever label you choose. Can you imagine telling my father?" I choked out, laughing with Alberto.

"Let me read your coffee cup," Alberto suggested. "We'll ask what will happen if you follow this path of magic."

I had turned my cup over, and not even realized it. Alberto examined it for a few moments, and then smiled broadly, turning it around for me to see. Jumping out of the cup was a perfectly-shaped, large, white dove. Near it was my name again, not as clear as the dove, but easily made out.

"I believe your way of peace is leading you in that direction, Mony," he said.

45. City of Prophets

We stayed in Mersin an extra day, as I tried to make sense of all that happened the day before. I felt weak and uncertain, my next steps unclear. Alberto was out most of the morning, and when he returned, he was in a clearly upbeat mood.

"A friend of mine just sent me an email about a place called Şanliurfa," he enthused. "I researched it on the Internet, and found out that it's an important site of pilgrimage. They call it the City of Prophets." I studied the map.

"It is four hundred kilometers east of where we are," I replied, seeing the end of Turkey, and not wanting to extend my time any longer than I had to. "We need to go south."

"We can take a bus," Alberto insisted. "It's believed to be the Biblical city of Ur, where the prophet Abraham was born, and where prophets like Jethro, Job, and Elijah also lived. It's even believed that Moses lived in the area, working as a shepherd before returning to Egypt. These were the greatest prophets, Mony, and each one had their faith in God, and in themselves, tested. Each had to find the courage to follow their truth. I'd like to walk in their footsteps, to feel the energy they left behind. It's no coincidence that I receive this message now."

My faith in everything that I believed in was certainly shaken, and perhaps I too needed to draw from others their secret knowledge, that invisible elixir that propelled them forwards even when mired in doubt. So often during this pilgrimage, they had led us to their hallowed sites, and I had felt uplifted without knowing why. I wanted this City of Prophets to do the same.

The seven-hour bus ride was grueling, but the reward at the end of that day was worth it. From our hotel room, we had an unobstructed view of *Halil-ur-Rahman*, the city's holiest site and destination of all pilgrims. It was a lush oasis of gardens and ponds, accentuated by two beautiful mosques; one venerating the cave where the prophet Abraham was allegedly born, the other the stuff of legend. It was told that the ruling pagan King Nemrud ordered Abraham to renounce his God, but when he wouldn't, the King commanded that Abraham be catapulted into a raging fire at the bottom of a tall cliff. In the spot where Abraham landed, the fire was transformed into water, and the firewood into fish. A mosque was built on that site. The fish are considered sacred, and the waters holy. It is here that pilgrims come to be renewed, and where we intended to join them.

Roses and flowers bursting with color greeted our arrival, their fragrance intoxicating. Short, quaint bridges arched over canals that connected several man-made ponds. Abundant fish swam freely in the waters, and clamored to be fed from the multitude of hands feeding them. We bought some bait from the many children selling them, and joined in the ritual.

The sound of the muezzin's voice suddenly filled the air, calling the faithful to prayer. My eyes inexplicably watered, and my body began to tremble. Something felt deeply familiar. I wanted to enter the mosque, to kneel in prayer, but not wearing a scarf and long-sleeved shirt at that moment, couldn't do so.

But we did, at sunrise the following morning, this time dressed appropriately. My steps already knew the way and instinctively followed the path leading to the mosque where Abraham fell. Alberto entered through the men's entrance, while I sought the women's entrance.

During my travels in Egypt, I had become familiar with the purification ritual that was performed before entering a mosque. Cleansing was part of the act of worship, not separate from it, and provided a transition from the outer world to the inner world, preparing a believer to stand before Allah united in body, mind, and soul. I did not perform the entire ritual, but took off my shoes and washed my hands and face before stepping inside.

The space was small, measuring no more than thirty square meters, and the walls devoid of decoration, as was typical in all mosques. Wall to wall carpet covered the floor. The few women who were there glanced at me with interest. I greeted them with the traditional *as-salamu-alaykum*[14], sitting down. They returned my greeting, warmth now replacing their curiosity.

Each woman stood in her own space facing the *mihrab*, a niche in the wall indicating the direction of Mecca. One older woman, dressed in a long dark gown, especially caught my attention, and so I watched her. She cupped her ears, her lips moving in reverent prayer. She placed

---

[14] Arab greeting meaning "peace be with you"

her hands on her chest, enfolding her heart. She bowed, and then kneeled, her silent prayers in synchrony with her graceful movements. I was amazed at her agility and watched this beautiful spiritual dance, this fluid motion of standing, bowing, kneeling, touching the forehead to the ground, and then rising again. Each ritual was unique, and as beautiful as the woman performing it.

The women finished their prayers and gathered at one of the walls. Speaking in broken English, one of the women explained that they were getting water from the spring that naturally erupted at the spot where Abraham fell. They filled my bottle, and saying goodbye, left me to perform my personal ritual.

I sat cross-legged on the floor and closed my eyes. I immediately felt a rush of energy course through me, vibrating and alive. It danced with me, causing my body to sway, filling me with a longing that I couldn't explain, and a certainty that all was well.

"*I lack the courage to follow this path you ask of me; to speak my spiritual truth,*" I pleaded, my deepest fear finding expression. "*I hear you asking me to speak this truth, to be faithful to it, to live it fully, but I'm paralyzed by others' opinions and judgments of me.*"

"Your courage will reveal itself at the right time and under the right circumstances," I heard reverberated within me. "The truly courageous are not those who lack fear, but those who walk through it."

I felt comforted in a loving embrace that I couldn't see, only perceive. The heavy sadness that so weighed my heart slowly lifted. I remained in that state for a long time, and eventually opened my eyes and sipped from the waters that faith created, completing my ceremonial renewal.

* * *

Alberto and I lay in bed, naked, cooling off from the day's heat. Alberto had just finished closing the curtains, and had grumbled once again that they didn't close perfectly, leaving a slight slit for anyone to peer through.

"There's a man there," Alberto yelled, pointing at the window. I saw a pair of dark eyes staring at us, the face hidden by dark hands, and shrieked, reaching for my clothes. Alberto hurriedly threw on his pants and rushed to the curtains, flinging them open, but the person had gone.

He furiously strode out to the corridor, but it too was empty. The corridor window right next to our door, however, was open. Alberto examined it.

"This window leads to a flat rooftop that goes around the hotel," he said incredulously. "I think they're the ceilings of the rooms underneath us."

I had always considered Alberto's obsession with our privacy to be unwarranted, but now wondered if he had been right all along. Shaken, we called security. Within moments, the apologetic manager and hard-eyed security chief were in our room, examining the area. They walked out of the corridor window and soon were at our window, peering in. As Alberto had suspected, there were rooms underneath, and their ceilings just happened to wrap around our room. Of the more than fifty rooms in this hotel, we were shocked to discover that ours was the only one where this was even possible. The manager offered to move us, but we thought it pointless, considering it was our last evening there.

The heavy silence between Alberto and I lingered as we walked to the gardens and, at the hill where Abraham was flung into the fires, we sat and watched the sun set.

"What happened back in that room was no coincidence," Alberto said, pausing for a long time before continuing. "I had so much faith in my path, in my pure intentions to create only positive experiences, that I didn't think my negative thoughts could also be creating. I thought if God is love, what purpose could manifesting my negative thoughts or beliefs possibly serve? I had made a pact to be an instrument of love, to only create good in the world, so I assumed that attracting in the negative didn't apply to me. I was mistaken. I see now that I am creating in the negative."

Alberto seemed to be thinking out loud more than speaking with me, and so I listened as he reasoned with himself.

"But if the Universe is love, then what is the loving purpose of negative experiences?" He went on. "If we create everything all the time, then where is God in all this? Why would we need him? What role does he play? Does God even exist? Is he unconditional love or a vending machine—make a wish and here it is—irrespective of what you wish for? Is the Universe that impersonal?"

He was touching precisely the key to my dilemma in following his path, of becoming a wizard. We seemed to be in an existential crisis, struggling with the questions that I'm certain have been asked by humanity since the beginning of time.

"I don't understand," he continued. "I don't see the whole truth, but I need to trust that there is a purpose to all of this, and that it will be revealed at the right time. That purpose is based on love, of that I have no doubt. I have felt the loving hand of the Universe so many times, asking me to be patient. It's all I can do now."

I heard the battle between control and surrender raging in his heart, and felt it in mine. Certainly full surrender to God's will was not the answer, otherwise why would we have free will? But being full creators of our lives, or wizards, without a higher context, seemed spiritually empty to me. We seemed to be getting contradicting messages. In the silence of our walk back to our room, the mind and heart of each sought that clarity.

46. Under Construction

The bus from Şanliurfa returned us to Osmaniye, two hundred kilometers north of the Syrian border. It was now October 19, 2002, and we walked with energy, breezing through towns such as Erzin, Dörtyol, and Iskenderun. Our steps were light, matching our mood. Our laughter and ease reflected back to us in endless greetings and invitations to eat and drink. I enjoyed those days of walking in a way that I had long missed.

We had started an arduous climb towards Belen when we came across a stretch of road that was under construction. At that moment, about fifty workers were sitting in a long file along the side of the road, enjoying their break. It was awkward enough being stared at under normal circumstances, but that day, despite Alberto's disapproving glance, I had chosen not to wear a bra because of severe chafing under my breasts. The wind was strong and blustery, and plastered my loose clothing against my body, accentuating every curve.

"Mony, walk behind me," Alberto commanded, his voice as tense as his face.

I charged ahead without responding, fed up with all of it. Alberto eventually caught up to me, and we walked into Belen together. The tension that had charged our prolonged silence was now replaced with fatigue. It filled our every movement in our hostel room that evening until it finally collapsed.

"I can't do this anymore, Mony," Alberto agonized, his voice cracking, his eyes filled with tears. "As hard as I try, I can't control my emotions. I can't stop my negative thoughts. I've lost my trust in people. I've lost my love for them. Worse yet, I expect the worst from them. This is not who I am. I can't live trying to control every part of our relationship, to make it the way I want. I can't fight my demons anymore because the harder I fight, the bigger they get. Whenever I think I've defeated them, they come back, more painful than ever. I'm so tired of fighting."

I looked at him in silence, weary on all levels.

"I'm so sorry," he whispered, gazing at me with such sadness. "You have a gift and a way of being with people that inspires their confidence. I don't want you to lose that because of my insecurities. It's not fair to you. I want you to be free to be your beautiful self. With or without me."

"So are you saying it's over?" I asked.

"I won't ask you to stay with me, but would like you to," he answered despondently. "The only thing I know to do right now is to surrender everything—my need to control and protect our relationship, my jealousy, my fears, even my way, all of it—to the Universe, and trust that all will be well."

We wept in each other's arms for a long time, for what appeared to be the end of our relationship. Our exhaustion brought sleep, from which I awakened all too soon. I found Alberto reading through his diary, in a contemplative mood. He looked over at me, and then from his diary, began to read in a soft voice:

"Nothing is more important than love. We are all brothers. I must see the good that's in every person. Positive attracts positive; negative attracts negative. What we most fear we end up hating, and this sum of negative energies is so powerful that it attracts more of what we most fear and hate. Without these experiences, we would not be aware of the quality of our thoughts and have the possibility to change. This is the process of growth, of love."

He then looked up at me and added, "I choose to trust in me. I choose to trust in people. I choose to trust in love."

* * *

We continued past Antakya and Harbiye, and now moved to the border town of Yayladaği, a few kilometers from the Syrian border. We were alone on this desolate road and crossed paths with farmers and villagers, all of whom stopped to offer us food and drink. The few drivers who passed us offered us a lift. Being so close to Syria, I was speaking in Arabic and feeling comfortable with people. Alberto was also relaxed, and encouraging me to be myself, which I took as a great sign of his recovering faith in himself and me.

With less than ten kilometers to town, we came upon a section of the road that was under construction. A car with two men pulled over and offered us a ride. We refused with our thanks, and asked if there was a bar nearby since we were out of water. One of the men, a tall, middle-aged, blond man with kind eyes said something about four kilometers away, and so we assumed he was referring to a bar. They drove away, but returned within a few minutes with a large, cold bottle of water. We thanked them profusely, but the blond man kept saying something about four kilometers away, and so we agreed to meet him there.

We finally arrived at an area with many flags, trucks, parked bulldozers, and several makeshift buildings; none of which looked anything like a bar.

"Would you like some tea?" A man's voice called out in English. He stood in the doorway of one of the buildings, motioning for us to enter. We followed him inside to a simply-appointed office, where we were surprised to find the blond man who had brought us the water. Our translator introduced him as Fethi, the manager of the company doing the road construction.

Our tea break turned into an invitation to dinner and an offer to spend the night. I had no idea in what conditions these men slept, but would not refuse their heart-felt hospitality. Clearly delighted with our decision to stay, the men accompanied us to another building and opened one of the nondescript doors.

In the clean space where we stood were two single beds separated by a simple nightstand. Each bed was made with clean white sheets and blankets tucked in around the edges. The modern washroom gleamed. Fethi smiled at my obvious approval, and told us to hurry to dinner. The shower was hot and invigorating, and after an almost forty-kilometer walk in the mountains, I desired nothing more than to crawl under those crisp white sheets. Alberto nudged me outside, following the sound of excited chatter to its source: a passionate game of *tavla*, backgammon. Watching their spirited animations and their attempts to engage Alberto in their revelry, I couldn't imagine a more fitting way to spend our final evening in Turkey.

The food was plentiful and delicious, and the company kind-hearted and authentic. More than welcomed, I felt loved. What made this experience all the more unforgettable was that we were among construction workers, all men, lost in the middle of nowhere. A month earlier this would have been unthinkable. Alberto had finally surrendered his fears and need to control, and the world had responded in consequence. On the eve of walking into Syria, this would stand out as one of the highlights of our time in Turkey.

Thank you, Turkey. *Tashekkur.*

47. Syria

"Why don't you have a visa?" The guard at the Syrian border barked, pointing at Alberto.

I was trying to understand his rapid-fire Arabic and asked him to speak slowly, but it only seemed to agitate him more. I was flustered and tried to explain that we didn't know we needed a prior visa, believing we could buy it as we had at the border of every other country.

"You can enter," he pronounced, pointing at me. "You have Lebanese documents, but for him it will be difficult. We must call Damascus. They can respond in two or twenty-four hours. You must wait."

We waited. We sat. We stood. We paced the small border area like caged animals, unable to move forwards or backwards. The officers occasionally called out to tell us that they had not heard from Damascus, and each time we thanked them for trying. Each time, they smiled a little more and spoke a little less curtly.

Four hours later, one of the guards came to our seats and asked if we were hungry. We had not eaten since breakfast at the construction site, and there were no vending machines or food kiosks at the border. We answered, "Yes." The man disappeared and returned shortly after, asking us to follow him. In a side room was a low table surrounded by cushions, and a large tray filled with foods that I recognized from my own home: a yogurt spread called *labneh*, a mix of herbs in olive oil called *zaatar* in which pita bread is dipped, boiled eggs, and olives. The man smiled slightly at my profuse thanks, and extended his arms out in invitation, before leaving.

The sun set and the stars came out, and we were still at the border. One by one, the various officers invited us to join them for tea, wanting to know more about us. I spoke in broken Arabic, explaining our walk as best as I could, but not specifying that we were ending in Jerusalem. We had been warned that other pilgrims had been turned away at this border because Syria does not recognize Israel as a legal state. Not wanting to jeopardize our crossing, I said that we were staying with relatives in Lebanon before deciding our next steps; but I had the feeling they knew exactly where we were going.

Later that evening, the more senior officials invited us to coffee which, in the Arab world, is a gesture reserved for guests. In the beginning, I had the impression that they thought us naïve idealists, but the more we spoke, the more I saw interest and respect emerge in their eyes, and their demeanor become ever more gentle, even kind.

"Can you call Damascus again and tell them to rush the papers for these people?" one of them yelled out. "They've been here for hours."

The night turned cold, and I began to shiver. One of the guards brought us green military jackets and blankets, which we deeply appreciated, and which they seemed pleased to provide. By 10:00 PM, it was clear that we would not be receiving Alberto's visa, and even if we did, we could not go anywhere without a map, tent, or sleeping bags.

As we tried to sleep on the bolted plastic chairs in the lobby, one of the senior officers called out for us to follow him. On the floor of the room where we had eaten were two foam mattresses laid side by side.

"Thank you," I said with sincerity. "I want you to know that this is Alberto's first time in the Arab world, and I'm happy to have him see this face of the Arab people."

He beamed, assuring me that the visa would arrive in the morning. As I began to fall asleep, I heard the sound of the fax machine, and the men saying that Alberto's visa had been approved.

* * *

"Alberto was granted a visa for only three days," one of the senior officials apologized the following morning. "You can renew it, but only for three days at a time, and only in major cities like Lattakia and Tartus further south."

It was Wednesday, October the thirtieth and the visa expired Friday, November the first. Government offices were closed on Fridays, the Muslim holy day. Even if we arrived in Lattakia the next day, the visa would expire before we could start walking again.

As Alberto and I contemplated what to do, a man entered the building and began speaking with the senior staff. They spoke in hushed tones, glancing at us, and eventually parted ways. The senior officer approached us.

"This man is a bus driver, and will take you to Lattakia," he said. "When you get there, go to the passport office and ask for Ahmed, telling him that I sent you. He'll help you."

The clearly contented officer shook our hands and hurried us to the waiting bus, while the remaining officers yelled out their well wishes. The bus carried us through narrow winding mountain paths that would have been challenging to walk, and an hour later, deposited us in the city center.

Although I should have felt thrilled to be in a country where I spoke the language and understood the culture, I felt surprisingly uneasy. Warnings about the Syrian secret police, mixed with stories of torture that I had heard growing up, replayed themselves in my mind, fueled by photos and banners everywhere of the current president Bashir Assad and his hardline father Hafez Assad.

I also didn't want to renew Alberto's visa every three days, and argued with him about taking a bus to the Lebanese border. In the end, we agreed that if his visa was renewed for only three days, we would take the bus. Otherwise, we would walk the short one hundred kilometer distance to the border.

At the passport office, we went directly to the contact we were given and explained our border experience. "I will do my best to procure a fifteen-day visa," he said, "but it is almost impossible because once a visa is granted, it can only be renewed, not re-issued." With his help, I completed the necessary paperwork, secretly hoping the visa would only be renewed.

In those days of waiting, we shopped for items that I didn't think we would ever need again on this journey: wool socks, sweaters, and light jackets. The days were still warm, but the nights increasingly cooler.

Many Syrians would often sit with us to tea, curious about the strangers in their land. On more than one occasion, anti-Semite sentiments were expressed, the passion of which surprised Alberto, but to which I was accustomed to hearing. I explained the little history that I knew about the region in an attempt to make him understand its complexities. The more I spoke, however, the more uncertain I became about the validity of our message. I had carried this peace for eleven months, and now that I was in the land that most needed to receive it, I wavered.

"*Am I being naïve after all?*" I wondered. "*How many others before me have shouted this same message, but what good has it done? Who am I to think I can get people to think differently?*" My quandaries produced no immediate answers, and only served to deepen my ever-increasing sense of uneasiness.

On the appointed day, we returned to the passport office. Our contact was not there, and no one seemed to know what to do. After three hours of going from one office to another, and procuring more signatures and stamps, we finally had Alberto's visa in hand. The administrator checked it several times before giving it to us, unable to explain how we had a fifteen-day visa, starting from the day we entered Syria.

That night, using the last piece of the yellow paper that we had bought in Italy, Alberto cut out the sign that we would now be carrying—*min ajl al salam*, meaning for peace—words that looked like beautiful scroll once Alberto finished with them.

On November 3, 2002, we started out of Lattakia, moving directly southwards along the Mediterranean coast.

I walked looking at the asphalt, mustering the courage to face the world with our sign, and our beliefs.

"*As salamu alaykum*," someone yelled out. I looked up just in time to see the disappearing face of a young man hanging out of his car, holding out his hands in the V sign for peace. I shouldn't have needed it. I should have drawn strength from my personal reserves, but that salute changed my stay in Syria.

More cars honked, and people waved in support. Some even stopped to offer us rides. Many invited us to cool off from the blistering heat and to offer us refreshments. Their kindness and hospitality overwhelmed us, not only with regular offers to pay for our meals, but repeated invitations to sleep in their homes. Even during Ramadan, the Muslim time of fasting which began November fifth that year, food and drink were offered us while our hosts abstained. We would forever associate our time in Syria with their unforgettable hospitality.

Despite these unforgettable experiences, I wasn't sure I was leaving Syria any more confident than when I had entered it. We would now be going to Lebanon, my home, carrying ideas of peace in a region strife with conflict and hatred. I didn't know if there was room for this humble message of peace, or if it would serve any purpose. When compared to the magnitude of the problem, our intentions, our walk, all of it seemed insignificant.

I had carried this message of peace through eleven countries and had faced rejection and ridicule, but carried on. Now the rejection and ridicule of those closest to me, from my family to my countrymen, terrified me. My heart believed in the truth of my words, but I didn't know if my courage was strong enough to guide my steps.

48. Coming Home

We entered Lebanon without incident, I with my Lebanese documents and Alberto with a three-month visa. It was November 10, 2002, almost one year of walking.

What most surprised me about that morning's walk was the general poverty that surrounded us: partially constructed homes, atrocious roads, and what looked like a large refugee camp with closely-huddled tents. I knew that the country was rebuilding from civil war, but wondered why it was taking so much longer here.

We spent our first night in the home of a most hospitable Muslim family who shared their Ramadan meal with us. The young man we met there insisted that we visit his high school the following day, and we did, meeting its remarkable principal. He already knew of our walk, and took us on a tour of his school.

"As you have seen walking here, this is an impoverished area," he said. "Most of the people living here are Palestinian refugees and mostly Shiite Muslims. I'm sure you've heard of their more militant arm, *Hezbollah*. The children here see no future in a country that they are continually reminded is run by Christians, for Christians. Their spiritual leaders, the clerics in the Shiite community, make them see only the injustice and futility of hope, and breed hatred and intolerance. I am here to undo their influence."

Young men and women passed by us, and he greeted each by name, asking about their families. Some of the girls wore head scarves, but all were dressed in modern street clothes. His caring for them was evident, and their respect for him even more so.

"I teach them the trades," he continued, showing us a classroom with car engines and another with electrical wires. "They learn to work with people whose ideas differ from theirs, and to befriend them. Here, they are not Christians or Muslims, Sunni or Shiite, poor or wealthy. They are students, and they are equal."

I couldn't help but feel inspired by this man's courage and tenacity, his determination to continue despite the odds against him. We accepted his invitation to stay at his home that evening, and to leave for my village of Kfarhazir the following day.

* * *

I saw my family home, and slowed my steps. I was happy to be there, but incessant thoughts plagued me. *"What will my family think about Alberto? Will he start talking about wizards and magic with them? How will they judge him? How will they judge me? Should I tell them we're engaged? How can I tell them if I haven't even told my parents yet?"*

I eased the kitchen door open. Yolla stood at the sink, washing dishes. Her eyes bulged open when she saw me, and she began to scream my name, clapping her hands and slapping her thighs. She rushed towards me and almost lifted me off the ground with her tight embrace. Her eyes sparkled with light and energy. Her face glowed with a healthy flush. I couldn't believe that this was the same woman I had left only eight months earlier. The only indication of her struggle was the patch of missing hair on one side of her head.

"This is Alberto," I said. "He is walking with me to Jerusalem."

She shook his hand warmly, repeating the words, "welcome," mixed with its Arabic counterpart *"ahla wa sahla."* She brought him to the bench to sit down, then excitedly rushed outside, calling out to our neighbor. Within moments, the house was full of well-wishers. Coffee magically appeared and everyone drank a small cup, celebrating our safe return.

The house finally quieted and Yolla began to prepare dinner. I showed Alberto around, and then led him to the upstairs apartment. "I think you'll be comfortable here," I said, reaching for the door.

"What do you mean, I?" He asked.

"I was thinking you could stay here while I stayed downstairs with the family," I replied awkwardly. Alberto glared at me.

"You're afraid to tell them about us," he accused. I looked at my feet, unable to see my cowardice reflected in his face.

"I'm sorry," I whispered. "I just can't do it."

"Is that why you took your ring off?" He asked sadly.

I had slipped my ring off just before entering the house, but I could still see its outline tattooed against my tanned hand. I felt ashamed for lacking the courage to speak about something so beautiful, and for betraying Alberto and myself. I turned and walked away, leaving him standing alone.

The days passed agonizingly slowly. Not only was I lying about my relationship with Alberto, but living a lie. I had become the superficial person I had worked hard not to be, hiding my true self, fearing my family's judgments. I was sick of hearing myself speak about banalities, but couldn't seem to stop. No one asked about our relationship, and I didn't elaborate, even when there were opportunities to do so. Everyone asked general questions about our walk, but never probed into our deeper intentions. I could have offered them, but chose to remain silent, entrenching myself even deeper in my inadequacy.

Everyone embraced Alberto and made him a part of all activities, including picking and pressing olives. One of my cousins even taught him a few words of Lebanese, and when he used them, he endeared himself even more to my family.

Our most memorable activity during this time was a visit to the museum and tomb of Khalil Gibran, the Lebanese mystic, artist, and poet best-known for his book *The Prophet*. He was buried in a picturesque village deep in the mountains of Lebanon, in an old cavern where hermits had sought refuge since the seventh century. His personal letters and belongings were on display, along with his paintings. I felt a tremendous peace being there, and knew that Alberto was enjoying his time too. I thanked this great Prophet for taking away my cares that day, and for bringing his brand of spirituality into the world rather than hiding it away. I hoped to, one day, be able to do the same.

In the gift shop, the attendant asked our names and where we were from. "Alberto?" She smiled. "You have the same name as Khalil. Alberto is Spanish for Albert; and Albert is English for Khalil. You have the same name as the Prophet."

Alberto smiled in contentment. I wanted his memories of Lebanon to be filled with moments such as these, to wash away the hurt that my fear had brought. Alberto had taken off his ring too, and it had hurt me deeply. The mark that he bore on that finger would be my reminder that I still had much work to do.

* * *

One afternoon, Yolla developed a fever that doctors worried would create complications that her body couldn't defend. The family prayed, while Alberto and I did our separate healing meditations. The following morning found Yolla seated in her bed, filing her nails. She greeted us cheerfully, telling us that she felt fantastic, before shooing us away to have our breakfast. Alberto sat beside me, humming.

"Why are you so happy?" I asked.

"Last night I meditated for her," he said conspiringly. "It was one of the most powerful visualizations I've ever done. I felt the energy shooting out of my hands and body. I feel as if I'm back on track again. I realized that, to perform miracles, I must choose what I want without fear of making a mistake. Fear robs them of energy. So last night I said to the Universe, I'm ready. No more fears. No more conditions. Only confidence. My will is God's will. And because of that my meditation was amazing."

"But who are you to choose that she should get better?" I interjected. "I think that's interfering in another life's path. We don't know her soul's purpose with this illness."

"Or it's a convenient excuse to not risk making a mistake and say it's God's will," he responded.

"I don't think it's up to me to decide whether a person should live or not," I countered. "In healing work, especially when I don't have that person's permission, I think my role is to be a clear channel for love. What that energy does in her body, and how it manifests itself in her life, is not up to me. That's God's will. That's the highest good we keep talking about."

"I think so long as you have God in your thoughts, then you are working with the highest good," he replied. "In that state, you are not only healing the illness, but passing along your intention that they awaken that healing consciousness within them. There are endless studies of patients who are prayed for without their knowledge, and who recover. I think what matters is that you trust the purity of your intention, and not fear making a mistake."

"I still believe that's playing God," I contested. "Perhaps if the patient collaborates in their healing, and not simply delegates the healing to me, then I can say that my will is that they heal because it is their desire too. I'm only augmenting their energy until they learn to do it for themselves."

"Until you can overcome your fear of offending God or infringing on what you believe is his will," Alberto said with finality, "then you will always delegate to a higher power and never claim the same divine power that is within you."

"In this, Alberto, I don't think we'll ever agree," I concluded.

49. Dangerous Territory

November 21, 2002. One year of walking, and the day that I announced my relationship with Alberto to one of my cousins, knowing it would reach the ears of my family. It wasn't the bold step I had wanted to take, but at least it was a step.

We continued our walk, much to my family's disappointment, who had wanted us to spend the Christmas holidays with them. But we needed to go on. Our route brought us back to the coast, where we passed Batroun and the historic Phoenician city of Byblos, believed to be one of the oldest, continuously-inhabited cities in the world, and pressed on to Jounieh, on the doorsteps of Beirut. That night, a torrential thunderstorm lashed the hotel where we were staying, and was still going strong the following morning.

"Let's practice stopping the rains," Alberto suggested.

Whereas a few short weeks earlier, that phrase would have sent me into an emotional frenzy, I now found myself responding, "How shall we do it?"

"I love you," Alberto replied, grinning widely. "Just do what feels natural. Remember, you are one with the elements, not separate from them. Let that feeling lead you."

It took a long time for me to overcome my own sense of ridicule, but I eventually did, and began to mentally repeat the words, "*I and the elements are one.*" I recalled Paolo Coelho's book *The Alchemist*, where the young boy Santiago speaks with the elements. It had captivated me then because it had seemed such a fantastic, yet wholly natural, thing to do. I imagined myself to be Santiago, and said the words that came into my mind at that moment.

"*Brother Wind, Sister Rain, you and I are one. We are created by the same hand, and all are living God's will. Thank you for cleansing the earth, and for nourishing the soil. Thank you for sweeping away the dead and decaying, and refreshing the land and air. You are doing God's work. You are living your purpose. I too am living my purpose, and need your help to fulfill it.*"

I trembled from the energy that coursed through my body, feeling its power but missing the loving sensations that usually accompanied it. I wasn't sure what was happening but didn't stop, my curiosity leading me.

"I ask that you hold your nourishing rains and purifying winds until we finish walking. Thank you."

"My will is your will," I heard Alberto pronounce in a low, deep voice that was filled with authority. "I am not afraid of making a mistake. You and I are one. I trust in the purity of my intention. I choose weather conditions that allow us to walk comfortably and complete our mission today. My will is your will."

When I finally opened my eyes, I saw a confident Alberto looking out the window. The waters were turbulent and the skies a dark grey. Patches of rain intermittently came down. "Let's go," he announced.

"But it's still stormy," I protested.

"Faith," he pronounced, preparing his backpack.

We walked under light showers, not heavy enough to make us stop, but steady enough that I needed to keep my head down. "*I knew this wouldn't work*," I thought disparagingly.

Almost imperceptibly, the rains began to ease, and within half an hour of our walking, completely stopped. The dark clouds began to disperse until, miraculously, the sun peeked out.

"You're a great wizard," Alberto teased.

"It was probably all you," I replied, unsure of what to make of it.

"No," he affirmed. "You just don't believe enough in yourself yet."

* * *

Before the civil war, Beirut was a cosmopolitan city that was described as the Paris of the Middle East. The various religious communities coexisted. Freedom of expression and tolerance were celebrated. The civil war revealed deeper schisms that the veneer of Beirut hid, and ahead lay the task of rebuilding the physical and emotional fabric of this city. Construction was plainly in evidence wherever we walked, but I wondered if the city's deeper wounds had been similarly healed, or simply built over.

The beauty of Beirut receded, and the freshly-paved asphalt highway that we were walking became a torn-up road. Partially constructed buildings, most unpainted and with the cement still exposed, filled the landscape on either side of the road. It was hard to believe we were only a few kilometers south of Beirut. Curious eyes now became suspicious. Those who made eye contact I greeted in the traditional Muslim manner of *as-salamu-alaykum*, but did not wait for a response. Most responded automatically, but their gaze burned against my neck.

Posters started appearing along our path proclaiming death to Israelis and their allies. The majority carried the name of *Hezbollah*, meaning Party of God. Many posters featured Muslim clerics denouncing injustice and calling men and women to arms for the liberation of their Palestinian brothers. I quietly raged at the mixing of religion with politics, but also felt afraid.

In the glossy beauty of Beirut, it was easy to forget that this was a city almost felled to the ground by the civil war. I had felt the disparity between rich and poor, Christian and Muslim, when we were in the north of Lebanon; but now, the further south we went, the more evident it was and the more radical the solutions being heralded. For the first time, I realized I was walking on land that had felt the rumble of tanks through its fields and tasted the blood of innocents. My fear intensified with every step.

We stopped at a roadside café to rest, our sign facing outwards. Two men at a nearby table kept glancing over and whispering. Finally, one of them turned around and, speaking in English, spat out, "Go tell the Americans about peace, not us."

I momentarily froze at the sudden outburst. Both men looked to be in their forties and had the typical dark Arab features. One was dressed in slacks and a t-shirt, but the one who spoke sported black slacks, black shirt, and colored tie. A diamond-studded gold watch glittered in the light.

"You are judging us before even knowing us," Alberto replied with calm authority. "We would be happy to sit with you and share our story."

The men stared hard at us for a moment, and then invited us to their table. With introductions made, we began to share the nature of our walk.

"We are not carrying this sign as a message to the Muslims," Alberto declared, impressing me with his confidence and directness. "We are carrying a message of peace for the world, based on seeking inner peace to create outer peace." The men quickly agreed, saying that the Koran also speaks of seeking this inner peace.

"This is not about individuals creating peace," one insisted. "It is about politics and American policies that prevent us from having peace. We are a peaceful people. We want to live in peace, but we cannot sit idly by while we are being attacked in our own homes." Openly weeping, he went on to describe massacres and other atrocities committed against the mainly Shiite Muslim population in this area by Israelis, Americans, and Lebanese Christians.

"*Hezbollah* is only defending our land and people," he asserted. "They are not murderers and terrorists. They are only responding to the injustice and terrorism committed against them. They are educated, well-informed professionals from all walks of life. It was they, not diplomacy, who pushed the Americans out of here. They responded to force with force."

I was in uncomfortable territory, facing every belief that I had grown up with. I believed so deeply that peace began within, but did not know how to extrapolate that belief to peace among nations. What words could possibly bridge my truth to these men's reality? How can I make this inner message of peace relevant to their outer world? How can my experiences of peace be relevant to them?

"You empower what you fight against," Alberto said. "I understand why you want to use force to stop force, but I no longer believe that's the answer. I read somewhere that an eye for an eye will eventually leave everyone blind. We've lived very intense experiences, and in every situation where we fought against what we don't want, we only made it stronger."

Alberto went on to share his personal experiences in Turkey, how in his attempt to fight and control the difficult situations, he only attracted more of them. It was a very candid discussion, an exchange that I never would have imagined possible with men who held such extremist views. I wasn't sure that we had changed their ideas about conspiracy theories and the need for radical action, but I was certain that we had touched them personally. Somewhere in that exchange, I hoped that the message of peace would work its way into their lives. We stood to leave, mentioning our excitement at crossing this final border into Israel and reaching Jerusalem.

"The border is closed," one said. "You will not be able to cross there. If you would like, we can get you into Israel. We know people in

Hezbollah who can smuggle you into the Palestinian side without a problem."

I thanked him for his generous offer, but told him we preferred to cross legally. They left us with their phone numbers should we require help in this part of the country, and asked us to pray for them in Jerusalem.

Among many things, our meeting did make me reflect on whether we needed a more universal message of peace, one that better communicated our intentions. Alberto and I spoke about it, and we finally agreed to use the symbol of peace, the pitchfork in a circle. When later we were asked if we were Americans, we decided to walk without a sign because it seemed that whatever we carried was open to misinterpretation.

Onwards we pressed past the coastal cities of Damour, Sidon, and Tyre, ever deeper into *Hezbollah* territory. At times, I felt like we were sitting ducks, passing through heavily militarized areas, uncertain of who the enemy was. We did meet many people, all of whom supported our walk and intentions for peace, and who kept assuring us that we were safe.

"*Hezbollah* is not roaming the streets shooting people indiscriminately," a young Palestinian man we had befriended one day stated. "It's true that their military wing carries out attacks into Israel, but the others are people of great influence who are highly respected here. Ask for help and you will receive it."

My perception of *Hezbollah* was still heavily skewed by how they were portrayed in the media, but I was opening to an aspect of them I had never considered. I did not agree with their military attacks or the mixing of religion and politics, but decided that I would keep an open mind should an occasion ever arise to ask for their help.

50. Final Crossing

A white kiosk. Scattered buildings behind it. Soldiers everywhere, machine guns slung over their shoulders.

"This is it," I enthused, continuing ahead. "Our last crossing."

"Stop," commanded the young soldier, his rifle at the ready. "You cannot cross here."

In Arabic, I explained that we were walking for peace and wanted to cross into Israel. The young soldier looked at us in confusion, and then motioned for us to pass and ask for the captain.

We were directed to what looked like a sitting area that was covered with a corrugated metal roof. Soldiers stopped and stared at us with curiosity. Under their watchful gaze, we slowly took off our backpacks, put them beside us, and sat on the plastic chairs. *"I wish I had our Arabic sign,"* I thought regretfully.

A large man with dark features and dressed in civilian clothes came striding across the mud. Walking a few steps behind him was a thinner man dressed in uniform. The larger man introduced himself as the captain. His manner was open and friendly, but his eyes were intense and searching. The other soldier sat beside him. "How can I help you?" He asked in French. The soldier translated into English.

The captain threw his head back and laughed heartily at our request, saying, "There is no way."

"You must understand," Alberto tried. "This message has crossed every border we have walked into. It is not about us crossing. It is about this message for peace crossing."

The smile faded and the captain now gazed at us with a look that I long ago had come to understand meant we were breaking through the façade. He asked a soldier to bring some coffee, and for us to wait while he called his superiors in Beirut. I smiled, feeling more hopeful. A soldier brought out a pot of coffee and encouraged us to help ourselves, but we politely refused, and waited for the captain.

"They refuse to let you through," he announced regretfully. "The border is physically closed with land mines, barbed wire, and cement barricades. If you had come by a few months ago, you may have been able to get a ride across with the United Nations, but now not even they can cross. It is impossible. I am sorry. Those are my orders."

I tried not to show my disappointment, and speaking in Arabic, explained that I was Lebanese. An audible buzz went around the compound, and soon our small make-shift hut was teeming with soldiers. One of the men stood in my line of vision, a soaring eagle boldly displayed on his t-shirt. I shared with them the nature of our pilgrimage, our beliefs about peace, and what we had learned. Translating for Alberto, he and I spoke, our words filled with sincerity and conviction. I kept glancing at the eagle, drawing courage from it when I felt my own faltering. The men listened attentively and were, as others before them, surprised that we had no religious or political sponsors, that we were two ordinary people trying to do something constructive for peace.

"All I can suggest," The captain offered, "is that you walk east over the mountains from here into Syria, and then enter Jordan. From there, you won't have any problems entering Palestine." I didn't have a map in front of me, but I knew that what he was suggesting was at least five hundred more kilometers of walking when Jerusalem was straight ahead of us, less than two hundred kilometers away.

"I don't have it in me to walk another month," I replied sincerely. "We're tired too." A murmur of understanding rippled through the gathered crowd.

"Another possibility," he suggested, "is to speak with the United Nations International Forces In Lebanon, in Sour. Sometimes, under extreme situations and very rarely, the UNIFIL people will cross the border to meet with Israeli officials."

I felt my heart lift. It wasn't impossible after all; it was merely difficult. We thanked him and stood to leave. The captain held my hands in his, his gaze tender, almost paternal.

"Please pray for me in Jerusalem," he said earnestly. With tears stinging my eyes, I promised to do so and mentally added his name to the long list I now carried with me. Pointing to a man beside a car, he added, "He is a taxi driver. He will take you to the UNIFIL office in Sour. It's all arranged."

We shook hands one last time and, to the well-wishes of the gathered soldiers, boarded our taxi. I felt tremendously upbeat. We hadn't crossed the border yet, but had touched people with our message and hopefully, although briefly, infused them and that whole area with the energy of peace.

The people at the UNIFIL office were phenomenal, making phone calls to the General's office on our behalf, and giving us the names of people who may be able to help us, including that of a senior official named Alejandro at the Spanish embassy who agreed to meet us in Beirut the following day.

"I'll try to get you to see the General himself," Alejandro promised, "but don't get your hopes up," he advised. "He's a difficult man to see, let alone convince. I will call you when I have news."

When Alejandro finally called three days later, it was to say that he was still trying, and to give us a contact at the Canadian Embassy and one at the Office of the Ambassador of the Vatican. We called them, but they too came back with the same rote response about the General. We even contacted *Fra* Ante, who remarkably knew people in Beirut, but they likewise were unable to help us.

The days crawled past. Signs kept telling us to persevere, but it was difficult. Our confidence ebbed and flowed with each call from Alejandro, who was exhausting his contacts. I begged the Universe for clarity, for a sure sign; but the silence deafened me, and only added to my confusion and frustration.

Our emotions were in turmoil. It had occurred so often during our walk that when one was down, the other was up; but those days found us both uncertain. We weren't sure what the way of peace was asking us to do. Do we stay and keep knocking on doors? Or do we find another way into Israel? The signs indicated for us to stay, but we doubted our interpretation of them.

To keep our focus on the way, we bought two lined windbreakers and a small backpack to accommodate the now bulkier clothes we were wearing. We emailed our friends, asking for whatever form of help they could offer. Along with the many responses of encouragement, my friend Johanna, the Dutch pilgrim answered, "This is the work of peace. The message is touching and influencing people in ways you cannot imagine right now. It is the process of peace that matters, not simply the result. Be patient, and never lose hope."

I resolved to try, and to do this work not in frustration and disappointment, but with the same love and energy that I put into walking with the message in the first place.

"I've been thinking about why we're unable to cross this final border," Alberto commented one afternoon in our room. "I'm reminded of some friends who, for years, were trying to conceive. They tried every treatment possible, all without success. They were so stressed and miserable, and finally decided to stop trying to have children and to live the life of a happily married couple. Two months later, they were pregnant."

"When they relaxed, nature could finally do its work," I added, familiar with several friends who had passed through a similar process.

"Exactly," Alberto concurred. "Perhaps magic is failing us for the same reason. Is it possible that for a thing to work we must love it and enjoy it instead of looking at it as an obligation, or a test of our abilities? Is it possible that magic, like conception, is something that flows naturally, but that we impede when we put pressure on it or attach our self-worth to its results? Maybe we just need to relax and trust."

"That may be true," I reflected, "but I believe we're going through this for a reason. I don't think it all rests on us. There's another hand at work here."

"Why can't it be both?" Alberto questioned. "I believe we can cross that border on foot, but with the doubts and pressure that we're putting on ourselves, we're creating obstacles to making that happen. Look at all the new possibilities that keep presenting themselves every day. I can't help but feel that our faith in magic created those possibilities and the signs that support them; but our doubts and insecurities undermined our joy and closed those doors."

"Surely not everything depends on us," I reflected. *"What a lonely road that would be. I'm here because I was guided here. Signs and coincidences led me to this walk. Then I made the decision. What Alberto is suggesting is the contrary, that once I choose, the signs support my decision and guide me towards it. I don't know what to believe anymore."*

"Why are we so attached to this result anyways?" Alberto went on. "In fact, why are we attached to any result? How important or fundamental is anything? If we believe that we are souls passing through this life to grow and to love, that life is only illusion, a theatre for the soul like in the movie *Matrix*, then why are we taking it so seriously instead of living it fully and joyfully?"

I didn't respond, and absently turned on the television. To my astonishment, the word *Matrix*, announcing the movie, filled the screen. *"Does this mean that Alberto is right?"* I pondered. *"Is the foundation of my beliefs completely wrong?"*

I watched the movie that night feeling more conflicted than ever.

* * *

It was now December 13, 2002 and we had been in Beirut ten days. Alejandro called that day to confirm that our request to meet the General had been denied, and that if we persisted in our efforts to cross the border, he would have us arrested.

We walked around the city for a long while, trying to decide what to do next. We passed a travel agency and stopped, pretending to be reading the promotional offers but, in reality, waiting for some sign to guide us. The miracle that we so desperately longed for, the definitive sign that would mark the way, never materialized. We finally entered and, after investigating several possibilities, decided to fly to Cyprus. From there, we would book another flight to Tel Aviv. Walking out of the agency, we noticed a poster on the door with the words that said: world of choices.

"Have we made the right choice?" I asked.

"I don't know," Alberto responded. "This sign seems to say that any choice we make is good. I need to think about it, but for now, it's time for us to move on."

51. The Wizards Fail

We landed at Cyprus airport, a short forty-minute flight from Beirut. Alberto left to get us breakfast at the open café, and returned shortly after, frowning. "What happened?" I asked.

"Nothing," he replied dismissively, "just two ignorant girls who took my order, laughing at me for not pronouncing the word *croissant* correctly. And stupid me, apologizing for my bad English instead of just disregarding them."

"Don't let them bother you," I said lightly. "There are ignorant people everywhere."

"No, I'm the stupid one for feeling ashamed and excusing myself," he replied angrily. "I'm realizing that the recent events in Beirut have really shaken my confidence. I knew that we could cross the border, but I couldn't make it happen. I feel like a failure, even though I know I'm not; but I still can't seem to avoid these occasional feelings. As hard as I try, they just appear when I least expect them."

We finished our breakfast and left for the customs area. Alberto stood in the line for the European Community, and I in the line for other visitors. Suddenly, I saw the customs official who was speaking with Alberto come out of his kiosk and storm ahead angrily, motioning for Alberto to follow him. Alberto caught my eye and shook his head in confusion, a look of shock on his face. I wanted to rush to him, but two people were ahead of me and no other kiosks were open. Alberto disappeared from my view. I waited anxiously for my turn.

With my passport finally stamped, I charged ahead, searching for Alberto. Through the large window of a small office, I saw him sitting across the table from a man who was gesticulating wildly and shouting. Alberto was trying to speak, but the man was cutting him off. Alberto's body was rigid and his face red. This man was clearly trying to intimidate Alberto, and for some reason, it was working. I knocked on the glass window and stepped inside the room, not waiting for a response.

"She can explain it to you," Alberto yelled, the rage choking his voice.

"Who are you?" The official shouted in a thick accent.

"I already told you we are pilgrims walking for peace," Alberto shot angrily.

"What do you mean working for peace?" He mocked. "What kind of peace do you work for? What is your business here?"

"We are walking for peace, not working for peace," I replied calmly. Alberto stuck out his palm in front of the man, and walked the fingers of his other hand across it.

"Then why do you have these Turkish stamps from Cyprus if you are walking?" He demanded, pointing to a page on Alberto's passport. "Do you not realize that the Turkish are occupying land that is rightfully Greek?"

"We are pilgrims," I explained slowly, holding my hands up in front of me and motioning for him to calm down. My heart pounded nervously against my chest. "We started in Rome and are going to Jerusalem. Our visas in Turkey expired and we were told to go to Cyprus to renew them."

"That is what is I was trying to explain to you," Alberto fumed, "but you didn't even give me a chance to explain. You didn't want to listen. You don't have the right to speak to people in that way."

"Hey, calm down," I commanded in Spanish, looking him hard in the eye.

"How do I know you are these pilgrims?" The official demanded. "How do I know you are not spies? What proof do you have?"

I slowly pulled out my letter from *Fra* Ante and showed him the various stamps we had received from Croatia to Macedonia. I pulled out my passport and showed him the stamp of every country we had walked in, pointing out the dates to corroborate our story. The man looked at Alberto's passport and then mine, matching the stamps.

"Then why are you in Cyprus?" He asked in a hard tone, but the anger had diminished.

"We tried to cross the border in Lebanon," I continued soothingly, "but were refused. The only way we can get to Israel is to fly to Tel Aviv from here." The man nodded, his expression stern. He opened a desk drawer and pulled out a stamp and ink pad.

"This Turkish Cyprus does not exist," he declared, inking the stamp and pounding it several times in our passports. "They are not a nation and do not have the right to stamp your passports." I explained that we had no idea about this conflict and certainly did not mean to offend him or anyone else. The man strode to the door and opened it for us.

"Welcome to Cyprus," he said politely, handing us our passports.

"Bye," Alberto spat, and stormed out. I thanked the man and ran after Alberto.

"I can't believe it," Alberto shouted. "This is exactly the kind of attitude that creates war and violence in this world. He didn't want to listen. He didn't want to understand. He only wanted to intimidate me, and he fucking did."

I quietly kept pace until he stopped. He opened his passport and in the same angry tone, stuck it in front of my face. "Look at this," he said, pointing at the stamp. Across the Turkish Cypriot stamp was the word CANCELLED in bold, red capital letters. I looked at my passport and saw that it was the same.

"What right does he have to do this?" Alberto fumed. "I am in the European Community where I should feel the most welcome, and it is precisely here that I have received the most disrespectful treatment." He stormed ahead again and I followed him until there was no more airport to stride through. He looked around like a caged animal.

"We need to get our tickets to Tel Aviv," I said gently.

He stopped and looked at me, but I wasn't sure if he saw me. At one of the agencies, we booked the first flight we could find, but it did not leave for another fifteen hours. We returned to the café and sat at a corner table, far from prying eyes. There were no words to soothe Alberto, so I left him and walked around the airport, occasionally glimpsing security forces glancing at me, unsuccessfully trying to be discreet. I returned a long while later, and found him writing in his diary. When he finally looked up, his eyes were filled with sadness.

"I was trying to explain myself in my bad English to that angry man, but he wouldn't let me," Alberto whispered, "and when I could open my mouth, I couldn't find words to say. My mind went blank, and I could feel my hands tremble. I felt a deep sense of injustice and impotence at not being able to express myself." His look was now tortured. "All this happened just when I was trying to stand up again, to find my confidence. What did I do wrong? I didn't mistrust anybody this time. Why did this happen to me?"

I felt a terrible aching in my heart watching him suffer. "I don't know," I soothed.

"I think the worst part was seeing my hands tremble," he continued, gazing at his hands, "and knowing that he saw it too. At that moment, Alberto the pilgrim, the wizard, all disappeared as if they had never existed. All I saw was the unpleasant and painful image of a frightened little child." His watery eyes locked with mine. "How easy it is to forget," he finally said, resting his head on the table.

The following hours until we finally boarded our flight seemed interminable. It had been an emotionally charged day capping an emotionally draining week. I had wanted to arrive in Israel full of light and energy, but rarely had I felt so depleted.

Alberto, however, seemed to be in better spirits and when I asked why, he simply said,

"If I can't love the wolf in me, how will I ever love it in others?"

52. The Holy Land, an Inner Journey

"Please follow me," the customs official said in English, taking our documents. My heart raced. Friends who had visited Israel had warned us that the Israeli security forces may not allow us to enter if they saw stamps from Syria and Lebanon in our passports.

We followed the official through the vast and modern airport that, at that late hour of the night, was packed with travelers. At a nearby office, she stopped and knocked on the door. Two young women, no older than twenty-five and wearing dark-green military uniform, answered. They exchanged a few words, and the official who had escorted us handed them our passports and left.

We stepped into a staid space with only a metal desk and several chairs. They flipped through our passports, examining each stamp. I thought my heart would burst through my chest, but tried to keep a calm demeanor. "Why are you here?" One of them asked in a professional tone.

My voice quivered, but quickly recovered when I saw the women smile at my explanation. They seemed surprised that we were refused entry at the Lebanese border. "I don't understand why they didn't let you cross," one said. "We have no problem with you entering our country."

I had assumed it was the Israelis who would not allow us to enter, and never considered that the Lebanese would not allow us to leave. I wondered what other misconceptions lay in wait for me.

The women were respectful, and although we spent a long time speaking with them, I wasn't sure we touched their hearts. I sensed a fatigue in them, of perhaps hearing one too many people speaking about peace.

On December 15, 2002 we officially entered the state of Israel with a three-month visa. The women guided us to a tourist information kiosk where we picked up a map of Israel and train schedules. From the long list of accommodations listed, we chose one at random and booked a room. We cleared more security checks before finally stepping outside the airport. The Tel Aviv night was damp, but not our enthusiasm. We had arrived.

* * *

The following morning, we boarded a taxi to the Tel Aviv train station. Our destination was Haifa, the most northerly Israeli town about forty kilometers south of Lebanon, and where our walk through Israel would begin. The message of peace did not cross the border, but it would come as close as it could.

What most struck me about Tel Aviv was just how green it was. I had always imagined Israel to be a desert, and was surprised to see manicured parks and colorful gardens among the vast streets and modern buildings. The crowds and traffic reminded me of any large city. However, the men and women with machine guns slung on their backs did not. Most of them looked like students, but carrying machine guns rather than school bags. Many were dressed in military fatigues, but the vast majority wore street clothes.

I had only ever seen the Palestinian face of the conflict, and their suffering. For the first time, looking out of the backseat of our taxi, I started to think about how this conflict was affecting the Israeli people. I wondered what it must feel like to live in terror every day, not knowing if the next bus they boarded or car that they walked past was going to explode. I began to understand their fear, and for the first time in my life, to feel empathy for them.

"So where are you from?" The taxi driver asked. We briefly explained. He glanced over his shoulder at us and laughed. "You are naïve," he said, shaking his head. "The Palestinians don't want peace. They only want us dead."

"Certainly not all Palestinians?" I asked.

"The radicals are the real problem," he pronounced. "You can't negotiate with them. It's all or nothing with them. We want to live in peace, but the radicals won't rest until we're all driven to the sea. The only solution is to terminate all those extremists." The intensity of his emotions took my breath away.

"Do you really think the conflict will end if you exterminate that minority?" Alberto asked intently.

The man did not respond or turn around. He drove us in silence, his jaw set and his eyes fixed ahead. At the train station, he surprised us with his well-wishes for a safe journey and even helped us to put on our backpacks.

I sat on the train, mesmerized by the number of people carrying machine guns. I had never seen a weapon up close. It looked like a toy. Sitting so close to them, however, I wasn't sure I felt safer. In fact, the longer I sat, the more unsafe I began to feel. None of them looked around nervously or seemed to be on the lookout for terrorists. They read their books and newspapers, stared out distractedly on to the passing landscape, or fell asleep while sitting. The scene could have been taken out of any train in Europe or North America. I glanced nervously at any person who boarded the train, wondering if they were a potential suicide bomber. Everyone was suspect. I began to feel claustrophobic, and wanted to get off the train. I expressed my fears to Alberto in Spanish.

"I don't think we've walked almost five thousand kilometers to get blown up on a train," he said. "If we do, then I guess our work here was done and it was our time to go." He was so annoyingly right sometimes.

I looked away from the guns and the people, and focused instead on the passing scenery. I was more relaxed by the time we arrived in Haifa, but hurried off the train. In the taxi that brought us to our hostel, the amiable driver enthusiastically supported our walk. "Your message of peace will be well received here," he assured us. "Don't be afraid. Go to Jerusalem. It is safe there."

My first day in Israel, this holy land that I had walked so far and so long to get to, was over. I had witnessed events that challenged my established views of Israel and its people, and revealed my prejudices. I could no longer claim with certainty that the Palestinians were the most afflicted in this conflict, or so easily dismiss as unreasonable the Israeli response. The most aggressive people I knew usually held the deepest fears, typically the fear of loss. It was easy to see how much Israelis had to lose, not only land but a dream that had driven them here through the centuries. It was easy to understand their desire to defend at all costs.

"Do you think we should carry the sign?" I asked Alberto.

"I'm not sure," Alberto responded.

"Me either," I added. "I don't know what's right or wrong any more. My heart is heavy and I feel like weeping at a time when I should be celebrating. When I first started walking, I only wanted to shout the message of peace from the rooftops. Now that I'm here, my voice is weak and my certainty shaken. I feel the need to listen rather than speak, and to walk in silence. I also feel nervous. This is an emotionally charged place, and I'm not sure how our message will be received."

"I have my concerns too," Alberto responded sincerely. "The emotions are powerful here, but more than that, I feel the need to reflect on my journey, and prefer to walk inwardly as well."

We agreed to walk without the sign, and to remain open to the possibility of carrying it again. For now, the outer way of peace would cede passage to the inner way.

* * *

On December 17, 2002, after more than two weeks without walking, we took our first steps out of Haifa. We cleared the city easily and followed the coast. We garnered many stares, but without our signs, we were two strange people walking along the side of the road. No one spoke to us. No one stopped us. We had as much tranquility as a busy thoroughfare could afford.

We stayed in a youth hostel in Tirat Carmel that night and continued southwards the next day towards Zikhron Ya'akov. Greenery dominated the landscape which, with the cool weather, made for an enjoyable walk. Security continued to be a visible force everywhere, even in places as ordinary as McDonald's.

We arrived at the turnoff for the town, and were disheartened to learn that it was five kilometers uphill, and away from the main road. Alberto mentioned he was receiving signs to pay attention. We stood at the bus stop, and waited. Within a few minutes, a small car bearing a young couple stopped.

"Would you like a lift to the top?" The driver, a twenty-something man asked in English. We immediately accepted. With our bags in the trunk, we got in the car and introduced ourselves. "Ah, you are from Spain," the man named Dvir replied in Spanish, going on to explain that he had back-packed all over Central and South America and so recognized Alberto's accent. "I stopped because I thought you were backpackers," he exclaimed when we told him we had walked from Rome. "With your funny white clothes, I didn't think too many people were going to stop."

We explained yet again the bleaching accident to a chuckling Dvir, a kind man with whom we felt immediately at ease. He drove us to a hostel, apologizing that his home was too small to accommodate visitors. We assured him that we were grateful for his help, and accepted his invitation to meet his family later that evening.

At the appointed time, Dvir arrived and drove us the short distance to his home. There, we met his lovely wife Anat and their toddler son. We were thrilled to discover that they were yoga teachers, and that they had traveled throughout India when Anat was pregnant. I sensed from our conversation fellow seekers, explorers walking a path of self-discovery just like us, so it came as no surprise that we shared similar open spiritual views.

"How can you live your open spirituality in such a religiously charged country?" I asked.

"Don't believe all that you read and hear," Anat declared. "There's a growing spiritual movement in this country, but it's underground for now. They are seekers like us, people challenging traditional beliefs and creating a new spirituality based on openness, tolerance and, above all, love. They are reaching across the religions and finding what unites us rather than what separates us. You are not alone in your beliefs, and not as foolish as you think carrying your message of peace."

Although Alberto and I had agreed not to carry the sign, our meeting with this young couple changed our minds. We saw an opportunity to add our voices to the voices of those creating a new spirituality and foundation for peace. Our sign would proclaim one word—peace—written in the three languages of the land: English, Arabic, and Hebrew. Peace, *Salam*, and *Shalom* would now share the same space on our backpack.

As the evening began to wind down, Dvir mentioned that his family owned an apartment in Jerusalem, and offered for us to stay there while they were out of town. We happily accepted, once again feeling the magic of the way and the forces of the Universe at work, facilitating our path in this divided land. I felt inspired as never before, and looked forward to carrying our new sign.

We pressed on to Hadera the following day, and then past Kfar Saba to Ramla, moving increasingly inland. In Ramla, we finally found the sticky paper that we needed to cut out our sign. It wasn't the attention-grabbing yellow that we had carried since Italy, but a light blue that contrasted against our dark plastic cover. Once cut out, the words looked spectacular.

We started eastwards the next morning towards Latrun, and if all went well, we would enter Jerusalem the following day. I walked excitedly, proud to be carrying our sign again. Our path took us along a quiet country road that cut through orchards, vineyards, and open fields. The occasional farm house and small village dotted our route but otherwise, it was the heavenly scent of flowers and the fresh breeze that carried it on that lovely December morning that accompanied us.

For some reason, I decided to walk behind Alberto for a while, and was appreciating the beauty and precision with which he had cut the letters. One of the letters was peeling off slightly, so I asked Alberto to stop, and pressed it back on tightly. I patted his backpack, and he continued ahead. Moments later, another letter began to peel off and was barely hanging by the time I reached it. I stuck it back on firmly, but within a few more steps, even more letters began falling to the ground. I picked them, and one by one, tried sticking them back on again, but they wouldn't stay.

"What is going on?" I moaned, the letters dangling between my fingers. Alberto shook his head in disbelief. Slowly, sadly, I took the remaining letters off, gingerly folded the covering, and placed everything inside the backpack. It was the first time it had ever happened, and I despondently wondered why it should happen now when we were so close to our destination.

We spent that night in a monastery in Latrun. In a fond return to our early days of walking in Italy, we had beds and a hearty meal, but no heating or hot water. It seemed that the closer we were getting to the end, the closer we were to the beginning. The monk who had shown us to our room stopped by to see how we were doing, and mentioned that we were in the ancient site of Emmaus, the place where Jesus appeared to two of his disciples after his resurrection. Something about that name was familiar and so, after he left, I searched through my diary.

"Do you remember Father Natalino in Venice?" I enthused. Alberto nodded. "He told us that we reminded him of a painting in his church called *Supper at Emmaus*. We are in Emmaus, and this is our last supper before arriving in Jerusalem."

"This is no coincidence," Alberto answered pensively.

"On top of that, tomorrow is Christmas Eve," I added.

"You know, I always wondered why the disciples never recognized Jesus after walking all the way to Emmaus with him," he reflected. "If I recall the story correctly, the disciples thought they were walking with another pilgrim. They were lamenting to him the events of Jerusalem and expressing their disappointment that Jesus was not the savior they had hoped for. In spite of all that Jesus had taught them, it was only at supper when he blessed the bread before breaking it that they finally recognized him."

"What do you mean?" I asked.

"I was thinking that this passage seems to be yet another parable that Jesus told, a metaphor that holds a deep mystical teaching: *the Christ was with them the whole time, but they were incapable of seeing it.* The story doesn't refer to Jesus per se, but to the inner Christ, the Divine consciousness that resides in each and every one of us. That is our true self that, invisible to the eyes, waits to be acknowledged.

Jesus was a great master who had fully unfolded his inner Christ. He overcame death as the ultimate demonstration of his control over physical matter, of his power to manipulate and transcend this illusion, a power that he promised we all had.

That's all a wizard is, someone who sees the world with the eyes of the soul, who seeks beyond this reality. It's someone who occupies himself with mastering his inner world and, once he does, his outer world changes in consequence.

That's why we both feel the need to walk in silence. We need to bring our message of peace to our inner world, to focus on the inner transformation. We have said these words so often, that peace begins within. Now, on the eve of walking into Jerusalem, we are being reminded in a very powerful way."

"Maybe that's why the letters fell off today," I reflected. *"Is it possible that this walk was never about peace in Jerusalem?"* I suddenly thought; *"That it was only a means to get me to create peace in my inner world?"*

53. Jerusalem

The rains fell steadily and the road climbed endlessly, but they could not slow our deliriously happy march into Jerusalem. The road eventually leveled off, and modern buildings and sidewalks appeared. I tried to hide my disappointment at not seeing the ancient city of my dreams. We followed street signs to *The Citadel*, hoping they would bring us to this old city. They did.

I stood at the intersection, staring at the imposing stone walls and ramparts surrounding ancient-looking towers and buildings. I wasn't sure how I felt. The traffic lights turned red and green several times, but my feet didn't move. The sight that I had traveled so far to see now frightened me. To touch its walls, to walk through its gates, meant having to end a journey that had defined my life for over a year. I had expected to arrive full of answers and revelations; but my revelations were minor in comparison to my even greater questions. The peace march that I had envisioned at the beginning of my walk now seemed so innocent.

I finally crossed the road, with Alberto alongside me. He had kept quiet, surely sensing my need to absorb this moment. I moved slowly, towards an arched entrance. I arrived, and stood under its protective dome. I caressed its walls, cold and damp with the rains, and then rested my forehead there. I wanted it to be the movie scene ending, me emotionally bursting into tears of joy and triumph; but the tears didn't surface. I felt numb, as if I was at yet another pilgrimage site, and tomorrow I would continue on my way. Alberto wrapped his arms around me and gazed at me tenderly. "We made it," he said.

I stood in his warm embrace for a long time, unable to give words to this moment. Then, hand in hand, we walked about the large entrance searching for any indication of where we were. A plaque indicated that this was the Jaffa Gate, one of seven gates into the Old City of Jerusalem. In Arabic, it was called Bab Al-Khalil. I stared at it in astonishment. Of all the ways we could have entered the Old City that Christmas Eve, I couldn't believe it was through *Alberto's gate*. Was the Universe nudging me to enter Jerusalem through the Way of the Wizard?

We learned that Bethlehem, which was normally closed by Israeli forces, was coincidentally open that night for tourists and pilgrims celebrating Christmas. We decided to go, considering it too important of a coincidence to let pass. Our Palestinian taxi driver brought us to the Israeli barricade, parking at a distance, and nervously saying he cannot come closer. We walked those few hundred meters, and were waved through by Israeli forces.

The road and surrounding fields were torn up. The few buildings that stood were riddled with bullet holes or missing entire chunks. Shreds of lamp posts kept a lonely vigil. The charred skeleton of a small car lay discarded nearby. I hurried my step, and in my fear, barely missed a barbed wire fence. We eventually began to see signs of life: lit streets, open stores, blaring music, people strolling about. We eagerly joined the growing crowd, and browsed with them the meager selection of the few stores that were open.

Our meanderings ended at Manger Square, the city's main attraction. It was teaming with pilgrims from around the world, gathered there to celebrate what is, for them, a holy night. Arab children mingled among them trying to sell anything they could. Desperation filled the air, and I found myself unable to remain impartial. My heart went out to them and felt their suffering.

We did all the tourist things one would expect at such a sacred site. We joined the crowds and television crews gathered in the Church of the Nativity to celebrate the internationally-televised Christmas mass; but it somehow didn't feel an appropriate way to end our pilgrimage or celebrate this holy night. We returned to our hotel room.

"I remember a conversation you and I had exactly one year ago about the meaning of Christmas," Alberto said.

"We were with *Don* Giovanni," I fondly recalled. "Father John. We talked about the birth of the Christ consciousness."

"And now we're in Bethlehem, the night that this inner Christ was born in Jesus," Alberto added. "That divine light continues to be born in the heart of each one of us. It is our true essence, and what I would like to acknowledge and celebrate on this special night."

He smiled at me sweetly.

"But first," he proclaimed, reaching for the $2.00 champagne bottle we had found in an open store, "a small celebration." He popped it open and filled our plastic water cups. "To the end of this way," he toasted, holding up his cup.

"And to the beginning of a new one," I added, clinking his cup. We crossed arms and drank from each other's cups.

We put away the cups and turned off the lights. The room glowed in the soft light of our candle. We sat on the bed facing each other, and lightly held hands. My eyes closed. In the stillness between us and within me, I felt the hand of love. It was beautiful in its simplicity, exquisite in its purity, and gentle in its embrace. I allowed this feeling to flower, this light to expand until it filled me completely. I didn't know what Mary and Joseph felt the night they witnessed the birth of their son, but I was sure its glow reverberated in their very beings as well. I gave thanks to that light, to the love that now brought tears to my eyes. When I finally released Alberto's hands, it was with the sense that we had celebrated the essence of what was truly born that night.

* * *

The following morning we walked around Manger Square. It teemed with trucks and cars bearing the logos of international television stations. Reporters with microphones and cameramen in tow roamed the multitude, randomly stopping people and interviewing them. We were successfully weaving our way through the crowds when an Arab-looking reporter caught my eye and smiled. He placed the microphone in front of my face as the cameraman began taping.

"Hello," he said in a friendly tone. The thundering sounds of my heartbeat cut out the rest of his words until I heard, "Can we ask you some questions please?"

"This may not be the kind of story you're expecting to report on," I answered.

"Why don't you let me be the judge of that," he replied confidently.

"OK," I said, inhaling deeply. "I am Canadian of Lebanese origins and my partner is Spanish. We just finished walking five thousand kilometers from Rome to Jerusalem, carrying a message of peace." The reporter scoffed.

"Peace? Where is the peace here?" he mocked, sweeping his arms.

"We've walked in thirteen different countries now, and more than ever believe that peace begins within you, me, and every one of us doing their part for it," I affirmed.

"What you are saying is so disconnected from the reality around you," he mocked. I bristled but kept my cool. After all, the cameras were still rolling.

"The message of inner peace is more relevant than ever," Alberto added. "We are all looking for the easy solutions, someone to create peace for us, but the key and the power to create peace lies within each of us and in the choices we make."

The journalist thanked us absently, his eyes roaming the square for another candidate. The cameraman smiled in understanding. His camera followed us as we turned away. Alberto took my hand in his. I leaned my head against his shoulder, and together, we disappeared into the anonymous crowds.

54. Ithaca

From the comfort of Dvir's family apartment, a short ten minute walk to the Old City, we explored Jerusalem. We lost ourselves in the labyrinth of streets inside its walls, and found hidden among them the city's timeless soul. We added our steps to the millions who had smoothed down its cobblestones, and left our imprint. Time stood still here, but the echo of this city's glory and turbulence still rang in every stone wall.

I was surprised to see the Old City divided into Quarters: Christian, Armenian, Muslim, and Jewish. The Jewish Quarter was the most modern, clean and quiet. Most of the shops were closed, and there was little sign of life in the streets and squares. Security forces were especially visible here, patrolling the streets in pairs, sporting bullet-proof vests, helmets, and machine guns.

The Muslim Quarter was by far the most animated, especially during the days of the open market. At those times, the streets were not filled with souvenir vendors, but with those selling necessities such as food, clothing, and household items. The smell of exotic spices mixed with the smell of sweat and packed humanity. Brightly colored fabrics reflected off brass and silver trays and pots. Young boys and old men walked the streets clinking small coffee cups, calling people to coffee in a ritual as ancient as the call to prayer. The City was alive to me then, and infused with a magic that I longed to see everywhere.

Beyond those days, however, the Muslim Quarter was as lonely as the other Quarters. Vendors polished and cleaned their wares. They perched on their store-front stools, greeting passersby in every imaginable language, inviting them to tea, trying to entice them to buy anything. Sadness and fatigue hovered in the air and tinged every contact we made, leaving me feeling melancholy.

We visited all the biblical and historic sites in and around Jerusalem. Everything was grand and beautiful, but I had seen enough physical structures during our walk, and now sought a deeper spiritual connection, something that would inspire new wisdom or a revelation about my next steps. In every place we went, I stopped and meditated, trying to feel the presence not only of Jesus, but of all the great prophets who had been there.

We reserved a special visit to the Church of the Holy Sepulcher, Catholic site of the crucifixion and tomb of Jesus, agreeing that it was the most appropriate place to leave the many objects entrusted to us throughout our pilgrimage: photos of deceased loved ones, a Croatian candle for peace, a silver heart from lovers now separated, a one Euro coin to light a candle for peace. A priest honored our request, also offering us candles to light for friends and family, which we did, and fulfilling our promise to all those who had entrusted us with their treasured hopes and wishes.

But I was still no closer to discovering what I wanted to do with my life. I had imagined arriving in Jerusalem brimming with confidence and answers for peace, and then working in projects that inspired me. Now that I was here, I wasn't sure that was still my dream. I scoured the Internet for peace organizations, and was surprised and impressed by the number of cross-cultural and multi-religious groups in Israel and Palestine working for peace. *"Why don't the media report on their efforts?"* I thought in anger.

The more I searched, however, the less interested I became. Their work was admirable but didn't inspire me as I had hoped it would. I felt weary and restless, desperate for a clear answer, and disappointed that I wasn't finding it in my ideals and dreams. Alberto was ever-supportive.

"You know I don't feel any attraction for living in Jerusalem," he said gently one night, after yet another marathon session at the Internet Café, "but if living here and working for peace was the dream that inspired you to start this walk, then keep looking until you find something that feels good and fits with who you are. I support you in whatever you choose." I had wept in his arms that night, comforted by his love and devastated by my indecision. I was free to live my dream. The only problem was that I no longer knew what that dream was.

Alberto's search was decidedly more inner-focused than mine, and delved into esoteric topics that I didn't understand. He seemed especially intrigued by a so-called White Brotherhood, who he explained were teachers and masters who once lived on earth, but then ascended from this physical reality and now, from the spiritual planes, helped humanity in its spiritual evolution.

"Do you remember my promise to the Universe, long before we met, to be an instrument of love?" He asked rhetorically over dinner one night, after enthusing about the teachings of yet another master. To my nod of affirmation, he continued, "I made this promise through a book that I coincidently received during that time and which deeply impacted me. In a spiritual ceremony that the book describes, I pledged to use my life in the service of love, and with that, opened myself to receive help from higher planes of consciousness."

In an enthusiasm that couldn't be contained, Alberto continued, "Mony, today, searching the Internet I learned that I made that pledge with this White Brotherhood. I realize now that the help I've been receiving during this walk, the invisible friends that I've often referred to, are them."

My wariness and lukewarm response did not dampen his interest or quest to learn more. While I dawdled and struggled with my next steps, Alberto seemed to be getting increasingly clearer messages about his path. One morning, he awakened and immediately reached for his notepad, writing furiously.

"Last night before going to bed," he said, "I asked to remember my dreams, and to receive through them any messages that I needed to hear at this moment. I just had a dream where I was digging somewhere in the desert and found a key. I feel my dream is telling me that I'm close to finding my grandest treasure."

The following morning, I woke to find a visibly shaken Alberto writing in his diary. "I had another dream," he said. "This time, in the dream, I once again found the key to the treasure. It was under the mattress where we're now sleeping. Don't you see?! The treasure that we had walked all the way to Jerusalem to find was always with us, but we needed to walk all the way to Jerusalem to discover that."

"Then, why keep searching if all the answers are inside you?" I asked.

"Because I want to find those who have discovered this before me," he replied passionately. "It's one thing to know that I am a creator, and another to live it. For example, I know that a master would have been able to cross the border into Israel. I want to know where I failed. Try to understand that, for me, it's not about crossing a border, but being able to transcend matter. On the Internet, I'm finding examples of so many masters who have done this, and not just Jesus and Buddha. The freemasons, theosophists, the Christian metaphysics movement, and many more groups have all had contact with who I believe are the Ascended Masters. They all teach the same thing, but in different ways;

one truth, many paths. They were all people like us who transcended this illusion—they ascended—and who are now helping us from the other side to do the same."

It was just all too out there for me. He was talking about ascension while I only wanted to know my next steps. We seemed to be living in different worlds.

Our favorite spot had become Dominus Flavit, where Jesus wept for Jerusalem. We spent a great deal of time there, enjoying the magnificent views it afforded. Perhaps I was drawn to it because I too felt that I was grieving a terrible loss, unable to comprehend why this Jerusalem I had walked so far to find was no longer inspiring me. It was during one of those visits, sitting on the rough stone ledge overlooking the city, our feet dangling into the valley below, that Alberto handed me a piece of paper.

"I found something on the Internet that might help you in your search," he said. "I carried the first paragraph with me the whole way, but only today found the entire poem by Constantine Cavafy. Read it."

> *"As you set out for Ithaka*
> *hope the voyage is a long one,*
> *full of adventure, full of discovery.*
>
> *Laistrygonians and Cyclops,*
> *angry Poseideon - don't be afraid of them*
> *you'll never find things like that on your way*
> *as long as you keep your thoughts raised high,*
> *as long as a rare excitement*
> *stirs your spirit and your body.*
> *Laistrygonians and Cyclops,*
> *wild Poseidon - you won't encounter them*
> *unless you bring them along inside your soul,*
> *unless your soul sets them up in front of you.*
>
> *Hope the voyage is a long one.*
> *May there be many a summer morning when,*
> *with what pleasure, what joy,*
> *you come into harbors seen for the first time;*

may you stop at Phoenician trading stations
to buy fine things,
mother of pearl and coral, amber and ebony,
sensual perfume of every kind—
as many sensual perfumes as you can;
and may you visit many Egyptian cities
to gather stores of knowledge from their scholars.

Keep Ithaka always in your mind.
Arriving there is what you are destined for.
But do not hurry the journey at all.
Better if it lasts for years,
so you are old by the time you reach the island,
wealthy with all you've gained on the way,
not expecting Ithaka to make you rich.
Ithaka gave you the marvelous journey.
Without her you would not have set out.
She has nothing left to give you now.

And if you find her poor, Ithaka won't have fooled you.
Wise as you will have become, so full of experience,
you will have understood by then what these
Ithakas mean."

55. The Return Journey

I sat in the window seat, watching Jerusalem disappear. Our three weeks there had passed quickly, and we now needed to return to our homes. Canada would be our final destination, stopping in Spain to meet Alberto's family. This flight, however, was bringing us to Holland, and my pilgrim friend Johanna whom I had visited before beginning to walk. It seemed a lifetime ago. With her, I hoped to have a decompression, an easing between our world as pilgrims and the world we were about to re-enter.

We spent several days with Johanna, trying to capture in conversation the feelings and experiences of a pilgrimage that still needed to be digested. She understood our many long pauses and contradictions, and listened, only advising us to be patient. She admitted her difficulty in fitting back into her own world, and in needing time to have reflected in her outer experiences and relationships the profound changes that had occurred within.

It had become our custom to have afternoon tea, and so we sat one afternoon with Johanna in her home enjoying this comforting tradition. A painting on her mantle of an American Indian man with a feather headdress caught my attention. I had seen the same painting in a bookstore earlier. Something about his presence, the way his eyes looked out with such compassion and love, compelled me to ask who he was.

"His name is White Eagle," Johanna said. I began to tremble. "He is a wise teacher and Ascended Master, and part of a group that serves humanity from the spiritual realms. They are called the White Brotherhood." I couldn't speak. Alberto looked stunned. Johanna suddenly stopped, and her eyes filled with tears.

"Oh, my God," she whispered. "He is here." Her eyes gazed beyond where we sat. "I see him standing there, and feel a tremendous outpouring of love, especially for you Alberto."

"Can you speak with him?" I whispered.

"I don't know," Johanna answered. "I've never seen him before."

"Does he know us?" I asked. Johanna slowly nodded, her eyes still fixed on the space beyond us.

"He says that he knows Alberto, but still not you, Mony." Then, in a voice filled with emotion, she said, "Oh, Alberto, I wish you could see him, feel the stream of pure love that he is directing at you."

Tears rolled down Johanna's face, mingling with a smile of contentment that now crossed her lips. "I'm sorry, I don't normally have these reactions," she said, drying her eyes, "but his presence was especially strong right now. I have had visions before, but never with him."

From her bookshelf, she pulled out several books, and from the guest room where we were sleeping, several more. "I had put these by your bedside today for some reason," she said. "Now I know why."

Emotion rushed through me when I read that White Eagle used as the foundation of his teachings the Gospel of St. John, revealing how to unfold the spiritual light, or inner Christ, that exists within each of us, so that we may uplift and heal our world with it. He refers to it as the Christ light, a universal light that is not linked to any one religion. He speaks of Jesus as a brother and great master who had come to the world to awaken the mastery within each one of us, and to be the living example of all that he taught. The symbol of that spiritual light, and of the White Brotherhood, was the six-sided star, symbolizing perfect balance and harmony between the spiritual and physical worlds.

The signs I had faithfully followed—the eagle, six-sided star, and John—had all come together in a most unexpected way, revealing a remarkable path that I would now begin to explore.

Final Thoughts

With time and distance, I would come to understand that I was indeed on an initiatic journey, one whose intent was never to create peace in Jerusalem specifically, but to begin the steps of unfolding my inner light by first removing the layers of fear and limitation that hinder its full expression.

I see now that my walk for peace was the laboratory for revealing the full extent of those fears so that I may finally heal them. The more deeply I am able to accept and integrate them as part of who I am, rather than reject them, the more brilliantly my light can shine. As I master my thoughts and emotions, I make room for my intuition and wisdom to guide me. As my concepts of peace evolve, as I find myself in greater moments of peace, so then can I bring that peace into my everyday situations. All teachings lead to mastery, but it is mastery of the self that is the ultimate destination. It is a journey we all share.

Like the Wise Men, I had followed a star to Bethlehem, and witnessed the birth of the Christ light; but that light was never outside of me. The Jerusalem I was walking towards was always within me too; a state of grace, perfection, and peace that I know will, one day, be reflected in the Jerusalem that I see in my outer world.

* * *

My aunt Yolla passed away in October of 2003, due to her illness.

Shortly after, my mother also passed away, in her sleep, leaving a contented smile as her final goodbye.

One month later, on December 5, 2003, exactly two years to the day after Alberto and I began walking together, our daughter, Sylvana Maria, was born. Our journey of peace now continues with her.

CPSIA information can be obtained at www.ICGtesting.com
Printed in the USA
LVOW082357170513

334423LV00003B/326/P